Music in the Secondary School Curriculum

Trends and developments in class music teaching

John Paynter
Professor of Music Education
University of York

CAMBRIDGE UNIVERSITY PRESS
Cambridge
London   New York   New Rochelle
Melbourne   Sydney

for the
SCHOOLS COUNCIL

Published by the Press Syndicate of the University of Cambridge
The Pitt Building, Trumpington Street, Cambridge CB2 1RP
32 East 57th Street, New York, NY 10022, USA
296 Beaconsfield Parade, Middle Park, Melbourne 3206, Australia
Published by Cambridge University Press for the Schools Council

First published 1982

Printed in Great Britain
at the University Press, Cambridge

Library of Congress catalogue card number: 82-4225

British Library Cataloguing in Publication Data
Paynter, John
  Music in the secondary school curriculum.
  1. Music – Instruction and study – England
  I. Title
  780′.76   MT10

  ISBN 0 521 24627 X
  ISBN 0 521 28860 6 Pbk

Cover picture: 'Aleatoric Rondo' by Andrew Dockerill, Richard Harbord, Matthew Russell, Barry Smith of Manland School, Harpenden (first appeared in East Anglian Centre for Music in Schools, Newsletter 3).

The author and publisher wish to thank the following for permission to reproduce material in their copyright:

Photographs on pp. 75, 129: Lynda Medwell, John Paynter and other members of the Project team.
Score on pp. 40–1: Michael Thompson, Manland School, Harpenden.
Sculpture on p. 97: photograph by courtesy of the Courtauld Institute of Art.
Magritte painting on p. 106: Statens konstmuseer Nationalmuseum, Stockholm.
Poem on p. 106: Penguin Books.
Stills from 'The Elf' on pp. 110–11: Madeley Court School, Telford.
Plans on p. 154: Crown copyright.

PN

Contents

Foreword

It has always worried me that music which, outside school, almost continuously goes in and out of young people's heads, which stirs their feelings and activates their bodies, becomes when presented – or as presented – inside schools, a 'dead bore'.

But I have now discovered, since working with the Schools Council Project for Music in the Secondary School Curriculum, that this anomaly need no longer exist.

That is why this book is so important. All my former professional colleagues, Heads of secondary schools in England and Wales, ought to acquire it, read parts of it, and then pass it on, rather insistently, to their music specialists. Or indeed the flow might well be reversed.

I realise that this will not happen in all schools, but if, by these few words, I could persuade some individuals to take the book up who would otherwise reject it, I would almost certainly be doing them, and their schools, a very good turn.

Music in the Secondary School Curriculum is important because it introduces schools, in some cases no doubt for the first time, to a possible approach to music which reaches all pupils, involves all pupils and enthuses all pupils.

The approach described and explained by John Paynter, which is generously backed up and illustrated by the materials produced and made available by the Project, is not at the moment very well known in our schools. Among some musicians, who will know better if they read this book, it actually arouses hostility.

Even music teachers who have read *Sound and Silence* by Paynter and Aston (1970), and who, through this or some other means, know about this approach, may have hesitated before adopting it in their schools. This book, and this Project should cause them to hesitate no longer, for here is both proof that it can be successful and guidelines to make it so.

The Project has involved hundreds of teachers and Music Advisers. They have met together over the years, discussed processes, made music, and contributed schemes, often – like Dr Paynter, the Director, himself – in their spare-time and unpaid. And they have produced a powerful instrument which introduces a new note, and promises a welcome 'crescendo' in the teaching of music in schools throughout the country.

Harry Rée
Chairman, Consultative Committee of the Schools Council Project,
Music in the Secondary School Curriculum, 1973–80

Preface

Although associated with the Schools Council Project *Music in the Secondary School Curriculum*, this book does not claim the objectivity of a conventional 'research report'. Based in part upon the Project's observation of ideas in action, but also upon the results of work initiated and developed at various times during a period of years prior to the establishment of the Project, it seeks to collate and present opinions (including, where appropriate, conflicting opinions) about the function of music in schools.

The Project did *not* set out to discover a 'better' way of teaching music. It did, however, try to promote widespread discussion on the subject of music's curriculum role with the object of producing among those with an interest in this topic – teachers, parents, educational administrators – a greater awareness of the contribution music could make to everyone's general education. It was expected that out of these discussions should be developed some guiding principles, and it is my hope that this book together with the Project's audio-visual materials will fulfil that obligation.

Right from the start the Project adopted a 'dissemination' strategy, organising courses and conferences, bringing together groups of teachers from various parts of the country and covering, geographically, a very wide area. The courses and conferences focussed on different aspects of music in schools but inevitably there was some overlap between topics. The chapters which follow *re*-present the Project's case for a new initiative in school music, and to some extent similar duplications occur from time to time. No apology is made for this since, in attempting to review a subject as involved as music in education, it is virtually impossible to examine any aspect in isolation. Decisions about one area may depend upon assumptions about another, and to explore the possibilities fully a certain amount of repetition is necessary. In this survey some matters are approached from a number of angles in order to take into account a variety of possible influences.

The pattern of musical activity in secondary schools is a complex one, but a recital of facts and figures would tell us very little since experience of music itself is primarily subjective and, in consequence, each of us has his own view of what is or might be considered 'important', 'useful', 'essential' or 'basic' in curriculum design. This book does not set out to 'prove' anything; nor does it propose a 'method' of music education. Descriptions of work in schools are offered as examples only, for the reader to reflect upon, not as 'lesson plans' to be copied slavishly. As with the Project's video programmes and films, the intention is first and foremost to provide a 'discussion document' which, it is hoped, will set people thinking and talking, and in particular will help teachers develop their own ideas for musical activities appropriate to the young people they teach.

Our aim has been to take note of and to learn from many different trends in class music teaching. Advice and comment has been sought widely throughout all areas of the country, and every effort has been made to achieve reasonable coverage of important issues and to suggest lines of action. But in the end a book like this cannot be a committee compilation; some*one* has to put it together, and inevitably the presentation takes on something of a personal view. Perhaps this is just as well since, if it is to promote further discussion, the book should be seen to be making some kind of case of its own. Nevertheless – or perhaps precisely because of this – I would not wish to claim for it anything more than that it is one of a number of possible interpretations of the information gathered. By the same token, although recommendations are made out of deep conviction and as a result of long and careful consideration of direct evidence from work in the classroom, there is absolutely no intention of presenting these views in an authoritarian spirit. In the end it is the teachers in schools who must decide for themselves whether or not the suggestions put forward here can usefully be acted upon.

John Paynter
Department of Music,
University of York
August 1981

Acknowledgements

A great many people have contributed, in one way or another, to the production of this book. It is my very pleasant task now to thank them. Because of the close relationship with the Schools Council Project, it seems both correct and appropriate to begin by thanking all the young people, school students during the years in which the Project was active in schools, for their exciting and imaginative music-making. Many of their compositions are featured in the films and the video tapes, or are described in the book. Allied to this is the work of countless dedicated teachers, Headteachers and Music Advisers whose efforts and achievements in music education have been at the very heart of the Project's work.

I am grateful to the officers of the Schools Council for their help and guidance, and in particular should like to mention Jasmine Denyer, John

Mann and Ian Parry (now Chief Adviser, West Glamorgan Education Department), as well as Jean Sturdy, Brenda Rowe and Toby Procter of the Publications Department.

The following, members of the Consultative Committee, generously gave their time and wise counsel over a period of several years, thereby helping immeasurably to ensure the Project's smooth running: Mr D. Allwood, Mr J. Ayerst, Mrs M. Ayling, Mr R. J. Blackford, Mr R. Bunting, Mrs H. Coll, Mrs E. Jones Davies, Mr J. P. B. Dobbs, Mr D. Frith, Mr D. Goddard, Mr R. Greenwood, Miss D. Griffith, Mr B. Harmon, Prof. B. Harris, Mr E. Hewes, Mr D. Hindley, Mr B. Kenny, Miss M. Maden, Mr L. Marsh, Miss K. Maynard, Mr R. O. Murgatroyd, Mr G. R. Pritchett, Mr G. Rolfe, Mr J. Sargent, Mr K. Sedgebeer, Mr G. Self, Miss M. Southworth, Mr J. Stephens, Mrs M. J. Venables, Mr J. Warren, Mr B. Wilks. In this connection I should also like to record my gratitude to Mr D. Hatliff, Deputy Finance Officer of the University of York.

Particular mention must be made of my colleagues in the Project Team: Roy Cooper, Assistant Director, whose inspiring and imaginative approach to our task cleared away a lot of cobwebs; Alan Vincent, Gillian Blake and Grenville Hancox, Schools Liaison Officers who between them travelled the length and breadth of the country visiting schools, organising conferences, lecturing, interviewing, filming and recording; Peter Syrus and John Bryan, Research Officers and editors of News Sheets and Working Papers; and Jane Allen and Wendy Nicholas, the Project's administrative secretaries without whom the whole operation might easily have fallen apart. I am particularly grateful to John Bryan for his help and advice in the early stages of preparing this book, for reading the first drafts and talking ideas over with me. Bob Fromer and Lynda Medwell were responsible for the audio-visual programmes and exhibition, and worked closely with the Team in originating those materials.

Professor Harry Rée nurtured the Project from its earliest days. As Chairman of the Consultative Committee he guided us through problem patches, inspired and supported in every possible way. I am especially indebted to him for the patience and good judgement with which he responded to the many demands I made upon him, reading the typescript of this book in its numerous 'final' versions and making many thorough and constructive suggestions which in every case brought about an improvement in the text. As if all that were not enough, he has generously contributed a Foreword.

To my wife Elizabeth I owe a very special acknowledgement. She has accepted the Project as a constant background to our lives for over ten years, and more than anyone else she has made possible my part in this lengthy programme.

J.P.

Guiding principles

The following principles were evolved by the Schools Council Project *Music in the Secondary School Curriculum* through discussion with teachers, Heads, Music Advisers and others interested in the role of music in education.

MUSIC does have a place as a time-tabled classroom subject in the school curriculum, and it should be available to *all* pupils. It should be seen as a part of a general policy for the arts in education, because the arts offer unparalleled opportunities for the development of imagination, sensitivity, inventiveness and delight – essential elements in a balanced curriculum.

MUSIC IN THE CLASSROOM is the core of school music activity; from there we can develop extra-curricular music-making. The content of the 'music lesson' should aim to develop musical understanding in all pupils.

MUSIC manifests itself in many different ways through a wide range of skills, styles and forms. In education our task is to reveal the breadth of music's expressive possibilities, not to restrict them.

MUSIC IS A WAY OF LISTENING to sounds, and musical experience is primarily a matter of *working* with sounds and of learning to control the medium. Because most pupils already have an interest in music of one kind or another, a variety of musical activities are possible which are not dependent upon formal musical training. These are starting points, and appropriate training should then follow from identification of the pupil's musical interests.

MUSIC IS A CREATIVE ART. All musical activity – listening, making, and interpreting – requires creative thought; the exercise of imagination influenced by personal choice and preference.

MUSIC-MAKING is more important than musical information – which is only a support for music activity. 'Theory' cannot, by itself, lead to musical understanding; it exists principally to explain what has already been experienced. Our first task is to involve young people with music itself. 'Knowing about music' can never be a satisfactory substitute for the living reality of musical experience.

'The opening up of . . . new realms of feeling has always been the artist's chief mission. A great deal of our world would lack all emotional significance if it were not for his work.'
Sigfried Giedion,
Space, Time and Architecture, 1956.

'There must be a more complete and widespread understanding of the fundamental needs of children during development – particularly their need to experiment both with the actuality of their environment in concrete terms and their need to create images through which they can explore its meaning and significance for themselves.'
Ernest Goodman,
Creativity and the Visual and Plastic Arts, 1971.

'I believe that music, being essentially a non-verbal form of expression, is best learned through non-verbal methods.'
Folke Rabe,
Music Education Goals, 1972.

'What educates is significant experience.'
James Mursell,
Human Values in Music Education, 1934.

'Subjects are also very likely to be found boring if pupils fail to see their relevance to their lives . . . Few could see any use in learning art and handicraft, *and fewer still in music.*'
Schools Council *Enquiry 1,*
Young School Leavers, 1968.

1 How did we get here?

A long-standing controversy

Throughout the spring and summer of 1872 James Arthur, Headmaster of a small church school hidden among the back streets of a northern industrial town, made an effort to bring some musical pleasure into the lives of his pupils. Probably very little of the spring or the summer managed to penetrate the city smoke or find its way into the classrooms through the windows set high in the walls, but Mr Arthur tried to make up for this by teaching his pupils songs about far away places and colourful characters. Week by week he recorded in his log book the songs taught and the progress made:

> Taught the singing class 'Over mountain.'
> Taught a round, 'The Bell.'
> Taught new tune, 'The Skaters' to the Singing Class.
> Taught the singing class 'The Swiss Toy Girl.'
> The Singing Class learned 'The Hero.'

Sometimes circumstances were against him:

> This week has been very wet . . . gave no singing lessons because I had a cold.

But as soon as was possible he did what he could:

> I taught them the first part of 'Lightly Row!'

And then, with renewed confidence:

> I taught them the whole of 'Lightly Row' this week.

In November the School Board inspector paid a visit and noted in the log that 'The school is in fair order.' However, somewhat surprisingly he added that, as a condition for an unreduced grant the following year, *'Singing should be taught!'*

What could he have meant? Had not Mr Arthur conscientiously taught singing for the past seven months? But an earlier, heartfelt entry may provide a clue to this apparently perverse recommendation – not without significance in the days of 'payment by results'. In June, James Arthur had written:

> I am trying to make them learn the modulator, but it's dreadfully uphill work.

After the November visitation he tried again with this 'uphill work' but the entries seem somehow less enthusiastic than his earlier list of songs.

> The Singing Class improves very slowly with the modulator,

he wrote in late November. And by January 1873 he was really quite depressed:

> I have been endeavouring to make the singing class master the Modulator rather than [he wrote 'teach them' but then crossed it out] acquire new tunes. So many of them are young that it is rather hard.

All of which suggests a difference of opinion between the Headmaster and the Inspector. We may easily identify with both points of view; with the teacher for concentrating upon the immediacy and the delight of simple music-making, and with the Inspector in his desire to see something of more permanent value learned. But reading between the lines of this more than one hundred year old school record we can see the elements of a dilemma which, in one form or another, has been a feature of music education for a very long time – and which to some extent is with us still. The history of music in schools is the continuing story of an apparent dichotomy between practice and theory; between the 'fun' of making music *now* and the hard grind of acquiring techniques which will (or should) make it possible to have much more musical enjoyment *later on*. Even today one may occasionally come across a school timetable which allocates for a class, say, two periods of music each week, labelling one period 'Singing' and the other 'Music'!

The implication that there is something slightly frivolous about the activity of music-*making* while the study of musical theory is academically respectable, is an echo of a controversy going back to the Middle Ages and having its origins many centuries earlier.

During the Roman Empire, academic study of music was purely a matter of philosophical speculation coupled with the theory of harmony, rhythm and metrics as a branch of mathematics, unrelated to practical musicianship. Meanwhile, there was both glorification for the virtuoso performer and, at the other extreme, the use of music as a crude background accompaniment to gladiatorial combat. With the growth and spread of Christianity, instrumental music in particular was anathematized – doubtless because of its association with the less pleasant aspects of Roman culture – and for a time even the academic theory of music was felt to be unworthy of study.

In the sixth century, when Boethius and Cassiodorus transmitted the ancient harmonic theory to the Latin West, the spirit of the earlier restrictions prevailed. Medieval thought divided music into three levels with *Musica instrumentalis* ('sounding music', both vocal and instrumental) at the lowest point and *Music mundana* (the 'music of the spheres') at the highest – the music of heaven itself. Musicians too were placed in categories, with the practical music-makers – the cantores – in a relatively lowly position. For it was not considered enough merely to know *how*; it was also important – indeed more important, in cosmic terms – to know *why*. Medieval philosophy regarded the numerical relationships of the harmonic series as a mirror of God's eternal order, and although the Boethian approach recognised the need for the practical as well as the speculative in music, it was the theory of 'number made audible' which lay behind all academic study of music, and which made the *musicus* ('he to whom belongs the ability to judge') more valued than the *cantor*. The curriculum of medieval universities was based upon the Seven Liberal Arts in two divisions: the *Trivium*, which consisted of Grammar, Dialectic and Rhetoric, and the *Quadrivium* of Geometry, Arithmetic, Astronomy, and Music. Although 'Music' may have included some knowledge of plainsong (and, of course, as a means of transmitting the corpus of the chant, singing was taught in the monastic schools), in the main 'Music' meant a theoretical knowledge of acoustics.

The division between theory and practice persisted, so that later in the Middle Ages we find a number of practical treatises emerging in parallel with those of a speculative nature modelled on Boethius. The practical 'manuals' were directed principally at singers and at the correct performance of liturgical music. In one of the most famous of these books, Guido d'Arezzo points out: ' . . . I have simplified my treatment for the sake of the young, in this not following Boethius, whose treatise is useful to philosophers but not to singers' (from Guido of Arezzo, *Epistola de ignoto cantu*, quoted (in translation) in Oliver Strunk, *Source Readings in Music History*, Faber, 1952, p. 125).

Throughout the sixteenth and seventeenth centuries in Europe the Church, both Catholic and Protestant, continued to provide musical training for its singers, and in secular life it was increasingly anticipated that educated people should have musical skills. The rise in status of music-*making* had some influence in schools and in sixteenth-century Britain there were educators, such as Sir Thomas Elyot and Richard Mulcaster, who were prepared to argue a place for music in the curriculum – though largely as a relaxation from more serious studies. Yet there were still plenty of people, then and later, who continued to see music as a wholly frivolous occupation and certainly not an area for serious study; an attitude which was not without influence during the eighteenth and nineteenth centuries and was effective in persuading many that music deserved no more recognition than as a 'polite accomplishment' for the upper classes. For example, the philosopher John Locke (1693) states: 'a good Hand upon some Instruments, is by many People mightily valued. But it wastes so much of a young Man's time, to gain but a moderate Skill in it; and engages often in such odd Company, that many think it much better spared.' (From *Some Thoughts Concerning Education*, Fifth edition, 1705 ¶ 197). And Obadiah Walker (1699) agreed with Locke that music took too much time to learn and 'little to lose it'.

Nevertheless, in England the establishment of universal education during the middle years of the nineteenth century awakened a new interest in music's educative potential. The poet Matthew Arnold was a Board of Education inspector, and in his 1863 report he recommended music as a means by which teachers could 'get entrance to the minds of children more easily than they might through literature'. Much of the impetus for music in schools from this time on into the early decades of the twentieth century was derived from educators such as Jean-Jacques Rousseau, Pestalozzi, and Froebel – all of whom advocated the use of music as a means to an end in a child's general education.

Although extensively involved with music, and active as an amateur composer, Rousseau had no formal training in musical techniques. Perhaps because of this he was able to bring a fresh and uninhibited mind to bear on questions of music and its role in education. Certainly, through his writings on these subjects, he exerted great and lasting influence. In many ways his theories were well in advance of his time and for the most part were developed from a 'back to nature' premise ('Retournons à la nature'). In his famous 'Treatise of Education', *Emilius* (Edinburgh, 1763, Vol. 1, p. 222 *et seq.*), he outlines a scheme for instructing his pupil (Émile) which stressed the need for substantial experience of singing and composition (the latter presumably by way of improvisation) prior to instruction in music reading:

> . . . you should endeavour to render his voice clear, equal, easy, and sonorous; and his ear susceptible to measure and harmony: but nothing more. Imitative and theatrical music is above his capacity. I would not have him even make use of words in singing; or if it were required, I would endeavour to compose songs on purpose for him which should be adapted to his years, interesting and equally simple with his ideas.
>
> It will be easily imagined, that, as I am not very pressing to teach him to write, I shall not be more so to make him learn music. No, we shall not require him to pay a very earnest attention to any thing, nor be in too much haste to exercise his judgement on signs.

At this point Rousseau admits to some doubts because in singing 'we make use of the ideas of others' and 'to express the ideas of others, it is necessary we should first be able to read them'. Nevertheless, recognising that music depends first and foremost upon what we can hear, he writes:

> . . . in the first place, instead of reading, we may hear them, [the ideas of others]

and a tune is more faithfully conveyed to us by the ear than by the eye. Add to this, that to understand music, it is not sufficient to be able to play or sing; we must learn to compose at the same time, or we shall never be masters of this science. Exercise your little musician at first in regular, harmonious periods; join them afterwards together by a very simple modulation, and at length mark their different relations by correct punctuation, which is done by a good choice of stop or cadence. Above all things avoid any thing fantastic and whimsical, nor ever affect the pathetic in your expression; but choose a melody always easy and simple, always naturally arising from the chords essential to the tune, and indicating the bass in such a manner as that he may easily perceive and follow it: for, to form the voice and the ear, it is to be observed, he should never sing to any instrument but the harpsichord.

Later the need for theory to supplement practice troubles Rousseau again and he describes a sol-fa method 'for the better distinction of the notes'. Interestingly Rousseau's is a moveable-doh system – as we should use today – and he spends some time criticising the French for having 'strangely perplexed these distinctions' with the fixed-doh principle! But in the end Rousseau is adamant that, whatever method is adopted, the pupil should not become so weighed down by the technicalities that he loses sight of the simple joys of music-making:

. . .you may teach him music in whatever manner you please, provided you only let him consider it as an amusement.

Both Pestalozzi (1746–1827) and Froebel (1782–1852) believed in a similarly simple approach that valued music primarily for what it could contribute to the general education of children rather than for its potential to make 'some sort of artist out of every pupil'. And they were convinced that singing – for Pestalozzi in particular, the singing of national songs – could have beneficial and harmonising effects upon character.

The pleasures and benefits of vocal music also found a place in popular (adult) education during the nineteenth century. Choral singing caught the public imagination, inspired in the first instance by the sight singing movement of John Pyke Hullah (1812–84). Even here music education could not avoid controversy! Hullah held classes for large numbers of people in a specially-built hall in London where (ignorant no doubt of Rousseau's strong words on the subject!) he taught the French fixed-doh system – and had great success. Many people who would never have thought they could acquire the skill, mastered the elements of sight-reading and grew to enjoy singing. But the Hullah method had severe limitations and was eventually displaced – not without a struggle – by the moveable-doh 'Tonic Solfa' developed by John Curwen and Sarah Glover. As so often happens in such controversies, the musical pros and cons were to some extent overshadowed by other matters. The more conservative musicians favoured Hullah, who was an inspector of music in teacher training colleges and seems to have used that position to wield influence.

Furthermore, the Curwen supporters were despised for their connection with non-conformist religion and the Board Schools, and were accused of lacking musical taste. In the end the Curwen system – intevallic and basically the method promoted by Guido d'Arezzo 800 years previously – was seen to be superior and more easily adaptable to music with complex key changes. Yet in spite of the argument and ill-feeling it generated, this was a genuine breakthrough in music education for the majority. It enabled vast numbers of people, who by social position would normally have been barred from access to musical training, to become proficient sight-readers. The dissemination of this skill in effect brought into being a new class of musical people and stimulated the enormous rise in the popularity of choral singing which was so characteristic of the late nineteenth century and early twentieth century.

Developing the curriculum

Understandably, those whose task it was to develop the *school* curriculum seized upon tonic-solfa as a means of extending the scope of music in education. The modulator became an essential piece of equipment for class music teaching, and the hope was that if sight-singing could be taught to *all* children as effectively as it had been taught to many adults there would be a clear line of continuation from schools into the ever more numerous choral societies, inculcating through music a love and understanding of 'higher things'. It was a convincing argument though, as we have seen, children generally lacked the motivation of those who attended the adult classes. For the adults, learning to sight-sing opened doors a world away from the drudgery of the daily routine, and produced a widespread enthusiasm similar to that which has characterised the brass band movement. For children in school, however, the modulator was just another 'subject'; symbols and formulae to be learned – possibly with difficulty and often, no doubt, out of fear rather than pleasure.

The universities went their own way, basing their music degrees in the main upon musicological study and 'academic' composition (orchestration, species counterpoint and fugue). Independently the Colleges of Music developed their own style of instruction, which for the most part concentrated upon performance. Although there was serious professional composition teaching in these institutions, most students, during the last years of the nineteenth century and throughout the first part of the twentieth century, went through a somewhat unreal study of written techniques – what came to be known as 'paper work'; harmony and counterpoint according to 'rules', the product bearing very little relationship to genuine music in any recognisable style. Interestingly, Ebenezer Prout (1835–1909), Professor of Composition at the Royal Academy of Music and later Professor in Dublin, a prolific writer of books on musical theory, whose name has so often (and quite wrongly) been associated with the 'dry as dust' approach, had a refreshingly enlightened view of these techniques. In his *Double Counterpoint and Canon* (§ 311), written in 1891, he makes a scathing comment about those who teach counterpoint as though it were a series of mathematical equations. Once more we seem to hear an echo of Rousseau when Prout writes: 'Music is meant for the ear, not for the eye; however ingenious these puzzles may be, they are not music.'

In time the influence of the universities was felt in the school curriculum through the matriculation examination and, later, the General School Certificate. These examinations were used to test a candidate's potential for higher education. Applied to music they never attracted large numbers of candidates, a situation which changed hardly at all when GSC and HSC gave way to 'O' and 'A' levels at the beginning of the 1950s; and it remains much the same today. The areas examined have normally concentrated on topics in music history (generally European and within a time-span of about 300 years – from 1600–1900 or thereabouts), together with elementary training in harmony and counterpoint on established ('traditional') models. The conservatoires' influence came mainly through the more wide-ranging development of graded instrumental examinations administered by The Associated Board of the Royal Schools of Music (with a corresponding series controlled by Trinity College of Music). These examinations have encouraged countless youngsters to persevere with piano playing and have stimulated many thousands more to take up orchestral instruments – an important factor in the growth of school orchestras and county youth orchestras, as we can see when we observe the dramatic rise in the standard of instrumental playing among young people since the end of World War II. Exciting and valuable as these developments have been, their influence upon music in the general curriculum of schools, both primary and secondary, has been two-edged. On the one hand there is little doubt that higher academic standards for music in public examinations coupled with an increase in performing standards have added to music's status in secondary education. But these same features have, by their very nature, tended to exclude large numbers of young people who do not have conventional musical talents and have no intention of pursuing music as a career. At the same time, the areas of music represented by the examinations have become major influences in teachers' designs for music in the secondary curriculum as a whole, which in turn has to some extent conditioned musical activity in the Primary schools. The understandable demands from university music departments that undergraduates should be proficient in basic musical techniques and have a reasonable general knowledge of music history on entry to higher education has strengthened the predictive nature of 'O' and 'A' level, but this has then become the tail that wags the dog, with the result that the place of music in general education has never been completely thought through. Even where attempts have been made to expand the scope of music in the curriculum, the influence of skills and accomplishments ultimately the province of the minority has generally prevailed, so that the ideals of majority participation have had to give way to the interests of the few.

Oddly, music seems to have suffered more than most curriculum subjects from the problems of ensuring adequate preparation for the specialists while not losing sight of an obligation to others. This is certainly not for want of trying. If we return to the early years of the present century we can see the diverse background of music education in the nineteenth century and earlier forming the starting point for a whole range of strategies, methods and systems for the expansion of music in schools.

Early twentieth century

A programme of work devised in the 1920s by Margaret Donington, music mistress at the Mary Datchelor School, Camberwell was specifically designed to expand music in the school. The scheme, which was worked out in great detail for an age-range of 4–18 and covered basic musical concepts, notation, music history, vocal and instrumental performance and creative work, received widespread recognition for its attention to the needs of the majority. Appearing first as a series of articles it was subsequently published in book form (*Music throughout the Secondary School/A Practical Scheme*, OUP, 1932). At the head of her introductory chapter Margaret Donington places a quotation from [Edward?] Dickinson: 'The teacher's business . . . is to help prepare the eager, joyous, personal acceptance of music as a living reality.' And she ends her book with the following:

> *Conclusion*
> The aim of the whole scheme is to treat Music as an ordinary class subject such as History. Every girl takes it as a matter of course whether she is gifted or not. The classes are *not* graded . . . There is no attempt at specialising in any direction whatsoever – the aim is rather to place within the reach of each child the opportunity of understanding and appreciating every side of the Art of Music.

The scheme drew unqualified support from the Headmistress, Dorothy Brock, who in her Foreword to the book writes enthusiastically about the development of music in the school curriculum 'in the last twenty years'.

From being an accomplishment for a young lady, a soft option for the dull girl, or an expensive extra for the technically gifted, it is slowly but surely winning recognition as a part of the education of a normal girl (and in some quarters also of a normal boy).

Margaret Donington's work is then commended because:

. . . nothing here described requires for its accomplishment a lavish expenditure of money, or impossibly ideal conditions, or extravagant timetable allowance . . .

That has an unfortunately familiar ring to it! But it is clear what is meant and, to be fair, the paragraph continues – with sound educational reasoning:

This is Music as a form subject, taught in class to every girl, not a course of specialised instruction for a selected few.

By 1931 and the publication of the Hadow Report (Board of Education, 1931), music had certainly become a topic for serious educational discussion:

The educative value of music has been often overlooked in the past. It has been sometimes mistakenly regarded as a soft relaxation . . . If taught on sound lines it should react upon the whole work of a school. In no subject is concentration more necessary; in no subject is there so much scope for the disciplined and corporate expression of the emotions . . . (p. 188)

High priority was given to the arts. They were linked with physical culture in the belief that 'the simultaneous development of physical and mental powers in harmonious interplay' produces 'poise and balance . . . qualities . . . intimately connected with intelligence and character,' and, it was stressed, 'Dancing, singing, music, the drama, are the means of cultivating them.'

Frequently the pages of the Report read like an inspired statement of belief:

. . . the curriculum should not be loaded with inert ideas and crude blocks of fact . . . It must be vivid, realistic, a stream in motion, not a stagnant pool . . .

a plan that has the arts at its centre:

Of music we need say nothing here except to indicate that we count it among the indispensable elements of the primary school curriculum. The subject enjoys a long established place in primary education, and its teaching in the schools shows a response to the present revival of the art as a constituent of the cultural life of the nation.

Neither does it stop at such general support; there is a substantial section of detailed proposals, together with comment on and evaluation of methods in vogue at the time. For example, the following in which we have italicised the key points:

The importance of good music teaching in the early stages cannot be too strongly urged. The facts of daily life do not form a corrective to poor teaching in music, as in some other branches of the curriculum, and unskilled teaching in the early stages may quite easily blunt the musical sense *that nearly all children possess.* . . .

The artist is strong in the child and it is to this side of the child's nature that the teacher should appeal . . .

Of recent years many experiments have been made in the teaching of the more theoretical part of music to young children. Many artificial aids in the form of pictorial representations of the stave have been found to be of doubtful value . . .

The subject of musical appreciation has lately occupied the attention of teachers, perhaps to the detriment of other branches of music teaching. At first undue emphasis was laid upon the importance of programme music or music with a story, or music that 'painted a picture'. Other and more important aspects were overlooked. The best results obtained when the children *have accomplished the music with movement* . . .

. . . if the child in the early stages learns a considerable number of songs of a simple character he has more chance of developing the musical sense. These songs should be carefully chosen. A song is not necessarily good, or even appropriate for children because it is childish. Good clear melody and good poetry are essentials . . . The importance of inculcating a sound melodic taste cannot be over-estimated. For this purpose *the use of national and folk songs is strongly recommended.* The melodic directness of the songs makes an instant appeal to the child, and forms an *instinctive and never failing criterion in after life.* (pp. 186–8)

The Hadow Committee drew much of its own inspiration from the writings of educationists such as John Dewey, whose own *credo*, 'Learning is active; it involves a reaching out of the mind,' may well have informed the Report's emphasis upon 'doing' – as opposed to the passive reception of facts. Thus music is frequently linked with dancing and with Eurhythmics. The watchword is 'participation'; providing something that everyone can do. And running through the entire Report is the recognition of our obligation to average children; the majority of children.

The twenties and thirties saw a great deal of enthusiastic experimentation with music teaching methods, most of it directed towards the younger child but almost all of it in some way concerned with extending the scope of music in education. In its detailed comments, the Hadow Report reflects this mosaic of different approaches. There was, for example, the Percussion Band which had much to recommend it, even with quite small children: a whole class could participate, it would draw upon and develop a child's natural rhythmic sense, it could be used to teach the elements of notation and ensemble playing, and – because the principal melodic and harmonic material was played by the teacher on the piano – it could be a way of ensuring that children heard, and perhaps remembered, some of the greatest melodies in the classical repertoire.*

As with the percussion band, so with folk songs and national songs; they could be seen as worthwhile experience in themselves but (and, in the view of some teachers, possibly more important) they could lead to the acquisition of musical knowledge. They were in effect 'a method' for teaching music:

> Such songs may form the basis of the early teaching of what is known as 'musical appreciation'. Elementary ideas of form, melodic outline, rhythmic balance, and climax can be learned from them. Every child should be steeped in the strong British idiom and musical flavour of these songs. Nothing can form a sounder foundation for a musical education. (p. 187)

The development of the gramophone and broadcasting gave impetus to the 'Music Appreciation' movement, which by the late 1920s had spawned an extensive literature but was also at the centre of an 'all-or-nothing' controversy, something of which may be glimpsed in the following extract from a chapter 'On Listening to Music' from John E. Borland's *Musical Foundations/A Record of Musical Work in Schools and Training Colleges, and a Comprehensive Guide for Teachers of School Music* (OUP, 1927):

> The last fifteen years have witnessed a veritable revolution in the teaching of music, and one important part of this revolution has consisted in the establishment of the subject known as 'The Appreciation of Music' in a large proportion of schools of all types . . . There has been a danger that teachers may neglect the thorough ear-training in favour of the 'appreciation' lessons because the latter appears to offer more immediate enjoyment both for teacher and for pupil. One supervisor of music in America calmly announced a few years ago that he was going to turn sight-singing out of the schools in his district and to teach the children to 'love music'. One wonders if such rubbish could be talked about any other subject. Imagine English children being taught to 'love' Shakespeare without learning to spell and read English. (p. 491)

The writings of Dr Thomas Yorke Trotter – notably *The Making of Musicians* (1922) and *Music and Mind* (1924) – had considerable influence at this time. His 'system for the practical education of children in the elements of music' had much in common with the methods of Émile Jacques-Dalcroze. Both made extensive use of improvisation and the child's natural feeling for rhythm, balance and phrase-length, and both

---

* The present writer can remember quite clearly taking part (on triangle!) in a classroom percussion band in the infant department of a London primary school in the mid-1930s. One piece in particular comes to mind; Schubert's famous *Marche Militaire* which the teacher played on the piano while the band added its rhythmic accompaniment. The Schubert tune remained strongly in the memory, to be identified many years later.

were, in a sense, the direct descendants of Rousseau's dictum: 'The sound first, and then the sign'. Subsequently Yorke Trotter's ideas were taken up by Gladys Puttick, who in her own work with children and in her training of teachers made an important impact upon music in schools in the 1940s and 1950s.

Meanwhile instrumental playing in class, from having been primarily rhythmic (i.e. the percussion band) took a new direction with the introduction of recorder-playing. A similar development, though on a less extensive scale, was the making and playing of bamboo pipes; an idea which had begun in America in the twenties and was fostered in some British schools throughout the thirties, largely through the energies of Margaret James, the founder of the Pipers' Guild.

Music in schools also received encouragement and stimulus from composers. Ralph Vaughan Williams, who in association with Cecil Sharp had done so much to promote the singing of folk songs in schools, also took an interest in the Pipers' Guild and composed for bamboo pipes. While, abroad, two major schemes of work were brought to fruition; the *Schulwerk* of Carl Orff (again linking music and movement) and the 'choral concept' devised by the Hungarian composer Zoltán Kodály. Orff and Kodály have had influence on music education in Britain and America, both directly – through the translation of their work – and indirectly by way of other schemes which imitate and adapt the originals. Notable has been the widespread adoption of the 'Orff' classroom instruments, independently of the musical materials in the six books of the *Schulwerk*. Indeed, many of the teachers who use the instruments and employ the basic elements of Orff's ideas have not studied the approach in any detail.

Although a large proportion of the ideas and methods developed between 1920 and 1955 were designed mainly for primary schools, almost all of them had some influence upon general music teaching in secondary schools. The establishment of Modern Schools after the 1944 Education Act presented teachers in the secondary sector with the challenge of working without the incentive of public examinations. In such circumstances the arts and crafts could have a new and vital role to play. With a background of many years of experiment and exploration in music education methods, including a substantial literature and any number of successful published schemes of work, it might have been expected that by the late 1950s we should see music in the very forefront of curriculum development. In fact, the opposite was the case. Although there was quite a lot of very creditable music activity in schools, there was also a certain amount of confusion. Music had not flourished *within the curriculum* as it might have done, and it was clearly not reaching a very large number of pupils. The severely subject-orientated curriculum of the Grammar Schools, together with the demands of GCE, generally worked against

music, and the introduction of GCE to the Secondary Modern Schools
soon produced a similar situation there. 'General' music classes tended to
feature less and less, so that by 1963 the Newsom Report noted that more
than half the schools in the survey had no provision for any kind of music,
and that 'music is the subject most frequently dropped from the curriculum
in boys' and mixed schools . . . the only subject in the practical group for
which one period a week is common' (DES. 1963. See particularly
paragraphs 412–20.) Newsom commented too on the shortage of *suitably*
qualified teachers for music:

> . . . not all music teachers who are highly qualified themselves are able to bridge
> the gap between the popular enthusiasms and the much more varied and
> demanding forms of music to which they rightly feel the school should be
> introducing the pupils. It takes a particular skill to use that initial interest, and
> without rejecting what the young people have spontaneously chosen, to sharpen
> perceptions and extend capacities for enjoyment over a wider field. (para. 416)

The Report also revealed the disadvantages under which many secondary
music teachers were working (criticism which may be applicable even
now):

> . . . music is frequently the worst equipped and accommodated subject in the
> curriculum . . . Of all the 'practical' subjects, it had the least satisfactory
> provision. Equipment is often similarly inadequate . . . the teacher has to begin
> with virtually nothing and build up very slowly through the years, with his
> equipment supplied by small grudging instalments, often of poor quality. (paras
> 418 and 419)

Paradoxically, this was a period of growth for selective extra-curricular
music activities:

> there are the individual schools, or whole areas where music flourishes,
> extending beyond the classroom to choirs, orchestras, brass bands, concerts . . .
> (para. 413)

But as a curriculum subject, even in the primary schools, music had not
kept pace. The Plowden Report (DES, 1967) acknowledged much
worthwhile progress, yet at the same time found 'the present position'
unsatisfactory; something that would have 'to be tackled systematically and
resolutely'. (para. 689)

The climate of opinion was 'favourable to musical education' but
equipment and time-tabling were still major problems; the teaching of
notation was not sufficiently related to active music making – '. . . it must
be functional, not theoretical' – and, significantly, 'The planning of music
as a creative subject lags behind work in language and the visual arts and
crafts'. (para. 692 (c) and (d))

This last criticism is particularly surprising, for, as we have seen,
'creative work' was a crucial part of class music training for Donington and

others forty or fifty years before Plowden, and rhythmic and melodic improvisation were central in the schemes of Dalcroze, Yorke Trotter, and Orff. What had gone wrong?

Ironically the answer may lie with the emphasis given to musical *activity*. It is true that we learn by doing, and music can have no meaning apart from its sounds. Moreover, to aim to involve all young people, of whatever age, aptitude and ability, in the direct experience of making music is surely laudable. But like every other art form, music alters with the passing of time and with changes in social outlook. Methods and lesson content appropriate in the 1920s become outdated and need at least a moderate amount of adaptation for children in the 1960s, 70s, 80s and beyond. The Plowden Report hinted at this and made some suggestions for new techniques (para. 692 (c) and (d)). What it did not sufficiently stress was the need for teachers to have a clear view of music's overall function within a programme of education *before* they started to work out specific methods and strategies. Understandably, the tendency has always been for us to skip the philosophy and go straight to the 'meat'; the 'things to do'. With hindsight, and fifty years on, we may now see that the Hadow Report provided all the stimulus needed for us to interpret and re-interpret its observations. The essential recommendations lay not so much in the detailed discussion of subject methods but in the underlying principles of its visionary general chapters. Had these been held firmly in the forefront of every music teacher's mind it is possible that the lagging-behind which Plowden noted might not have occurred. Moreover, had the educational rationale for music in the primary school been clearly understood and strongly maintained, the position of music in the *secondary* curriculum could now be much more secure than it is.

1960 and beyond

There have, of course, been many heartening developments in Primary school music in the years since Plowden. The range of activities is wide, as is so admirably indicated in the 1975–7 survey of primary schools (DES, 1978). Even so, in that document it is still the 'things to do' which receive most attention, and one may look in vain for clear indications that all these exciting and enjoyable activities are indeed the diversification of an *Urlinie* of educational principle which is understood by everyone and which will be capable of *re*-interpretation and *re*-development as the years go by. But for the time being, at any rate, the Inspectors' view of primary school music is a sunny one and full of hope.

Much less encouraging is the corresponding survey of the secondary sector (DES, 1979). If the picture drawn by the Inspectorate is a characteristic one (and we must assume that it is), then examples of the diminishing role of music in general education are not hard to find:

> . . . the price usually paid for the introduction of a second language into the second and/or third years is the loss or severe reduction of contact with the creative/aesthetic area of the curriculum (art, music and the crafts) for the able pupils concerned. (p. 19, 3.12)

In the timetabling of options music quickly becomes the exclusive province of those who receive help and stimulus outside school (e.g. those having instrumental lessons):

> . . . music . . . tended to be chosen by well-motivated pupils, *producing groups of less diversity.* (p. 27, 9.1)

> Whatever the reason, groups of fewer than 12 pupils occurred most often in additional second languages *and in music*, in all types of school . . . (p. 33, 11.2)

This is also a subject where pupils with particular aptitude are likely to be given special attention, perhaps at the expense of continuing general classes for the majority. For example, *Aspects of secondary education* notes that:

> Talent of a particular kind was most frequently mentioned with regard to sports and athletics. *Next came music.* (Appendix 4, 2)

> with regard to the identification of pupils with particular talents . . . examinations of the Associated Board or Royal Academy of Music were mentioned . . . (Appendix 4, 3)

But only about 8% of the schools visited included non-examination music in the fourth year. Where the survey does specify types of musical activity it is the 'out of class provision' of 'choral and instrumental music' with which 'The formal curricular programme was . . . supplemented'. (*Aspects*, p. 258, 5.6) It is to be hoped that, at least in the school described there, the choral and instrumental activities produced useful and exciting feedback into the class lessons. Unfortunately, details are not given. In many schools there is often no connection between 'in class' and 'out of class' music. Indeed, in the secondary sector, unless we take very determined steps to prevent it, the law of diminishing returns works with a vengeance as far as music is concerned. The more we exploit the opportunities for extra-curricular ensembles and encourage the talented pupils to increase their skills, the less spin-off there may be within the curriculum as a whole. As we have seen, other pressures may force teachers to give extra attention to the musically talented and so slant the programme towards the 'out of class' activities anyway. Where this happens it is not uncommon to find that, far from causing others to want to join in, musical activities assume an exclusive appearance, with a correspondingly weakening effect upon general class music.

Obviously, it is easy enough to fall into the trap of thinking that, because we commonly refer to choirs, orchestras and bands as 'extra-curricular', they are not part of the curriculum at all: they are indeed part of the school curriculum, and an important one. But at the same time, we cannot ignore the fact that they cater for a minority, and if we allow our efforts on behalf of that smaller group to impair what we are able to do for other pupils, we should at least recognise this as an educational decision, even if it is not one with which we feel completely happy. There are, for example, areas of the country where the Youth Orchestra figures so large in the Authority's view of 'school' music that individual teachers can be forgiven for thinking that their prime duty seems to be to ensure the continuing supply of suitable recruits for the orchestra. This should not be taken as a criticism of 'extra-curricular' music, nor of Youth Orchestras (about which we shall have more to say later on), but it is an indication of the continuing state of indecision about the place of music in the curriculum and there is no doubt that some teachers are puzzled by it. For example, in one Authority with approximately 75,000 pupils in its secondary schools and a justifiably renowned Youth Orchestra, the Project met teachers who felt that insufficient attention was given to the needs of class music teaching. It seemed to them that a decision had been taken to give priority to the orchestra, and that the LEA regarded that group of 100 players as the main justification for music in education. So, in a sense, it might be argued that 'school' music was geared to 1 in every 750 pupils. The point is that, whether or not this was actually so, there was the impression of a bias in that direction.

One of the strongest indicators of a tendency to emphasise selective 'out of class' music-making at the expense of 'in class' work with the whole ability range is the *Aspects* survey itself. In the whole of this 307-page document (approximately 60,000 words and more than 60 statistical tables) there are only 10 very minor references to music, and in the main these point to specialism in music rather than to the development of a broader 'general curriculum' approach.

GCE, CSE and 16+

Currently the discussion is again focussed upon examinations, in particular the proposals for a single examination at 16+. Inevitably this has aroused much controversy, and music teachers have not been slow to express their feelings on the subject. Certainly, 16+ raises questions which, if they are not satisfactorily answered, will only aggravate the indecision about music's education role.

Examinations evaluate educational processes; they also *create* educational processes. The implications of any form of assessment are inescapable, for whatever system we adopt it must influence curriculum design and content and teaching method. Examinations *compare*. They compare students with 'norms', students with other students, students present with students past. Comparisons are odious – and that is the root of our problem!

Matriculation was needed for university entrance so, by arrangement, the General Certificate of Education – intended primarily as a summation of 'general schooling' – was allowed to carry with it 'matriculation exemption' if the candidate achieved the necessary number of passes at one attempt. This was then seen to create an unfortunate comparison between those who achieved matriculation exemption and those who 'only' got a School Certificate. The change to GCE modified this and made it possible to collect individual subjects. Even so, there was still the vast majority of pupils, those who attended Secondary Modern Schools, who had no opportunity to take any kind of public examination from school. Some LEAs devised their own 'school leaving certificate' to encourage the Secondary Modern pupils, but this only emphasised the differences between Secondary Modern and Grammar. So GCE was introduced to the Modern Schools. Immediately this created another unfortunate comparison. Many of the Secondary Modern pupils were achieving no more than one or two GCE 'O' levels, whereas their Grammar School contemporaries were generally taking nine or ten subjects and, on the whole, realising higher grades. Even the development of Comprehensive schools did little to remove the stigma of the 'less able' when it came to GCE. So the Certificate of Secondary Education was devised; an examination in which everyone gets a certificate.

The implications are now very clear; GCE is the predictive examination, the direct descendant of Matriculation, while CSE is a summative examination, intended to give candidates a sense of achievement at the close of their school career. (Admittedly the position can be complicated by the attention which employers may or may not pay to these qualifications.) But there is also the unavoidable comparison. Out of renewed efforts to improve the entire assessment process, and if possible to avoid the implication of comparison between school students of different abilities, the idea of a single examination has been born. But how do we devise an examination for everyone that will be a useful prognosis of some students' potential for more advanced work and, simultaneously, act as a meaningful record of achievement for students of quite different ability who are unlikely to want to go further? Apart from the obvious problem of the very wide range of ability which must be *suitably* tested, there are far-reaching implications for curriculum content.

Music presents a particularly pertinent example of this problem. It is regrettably one of those subjects about which it has sometimes been said we have 'made important what is examinable instead of making examinable what is important'. That is, perhaps, a trifle glib, since certain types of skill are essential for those who intend to pursue conventional musical studies even if those skills are not in themselves of the essence of musical experience. Nevertheless, as far as music's place in general education is concerned, trends in recent years have been towards a much broader view of music. Where development along these lines has taken place, it is now clear that the range of work produced can be very wide indeed. Were we to dodge the issue of assessment with such work and continue to limit 'examinable' music to those things which are most conveniently tested (i.e. more or less 'the mixture as before'), we should perpetuate yet another unfortunate comparison between 'real' (= examinable) music and everything else. If that happened we could find ourselves in just the same position as the unfortunate Mr Arthur whose story was told at the start of this chapter. He thought he had been teaching 'singing', only to find that what he had done was not considered 'real' singing.

Yet there is much to be hopeful about. The DES and Schools Council have published their declarations of good intent for the future of the curriculum and for the 16+ examination, (DES/Welsh Office, 1981 and Schools Council, 1981) and although it is to be regretted that neither paper does much more than pay lip-service to the place of the arts, the principle is clear enough. Coupled with what we have learned over the past ten years from our attempts to 'refresh' class music teaching and to find new approaches suited to the changed and changing attitudes of young people, the DES and Schools Council ideals could provide just the sort of stimulus we need to make sense of music in schools. The Project *Music in the Secondary School Curriculum* observed a great variety of music-making with many hopeful signs for the future. Some of this work is described in the chapters which follow. There are topics which have been at the centre of vigorous debate among music teachers; a debate which continues, sometimes resulting in unfortunate misunderstandings, sometimes producing bitterness and polarized arguments. The tendency to concentrate upon 'things to do' is still strong, but there is also a much greater awareness of the need to seek out and discuss sound educational reasons to guide decisions about the music curriculum. The establishment of regional centres for music curriculum development has assisted this process and could do much to bridge the gaps between differing viewpoints as well as drawing the primary and secondary sectors closer together. And if we can distance ourselves, for a short time, from the 'What-do-I-do-next-Monday-morning?' problem, we may also take heart from the evidence of the past. For in spite of all the arguments about what aspects of music are appropriate, virtually every scheme for general education, from Plato to the latest DES pamphlet, has included music somewhere. If that is what people want, then that is a really hopeful sign.

2 Music in school and society

The many sounds of music

Music in school has to serve many different purposes – just as it does in society at large. It offers relaxation and entertainment; it supports and integrates with other experiences (art, dance, theatre, film); it can give us a sense of achievement through the mastery of skills and provide a satisfying group identity (through membership of a choir, an orchestra, a rock band or whatever). Music enlightens and inspires; it can give pleasure or it can disturb. Whether we play or sing, invent or listen, music may excite and move us in many ways and for many different reasons. All these experiences can in some sense be said to be educative.

School also serves a variety of purposes, not all of them 'academic' in the conventional sense but all in some way potentially educative. There could be a number of answers to the question 'What is school for?' but whatever basis we adopt, the aims are surely the same for *all* children; to help them make the best use of their particular talents in school and later in adult life.

Although we would probably all acknowledge the educative nature of the total school experience, we may also have a notion of a centrally educational curriculum which we regard as the real core of schooling. What goes into (or is left out of) the curriculum is significant. As we have seen, the definition and development of the secondary sector curriculum has been fairly haphazard. Although there seems not to have been much doubt about the basics, literacy and numeracy, in areas beyond those basic skills, curriculum content is largely the result of opinion and historical accident. Moreover, as far as these other areas are concerned, we have been influenced largely by the procedures adopted for those already agreed 'basics'. Rarely have we questioned this or asked ourselves whether the system which has grown up is always appropriate for subjects which involve different ways of 'coming to know'. There would appear to have been an unwritten assumption that all subjects worthy of a place in the curriculum should be seen to operate and to be studied in the same way, and that the prime task is one of imparting information, inculcating clearly defined skills, and testing to see if the imparting and inculcation has been successful.

Perhaps more than anything else, these assumptions have been responsible for the uncertainty that surrounds the arts in education. Music especially is in a difficult position. By its nature it is intangible, abstract and mysterious. Whereas most people would feel they could understand painting or sculpture (particularly if it is reasonably representational), precisely what is involved in 'understanding' music is for many a mystery in itself. With the apparent complexities of notation on the one hand and exacting instrumental skills on the other, it is small wonder that the general conclusion has been that 'music is what musicians do' – and what non-musicians may listen to. As such it has no obviously useful role in general education. This has been aggravated by the long-standing belief that the most valuable aspects of education are those that express ideas in words or numbers. Obviously books are and always have been important tools in education, but to some extent we have been blinded by discursive prose, by verbal reasoning, rational explanation, and the power of facts and proof. In consequence we have educationally downgraded imagination and feeling, poetry and the non-verbal means of expression – music, painting, dance and dramatic gesture. These things offer experiences which are essentially different from the world of facts, theory, explanation, measurement and proof, but they are no less important. Our attitudes to the arts in education would appear to flow from this difference in character. The arts are considered to be of lesser importance simply because they are not based upon the same kind of 'evidence' as, for example, history, geography, mathematics and the sciences.

Yet a very large number of people have a *use* for music. It is all around us and in one way or another most of us 'receive' some music almost every day; through radio or television, in the supermarket, in the cinema, in cafés and restaurants, in discos, in church – even in railway stations and in the streets. Some people, with the help of transistor radios and cassette tape-recorders, literally carry their music with them! The extent to which we are attentive to the music or even aware of it in these differing circumstances will vary, of course. Nevertheless, most people would probably acknowledge a use for music more readily than they would recognise the usefulness of painting, sculpture, dance, drama and poetry. Music, even though it may be no more than a background, does appear to have some significance in our lives. Clearly, then, it should also have a place in school education. But what place?

Should it be the traditional 'academic' study of music as it was developed in the past by the scholars and theorists of the older universities and the conservatoires? In school that would surely have limited application. Those techniques were designed primarily for students who are already 'far gone' in music. Even if we extend that approach to include various vocal and instrumental activities, unless we are prepared to break through the whole theoretical basis of music and admit many aspects of music-making which did not find a place in the traditional university/music college courses, the appeal will still be a limited one, leaving out a vast amount of the music most of us meet day by day. Yet school is a microcosm of society, and if education is to meet the needs of those for whom it is designed it cannot afford to pretend that some things do not exist. If music has something to offer to all pupils ought we not to recognise music as it is – with all its variety of style and purpose – and not take arbitrary decisions about what we can admit into the classroom and what we must, for 'academic' reasons, reject?

The demands on the music teacher

If we decide that we cannot accept in school and in the general curriculum music 'as it is', may this not raise some questions about our role as *school*-teachers? For example, can we justify limiting the application of music, in the main, to those pupils who are already motivated (such as those who are having private instrumental lessons) and for whom 'music' can safely be encompassed within 'O' and 'A' level syllabuses and the lists of instrumental 'Grade' examinations? Is this how we see music in education – apart, possibly, from some general class lessons in the lower school principally of a 'cultural' nature; singing and listening to standard repertoire works on the gramophone? As an experience of music this has obvious limitations and tends to ignore the interests and potential of a large number of pupils simply because it recognises only a small area of music activity. Would we be prepared to argue that music in school *must* be limited? That it is a highly specialised field; and that we can only afford time to address ourselves to a very clearly-defined area of musical experience and expertise, regrettably having to ignore those huge areas of music-making which do not have the definition and confirmed 'standing' of the traditional courses of study? Even when we add the participation in bands, orchestras and choirs, a music programme which is geared to the conventionally 'musical' minority (on average not more than 10% of secondary school students) is hard to justify in general curriculum terms. Eyebrows would certainly be raised were we to suggest that for roughly 90% of school students mathematics was more or less irrelevant. But if music doesn't seem to matter like mathematics, perhaps we should accept some of the blame ourselves. For if our curriculum planning has suggested to pupils and colleagues alike that only a limited range of established music is 'suitable' for school, it is hardly surprising that some (perhaps the majority) will not find our musical choice immediately relevant.

For many people 'school music' means 'special occasion music'. The model is in the tradition of the independent Public Schools where music has often been an 'extra' academically, coming into prominence only once a year as part of the public display of Speech Day or Founder's Day. This is still the most widely accepted image of music even in comprehensive schools. Indeed, quite a few Headteachers have been known to defend this use of music on the grounds of its 'public relations' value. The appointment of a music teacher carries with it the expectation of a high standard of termly/annual concerts, the occasional Gilbert and Sullivan (or some suitable equivalent: 'Oliver' or 'West Side Story'), the school band playing at morning assembly, and so on. You do not need a dedicated class music teacher for that kind of work; you *do* need a gifted and skilful musician who can produce publically acceptable music from amateur players and singers. If it is a question of priorities, the general educational values of music (that could be applied in the classroom for the benefit of the majority) may have to give place to demands of a specialised and musically restricted extra-curricular programme.

True, it doesn't have to be either/or: it *is* possible to do both things. But it is extremely hard work for the music teacher, and if the unspoken assumption seems to be that the priority is working with the select choral and instrumental groups who will blame us if, almost without considering it, we place the emphasis there? For apart from anything else, it has to be admitted that in the majority of cases our training as music teachers will have disposed us towards the organisation and direction of choirs and orchestras, and we should not be musicians worthy of the name if we did not enjoy those activities. Then again, our training will probably have concentrated on standard repertoire works and established music techniques. Very few training courses seem to encourage much in the way of adventurous exploration or experiment, or even a passing acquaintance with music of our own time. The tendency is to stay within the safety of the traditional and the well-known. Moreover, those same courses often strongly suggest priorities in such a way as to make choices for us and so 'enclose' our tastes. As a result it may become difficult for the music teacher to remain open-minded or to be enthusiastic about unfamiliar music. His dilemma is that he must be a skilful and perceptive musician, aware that some kinds of music will mean more to him than others, yet at the same time avoiding the inhibiting effects of those preferences.

Listening to music

Furthermore, we are also, to some extent, handicapped by popular misconceptions about our art. Much of the uncertainty about music's place in education probably stems from characteristics of music itself. Although music is constructed with logic, precision and often with incredible ingenuity, to the average person it is not generally clear what it *does*, beyond producing a (possibly) pleasurable effect. The common assumption is that music is an experience we should allow to flow over us, taking charge of our emotions ('. . . charms to soothe a savage breast', and so on). This may to some extent explain why it is relatively easy to get an audience for a standard repertoire symphony concert but extremely difficult to fill a concert hall if the programme contains new music. It isn't that the audiences necessarily find the familiar works more exciting or musically interesting, but rather that these works are precisely those that most easily permit the 'flow-over' idea to operate. New Music, on the other hand, speaks with an unfamiliar voice and therefore forces itself upon our attention. If we are at all uncertain about *how* to listen to music that can be a depressingly uncomfortable experience – whereas it should be a delightful adventure, exciting and invigorating.

Regrettably, instead of helping uninitiated listeners to deal with the *sounds*, the 'specialists' have tried to translate the experience into words. So, audiences are provided with elaborate and scholarly programme notes which seek to explain retrograde canons and '*sui-generis* serial procedures'; the kind of thing of which Bernard Levin once wrote, 'The trouble with this stuff is that the people who can understand it don't need it, and those who need it can't understand it'. Such description helps very little, even though we may persuade ourselves that it does. We do not listen to music analytically. Some recent experiments have suggested that the part of the brain which 'processes' musical experience has been developed primarily to deal with *whole* sensations; with the integration of many inputs and overall patterns of relationships rather than the linear, analytic thinking which is needed for speech and language functions, for reading and writing words and for decoding symbols (Galin, 1976, pp. 28–9). Although music is a logical process, with the exception of monody its logic is used to combine a number of different parts, patterns and connections which the brain must perceive simultaneously. We have only our ears to help us. Information may possibly, in some roundabout way, motivate us to listen more attentively, but it will not of itself aid us in our perception of music. There is nothing that can be said that will equal the direct experience of the sound. The gateway to musical understanding is to work with sounds; to try things out for ourselves. We have to learn to receive music on its own terms. To be told about music is no substitute.

Unfortunately the damage has been done. Many music teachers, blinded perhaps by the tradition of programme notes, continue to follow the 'soundless' path of old-style musicology. Thus the 'O' level bar-by-bar description (falsely called 'analysis') persists as a norm in music teaching, and, incidentally, does much to support the layman's belief that music is not self-sufficient: to be understood it must be explained or linked with some more tangible and familiar form such as a visual or literary image. Intentionally or not, this view acquired prominence in the Music Appreciation movement with its attendant efforts to find a cultural and 'improving' role for music in schools (see p. 11). But although the aim of this information style of music teaching is a laudable one – to produce more informed and intelligent listeners – it has often had the opposite of the desired effect. Children, aware in an uncomplicated way that the sound of music is something they can get excited about in all its complex simultaneity if they open their ears to it, and sometimes allow their bodies to move to it, are inclined to reject the complicated explanations, the wordy descriptions, discourses and dictated notes, which are so far removed from the first-hand reality of the sound which they *know* and enjoy. Their rejection of what is offered in the music lesson may be interpreted by the teacher as lack of interest or simply philistinism. Unconsciously he gears his lessons to those most likely to respond – the pupils who are receiving instrumental tuition. Before long we are back with the old problem; for the majority the lesson content is irrelevant and 'unreal', confirming their suspicions that music, as it is presented in school, is not for them. Boredom sets in, and music as a 'subject' loses credibility.

Whilst we shall, naturally, want pupils to hear as much music as possible, paradoxically it is the excessive use of recorded music which so often seems to generate a feeling of 'unreality'. We should look closely at the common assumption that music can be passively absorbed from recordings if it is sufficiently explained. Obviously, to the teacher it makes good sense to play records of the music he is introducing to the class. But *he knows the music already*, and when he listens to the recording he automatically makes the necessary 'transfer' which compensates for the missing 'live' elements: the subtle inter-action of performers and listeners in the same room re-creating the music *together*. For a concert performance is (or should be) a creative act in which the listener plays a part. Listening is an adventure of the imagination in a world of sounds and to anyone who has not been involved with such first-hand participation, to approach music first by way of recorded performances can present difficulties. A recording has about the same amount of value as a photograph of a painting: it is a useful tool for further study if we have already had the direct experience, but without previous and substantial encounter with the reality of music in performance – either as listeners or as singers/instrumentalists – a recording conveys only a small part of the whole. Those of us who cannot remember what life was like without practical musical involvement may find this difficult to accept. It is easy to see why, given that other barriers have been overcome by our explanations and pupils are reasonably motivated to listen, we should think it logical that they should be excited by the music on record as much as if they heard it live. But understanding music is a subtle combination of feelings and circumstances. Teenagers are aware of these things no less than adult concert-goers. A disco, for all its atmosphere, does not attract the same kind of enthusiastic support given to live performance, for example at open-air rock concerts and pop festivals. No matter how good a recording is technically, as an experience of music it is limited. The position becomes even more confused with the increase in music produced 'for the disc' and intended primarily to be heard through loudspeakers. This is the case with a great deal of 'top ten' pop music, and is more obviously so with electro-acoustic music produced directly on to tape for which the only 'performer' needed is the engineer who presses the 'play' button of the tape recorder. The difficulty which even some regular concert-goers have in listening to electronic music in concert halls is possibly due to the disturbing absence of the rhythm and movement that is normally visible in the actions of performers. A listener who has had experience as a performer will probably find it easy enough to compensate and immerse himself in the sounds; one who has not may well find the 'music from loudspeakers' experience unsatisfactory.

For although music is fundamentally an aural sensation, in its origins it must surely have been a corporeal art, inseparable from bodily movement and gesture. Public performance before an audience is a relatively modern invention, but at least we *see* the musicians' movements and we feel with them the rhythmic direction of the sound patterns and textures. It is simply unrealistic to assume that, by explaining structure and background history, we can ensure an interaction between recorded music and a cross-section of young people sitting in a classroom having had little or no previous experience of live musical performance.

Music in and out of class

In summary, then, it would appear that, in trying to determine strategies for music in school, we face some fairly daunting problems. Music has significance for almost everybody, but there is evidence that its functions are only imperfectly understood. The popular misconceptions and the historical accidents have been compounded and transmitted through higher academic training to school courses which then seem to have little or nothing to offer the majority of pupils, and even for serious students of music frequently appear to concentrate on the wrong things. The aims of the music teacher may sometimes conflict with the aims of the Headteacher. And what passes for music in schools often seems to be out of touch with music as we find it in a multiplicity of circumstances outside school.

Yet since, in one form or another, the experience of music matters to so many people, it is clear that it ought to have a role in education. How then can we capitalise upon the *reality* of musical experience and avoid those methods which have alienated so many young people and left music in a curriculum backwater?

One of the biggest obstacles to progress has been the conventional, limited and relatively fixed image of 'The Musician'. For many of us that image has become a goal in itself and we have seen our task in schools primarily in terms of producing more Musicians (with capital *M*s!); an outlook appropriate enough for a specialist music college, perhaps, but unsatisfactory for normal schooling where the curriculum must be constructed with all pupils in mind.

Obviously music can be an 'out of class' selective activity for those who enjoy playing and singing together in choirs, orchestras, brass bands, rock bands, recorder groups, steel bands, or whatever. It can also be a formal subject of study for those who are going to want to take it further into Higher Education and the music profession. We must not neglect those with musical talent: they need our encouragement and we must provide opportunities for them to develop their skills. But they can also contribute in general music lessons if we devise activities in which their special skills can be used alongside the non-specialist work of other pupils, and for the talented pupils this experience could add something of musical worth normally absent from the standard 'O' and 'A' level courses. The core of our work should be in the general class activities offered throughout the school, because music is not exclusively for the classifically-trained musician, nor even for any one kind of musician! Everyone can respond to it and in some way be involved with it. Music stimulates the imagination; it engages the intellect. And it does this through *sounds*, not through words about sounds.

This is all part of the much needed broader approach; one that sees music as 'an education' and our task 'to educate *through* music'. Our goal should be musical understanding (in the broadest sense) because musical experience, when it is properly understood, is concerned with 'wholeness' and provides an essential complement to the sequential, linear and analytic aspects of schooling. Many writers have identified this need for a balanced education but none has expressed it more succinctly than Robert Witkin in his concept of 'the intelligence of feeling' (Witkin, 1974). If we fail to educate the feeling side of understanding, we educate only half the person. Music has a vital role to play here in the complete education of all school pupils, and music teachers are the only people who can provide what is necessary.

Our task is to find a way of working which will accommodate the widest diversity of talent and musical awareness, and which will also allow for changes of direction. For if we concentrate too strongly on one manifestation of music or musical technique, or upon certain kinds of instrumental talent while ignoring all others, we may easily fail to recognise the presence of musical perception in those outside our prescribed area. This may be a considerable challenge for some who teach music in schools. But if we are to see a broader and more successful application of music in education it must be possible for all the pupils to feel that what they experience in a 'music room' is part of the universal *reality* of music.

Any musical styles may find a place in our work. But 'reality' goes much deeper than the outer shell of style and fashion. Classroom work should be based upon music-*making* (performing, improvising, composing) and, in the forefront of all activities, the development of aural sensitivity and awareness. Keeping our ears open to sounds – all sounds, any sounds – is the most basic and therefore the most 'real' of musical skills. From there we can develop activities which are inventive, interpretative, and perceptual in whatever styles, forms and structures are appropriate for the pupils we teach. In this way the gap between music in school and music outside school may be narrowed so that the understanding derived from either sphere will react with the other.

Links across the curriculum

In the chapters which follow we shall examine in greater detail the practical application of these proposals, but before we do, perhaps we should remind ourselves that the problems we face are not confined to music. There has long been widespread misunderstanding about the role of all the arts in education, but progress is being made (see Ross, 1978), with potentially exciting developments such as the establishment of creative arts 'faculties' in some secondary schools.

Unfortunately music has lagged behind and even stood aside from many of these developments. Our colleagues in the visual arts and in dance and drama focussed their *educational* sights long ago and struck the right mark. Far from resting on achievements, they have continued to extend their classroom techniques individually and in association. We have a lot to learn from them. Although each art form has its own integrity, there are substantial regions of common ground; good reason for us to try to work together – not necessarily always in integrated or combined arts projects, but certainly in efforts to foster more positive attitudes to the arts in the curriculum.

No-one will take us seriously in these things unless we ourselves treat them as serious matters. That means going a lot further than merely a desire to pass on a limited range of musical skills. It is first and foremost a question of our attitudes to education and to the value – in educational terms – of what we do. Concepts of schooling tell us something about people's aspirations for the kind of world they want to live in. This is where we shall find the most telling clues to our responsibilities in the inevitably new world of tomorrow.

Looking to the future

Technological development of an order that would have been unthinkable seventy years ago has released masses of new information in every branch of knowledge. It has also made possible the extensive information storage, retrieval and communications systems which underpin yet more scientific and technological advance. Education as a whole must change to meet new social needs, and individual subjects in the curriculum must face problems of content. There is now so much to know! It is difficult to tell where we should begin, what we should include, and what we should leave out. One thing, however, seems certain: we can no longer rely solely on *received* values and inherited wisdom. Such things are important, of course, and must still find a place in the school curriculum, but education must also enable people to develop their own wisdom to deal with totally new problems. It should equip them to take decisions and to use imagination so that they can cope with the rapid change which is characteristic of our time. Education must try in every way possible to provide opportunities for young people to interpret information as well as simply to receive it. For in a society which relies heavily upon technology and automation, the sparks of insight which mark human individuality may easily be distinguished.

There are complications and problems ahead, and all educators should be prepared to face them. Technological developments may produce for some less job satisfaction, and for many as we know already in the more traditional areas of work, widespread unemployment – experiences that can be deadening to the spirit and damaging to self-respect. But, serious as these difficulties are, we should be losing sight of education's function if we allowed them to force out of the curriculum anything that was not obviously going to lead directly to employment. Indeed, as many people have foreseen, it is probable that before long we may have to take a different view altogether and re-orientate the curriculum towards a life of greatly extended 'leisure-time' instead of the present bias towards a life of 'work' for everyone. One very obvious possibility is to modify our ideas about the meaning of 'work' and 'leisure'.

Education cannot hope to find an answer for every social problem, and it would be a pity if we made that an excuse for ignoring the humanising influence of certain areas of the curriculum. Whatever the social, financial, and industrial problems we have to face, educators should give high priority to safeguarding independence of thought and those vital opportunities for the development of sensitivity and imagination which go hand in hand with the expression of ideas and feelings. To acknowledge the importance of the individual is not to advocate an anarchic society in which everyone 'does his own thing'. It is simply to recognise our responsibility in helping people to maintain self-respect through self-realisation.

Artistic experience offers something special here; something which is not precisely equalled by any other area of the school curriculum. It is not without significance that we speak of 'the creative arts', for although the artist does not have a monopoly of creativity it *is* the principal characteristic of what he does. Because the creative element is so strong in artistic activity it is this, more than anything else, that justifies a place in the curriculum for the visual arts, for dance, for drama, literature, poetry – and for music.

3 Action and reflection: what, how and why?

'What do I do on Monday morning, and how do I organise it?' For most teachers these are the key questions. But most would agree that there is also a need for a strong underpinning of educational philosophy; a need to define the *role* of the subject in the curriculum.

The project did try to deal with both these questions, though without providing a set recipe to deal with the first. Nevertheless, later in this book and in the tape-slide programmes and the film *A Place for Music*, we provide what we hope are usable guidelines. The question of a fundamental philosophy – a 'rationale' for music in the curriculum – is one we regarded as vitally important, and the arrangements made for dissemination, development and 'after-care' of the Project's work place emphasis upon this. For whilst we fully appreciate the need for help with current problems, we also recognise the importance of evolving long-term policies that will enable teachers to cope with their subject in the context of education's cycles and fluctuations – the 'swings' of schooling (see Carter *et al.*, 1979).

Music teachers rarely have the time to reflect deeply on the purpose of their job. Moreover, they are often in a less enviable position than teachers in other subjects, where colleagues in large departments can and do discuss, not merely their day-to-day work, but occasionally their aims and ideals. All too often the music teacher is alone.

This increases the need to create for music teachers opportunities for discussion, and here experience during the seven years of the project has provided us with hard evidence of the value of teachers' meetings. We do need to get together more often, to share our views on music education, and to talk about the work we are doing in the classroom. Probably teachers are asked to teach too much, and serious consideration should be given to making it possible for teachers to be released for further study at reasonably frequent intervals, and to offering more opportunities for reflection, reading and discussion as a recognised part of a teacher's working time. It is doubtful if we shall make much real progress in the development of the music curriculum without a satisfactory and properly understood rationale for music as part of the general curriculum. In this chapter we shall be looking at the practical issues, as teachers have raised them with us, and examining the necessary links between content, method and philosophy: What, How and Why?

Part 1 : The content of the music course

How realistic is an 'agreed' syllabus?

A County Music Adviser writes:

> You cannot structure the development of the imagination and its expressive stimulus, and cannot therefore create anything faintly resembling a syllabus of work (although it is essential to know what work can be done at various ages/ stages).

This is a salutary reminder of what we all know but are sometime loath to admit to ourselves: that no one method or syllabus will work in every given circumstance and that, in the last analysis, every teacher must develop strategies appropriate for his/her circumstances and suitable for those pupils in that school. It is part of our professionalism to be able to do this. An 'agreed syllabus' in music, laying down precisely what should be taught at any given point, would be unsatisfactory for anything other than standard techniques. And how do we decide what is 'standard'? Even the music colleges and the universities have gone through a great deal of heart-searching on these points; and they, after all, are concerned specifically with training musicians. Our work in schools is on a much broader front. Whatever the conservatoires and the universities may decide about their specialised courses, for us music is clearly not something we can restrict and channel into easily determined formulae. It is not one thing but many, many things, and provided that we teach it *musically* (i.e. in terms of its *sound*) there are any number of paths we might usefully take. This is, nevertheless, an area where feelings can run high and where there is frequently disagreement. It may therefore be helpful to examine more closely some of the conflicting points of view.

Established standards

> Should the teacher be seen as . . . the channel through which received traditions and techniques are passed on; as the arbiter of *standards*?

This is the view of the teacher as Master Craftsman. The content of his teaching is principally what he himself has learned and his job is to pass on the information and the skills so that the pupils will eventually be equipped as nearly as possible in the same way as the teacher. The skills and

techniques thus absorbed become established simply by the fact of being
handed on intact from one generation to another. They may then be used
as a touchstone against which to evaluate new developments. In craft terms
alone this makes a lot of sense. But although craftsmanship is important in
the practice of music, music is more than just a craft. Unlike artefacts
which have clearly defined purposes and which, with those purposes in
mind, can quite satisfactorily continue to be made more or less in the same
way from generation to generation, artistic expression is inseparable from
social characteristics and from the changing ways in which people see
things and think about things. Thus the techniques of expression must also
change.

This is not to say that there can be no standards or that there will be no
place for received traditions. Every generation builds on the past and to
some extent carries the heritage with it. New techniques are developed;
new disciplines and new standards determined. Older techniques will
continue to find a place so long as they are relevant to the expressive needs
of the time. But there can be little virtue in trying to keep alive a manner
of expression which does not meet present needs. One has only to look at
nineteenth-century *Punch* cartoons, with their lengthy and often elaborate
captions, and compare them with the succinct style of today's cartoonists;
or compare the pace of an old comedy film with that of a modern
television show. We can admire the old style of humour and comedy *in its
own context*, but as a manner of expression it would almost certainly not
work for the kind of things we laugh at today.

In music teaching it is all too easy to persuade ourselves that we are
guardians of a sacred flame, and thus to create artificial standards simply
by preserving certain techniques long enough for it to seem that they have
always been there. Are we afraid to admit that the things we revere were
once new; were not 'traditional' but were related to specific expressive
needs of a certain time? In his training a musician must acquire
craftsmanship, but in the end he is an artist primarily. This is not to belittle
craft skills but merely to recognise that artistic skills are different. There is,
for example, the question of 'transfer'. Although we may not *like*
everything we hear, nevertheless our training should make us sensitive to
all music, not simply to a limited area of it. Understanding and appreciating
music is not just a matter of mastering certain technical tricks; it involves a
feeling for the medium so that we can apply the insights we gain as widely
as possible to help us deal with any music we hear. These insights should
tell us whether techniques applied to specific problems of musical
expression 'work' or do not 'work'. The teacher is indeed an arbiter of
standards. But immutable standards based solely on the techniques of past
generations are insufficient. We have to be able to deal with a variety of
musical styles – some old, some new and it is this variety for which our
training must equip us.

Musical concepts and musical knowledge

> What do we expect adolescents to know, in conceptual terms, about music? (Pulse, rhythm, harmony, timbre, etc.)?

This question, like the previous one, sees music education as 'things to be learned' and, therefore to some extent, as 'techniques to be passed on'. But it is worth noting that it defines musical knowledge in broad conceptual terms rather than specific craft skills to deal with a limited range of problems. It is as though one might say of an apprentice joiner not only 'I would expect him to know how to make butt joints, ledged joints, mortice and tenon joints, etc., etc. . . .' but also 'Does he understand the concepts on which *all* these techniques are founded?' Thus, the teacher is more than merely a channel for passing on skills. The expectation is that the student will acquire general insights into how things function, and be able to apply them to new material in forms he has not so far met. (See Gertrude Hildreth: *Introduction to the Gifted*, p. 223. 'The facts are more easily learned and retained when they are meaningfully organised in terms of basic concepts and generalizations.' [Hildreth, 1966]) This in no way restricts the music curriculum or the way in which it is taught, because pulse, rhythm, harmony and timbre are facets of world music in an amazing multiplicity of styles, and are fundamental to the construction of music.

However, there is in this question a further implication: 'What do we expect adolescents *to know about music?*' It is not easy to answer that without considering *how* we shall cause them to learn. Content and method are linked and are an expression of educational attitude. It would be possible to 'feed' young people with information on virtually any musical topic or technique, and by frequent testing we could try to ensure that they 'knew about' these things. Musical experience need not be part of the process at all. But there is little virtue in knowing about pulse, rhythm, harmony, timbre, etc. unless we can make musical (i.e. artistic) use of these concepts, and unless the insight derived from the experience is such that it enables us to deal with other and varied uses of rhythm, harmony, timbre, etc. as and when we meet them. Obviously it is impossible to cover everything within the limitations of any one course. Nevertheless, we should try to include a reasonable range of possibilities, both geographically and historically, drawing examples from various ethnic musics and from the music of the Middle Ages and the present *avant-garde* as well as European classical and baroque styles. Students should have opportunity to try things out and 'make them their own', so that they are left not with a view of music as a closed and immutable system but with at least a glimpse of the almost endlessly extendable possibilities that arise from varied combinations of the basic musical elements. Clearly a wide range of examples is possible, and it is unlikely that any one teacher, or any one school would be able to offer pupils a whole panorama of musical styles and experience. A selection has to be made, and no doubt this will be based on the predilections of the teacher and on the inclinations of the pupils. Encouragingly, the Project has been able to show that in a number of schools pupils are experiencing not merely 'their own' music, but new music not closely related to the traditional field.

One of the more worrying features of music education in our schools has been the tendency in some quarters to promote 'knowing about' without 'experience of'; as though 'knowing about' had a value all of its own. This has arisen partly from too strong an emphasis upon selected techniques and points of musical history for their own sake. If we want to encourage musical understanding there is no substitute for first-hand experience of music itself. A well-structured course is essential, and for this *musical concepts* will form a very satisfactory basis. They offer a framework for a variety of music, though we have to remember that it is difficult – and hardly profitable – to separate the elements from one another. Melody, for example, so often has harmonic implications, and a study of harmony can quickly lead us to consider density and texture. Even so, these concepts are useful points of focus, and through them we can explore music from a number of different angles.

Suggested approaches

The following ideas have been found successful with secondary age pupils. *They are offered here only as suggestions for further development, not as 'cast iron' schemes of work which can be applied without reference to the particular needs or circumstances of a given school. These suggestions must be interpreted by individual teachers.*

An approach based on musical concepts

(i) Begin with exercises and experimental projects which investigate various possibilities in *pulse* and *rhythm*, e.g. repetition as a basis for structure; repeated rhythmic 'cells' in 'primitive' music; rhythmic ostinati, including riffs in jazz and rock music; divisive and additive rhythm patterns; the rhythmic techniques of non-western musics, e.g. Indian classical music, African drumming techniques, Balinese gamelan music with 'resultant' melodies based on interlocking rhythm patterns and the influence of these ideas upon pop and rock styles, e.g. reggae, rhythmic canons, 'phasing' principles in clapping pieces (see the music and writings of Steve Reich), free rhythms in indeterminate music, duration.

(ii) Taking as the next starting point one of the simpler ideas from the rhythm part of the course (e.g. rhythmic/melodic 'cells' in primitive musics) emphasise the *pitch* content and draw the experimental projects towards greater consideration of *melody*, e.g. one-note riffs developing into more elaborate ostinati; improvisation within a mode or note 'set' over given ostinati; antiphonal ostinati; 'call and response' melodies in work songs, sea shanties, etc.; rounds (another use of repetition); modes, scales, intervals and tone-rows (permutation as another form of repetition to create unity as well as diversity in music); different melodic styles (how a tune can be built up by 'working' a rhythmic/melodic motif); 'vertical' variation of nuclear themes in Balinese gamelan music; 'standard' popular songs and different versions of them; pupils making melodies which exploit the characteristics of different instruments.

(iii) Leading on from the relationship between instruments and melodic characteristics (e.g. sharply disjunct and 'jagged' melodies on 'dry' instruments such as xylophones; flowing conjunct movement for wind or strings or the 'sustaining' sounds of the metallophone) concentrate next on *timbre*. Explore the different 'colour' effects of whatever instruments are available in the class. Try out various effects in the contrast and combination of timbres, and in the articulation of sounds (different ways of making sounds – e.g. different ways of striking percussion, variety of beaters, etc.). Making improvisations and compositions for single timbral ensembles (e.g. a piece for a group of cymbals of different sizes or various kinds of drum; a piece for as many *different* metal sounds or glass sounds or wood sounds as can be assembled). Explore different kinds of *vocal timbre* – relate this to style in songs (e.g. voice qualities most suitable for folk song, c.f. the techniques of folk 'revival' singers such as The Watersons; scat singing in jazz; 'toasting' in reggae); other uses of voice sounds (not necessarily singing voices, e.g. in the music of Luciano Berio, Bernard Rands, *et al.*).

(iv) Timbre is linked with *texture*. Try out various different textural effects. This could lead to a discussion of *density* which is the basis of *harmony* and *counterpoint* – two or more sounds occurring simultaneously in relation to one another. Questions of density and balance are fundamental to our understanding and appreciation of harmonic effects. Anyone can explore these ideas by working directly with sounds of various kinds in combination. Improvisation is the first stage. From there we can go in whatever directions seems most suitable for the pupils. It is surprising how often students work their way through 'A' level harmony papers and present themselves for university entrance knowing all the 'rules' about consecutives, doublings, spacing, and so on but without any really musical appreciation of *why* these things have been learned. Some elementary exploration of density and balance in combining sounds of various kinds will make all the difference to students' understanding of four-part harmony or string quartet style.

What has been suggested here is, of course, only one of many possible models for a course based on musical concepts. In the first place the order *pulse/rhythm/duration, pitch/melody, timbre/texture, density/harmony* could be changed to suit the teacher's preference or the availability of equipment. It is important to capture interest quickly, so that if melodic instruments were scarce it might be advisable to start the course with an exploration of timbre for which *any* sound sources could be used. Or we might begin with voice sounds of all kinds, exploring speech sounds and 'vocal gestures' (Oh! Ah! Ooo! etc.) before going on to the singing voice. No equipment would be needed there beyond what the pupils brought with them. We could have other reasons for changing the order of topics. Some teachers like to start with the concept of *timbre* because it offers scope for pupils to invent 'atmospheric' or 'impressionistic' music. Provided we structure the course so that there is clear musical development through other concepts from that point, and it does not remain at the level of mere sound effects, there is a lot to be said for that approach.

In addition to considering exactly what musical material we shall include in the course (and there is obviously an enormous range of possibilities), there will be important decisions to be taken about timing and duration of chosen topics. We could work through all the selected ideas around one concept before moving on to the next (i.e. as the suggestions have been laid out above). Alternatively, we could take the simplest ideas within a section first, returning to that same concept but with more elaborate or advanced examples and projects for the older age groups. Much will depend upon whether we set out the course over a period of three years, or four or five, or see it as a general music course that will carry right through the secondary school. This will affect the degree of depth with which we explore each area. There will also be variations depending on the time available in a week, and on the opportunities for concentrated periods – perhaps geared into other subjects with the same time demands.

In the matter of timetabling, the Project has come to the conclusion that it is extremely difficult to give effective musical experience if only one short lesson period – or two short periods can be allotted to music each week. Music teachers need long sessions (and need to fight for this, as games teachers have done!).

Most importantly we must ensure that pupils have ample time to explore ways of using these concepts musically. If the course has to be covered in the first three years it would be preferable to reduce the variety of examples – so long as there is still reasonable breadth – rather than cutting down the class time for work with sounds. Musical insight comes from first-hand exploration of the medium; trying out ideas, working within limited objectives to construct solo pieces and pieces for small groups or the whole class by a process of 'empirical composition', performing these pieces, discussing them, wherever possible performing pieces by professional composers which link with the themes or techniques explored by the class groups, and hearing recordings (or better still, live performances) of works by professional composers – again in related areas and *after*, rather than before, pupils have tried out their own ideas.

Proceeding in this way over the first three or four years of the secondary school we could cover the principal concepts of music by working from the creative impulse of the pupils themselves. How much or how little of detail we could include would obviously depend upon time and our own decisions or priorities. In this connection it is important to be clear in our own minds about the question of notation. This is a topic which is dealt with in greater detail on page 58 but we should perhaps consider it very briefly here in the context of the course suggestions outlined above.

It would be perfectly feasible to teach this course and to ensure that pupils had a working knowledge of musical concepts such as pulse, harmony, timbre and melody without recourse to notation of any kind. Improvisations can be worked carefully and kept in mind by individuals and groups, or tape-recorded for later discussion. This procedure is especially suitable where we are dealing with less-motivated pupils for whom laboured exercises in notation can so easily kill interest and involvement. We may well be using as illustrations or as starting points music which stems from an aural tradition in which notation plays a very small part – if indeed any part at all. In particular, those who teach in schools with a high immigrant intake will need to take account of this. As one teacher puts it:

> Environmental and cultural differences play major roles in determining what will be acceptable and of value to different groups of young people. In a multi-cultural society it is often necessary to adapt materials to allow for an equal contribution from the musical experience of diverse cultural heritages.

It would be unfortunate were we to give the impression that notated music is in some ways more important than (or 'better than') music within a purely aural culture. Musical concepts are essentially concepts of *sound* organisation. We should at least approach them in that way. However, this is not to say that we should ignore notations altogether. In the right circumstances (i.e. given the necessary amount of teaching time and with pupils who are motivated to take an interest in the use and possibilities of notation) it would be easy enough to run side by side with the experimental and compositional activities discussion of the appropriate notation systems.

A different approach: techniques and structure as starting points

A programme based on musical concepts offers the scope we need and it can be adapted to suit virtually all circumstances. A similar approach is one which selects *techniques* and *structural procedures* from the works of professional composers and uses these ideas as starting points for expressive exploration. A course on these lines has been evolved and taught with great success by Tom Gamble at The Manland School, Harpenden, Hertfordshire (see Appendix 1). His pupils' work is demonstrated in the Project's tape-slide programme *Music at Manland* and music made by these students can be heard in full on the music-track tape associated with that programme.

Tom Gamble believes that 'Whatever we do in class music we must aim to involve all the children, and to involve them in real experience of music.' With this as his objective he has devised a programme of creative work in music which is certainly not a matter of trial and error. It is carefully controlled and planned because he further believes that:

> If creative activities in the secondary school are to have educational value they need to be structured over a three- or four-year period to ensure continuity and development, while at the same time retaining some flexibility.

Tom Gamble's work takes its inspiration from a wide range of music: '. . . historically from the Middle Ages to the present day and geographically from Bolivia to Bali'. But a bias towards twentieth-century music is unmistakable. He explains why:

> Music of the twentieth century, and particularly the past twenty-five years, will have a special relevance to children's work in class – not only because of the emphasis on timbre and texture but also because the new solutions which young people adopt to old problems are so often refreshingly original and imaginative. There is a level of generality at which the parameters of music are used, not only by pupils and contemporary composers, but by composers of all periods. They are all working with sounds; ordering, developing and shaping them to form a coherent sound object which is musically expressive and interesting.

Development over the whole period involves an increasing complexity of the musical ideas and experiences, of the musical concepts employed and of the notation used. There is also development in performing and listening skills, so that a pattern emerges on the following lines.

Year 1
Work with 1st-year pupils begins with exploration and experiment with one type of sound-source at a time, and leads to a short composition.

> I believe that limiting the use of instruments in this way helps focus concentration and aural imagination.

Group compositions for voice allow pupils to experiment with the range of vocal sound they can produce. The piano can be explored in the same

adventurous spirit using chords, clusters and melodic patterns. A totally
'new' instrument can also be a powerful stimulus to imagination. For
example, a piano-harp (the frame with strings taken from an old and
unwanted piano):

> Children approach this instrument without any inhibitions about technique, for
> they have no preconceived notions about how it should be played.

When a piece has been thoroughly worked out by a group, a score is
constructed using a standardised simplified notation (as shown below).
With the aid of this kind of notation pieces can be preserved and may be
brought out for further discussion at a later stage of the course (i.e. 4th or
5th year).

Many group compositions explore instruments of the same family (e.g.
strings) and may be based on simple technical procedures such as a
contrast of long and short sounds. Wherever possible, reference will be
made to other composers' use of similar techniques. For example, the long
sounds/short sounds idea for strings may lead to discussion of the same
principle as applied with wind instruments by the contemporary composer
Xenakis in his work *Akrata*.

Provided that the recorded music is used to link ideas that have been
explored by pupils directly in 'live' sound Tom Gamble believes that:

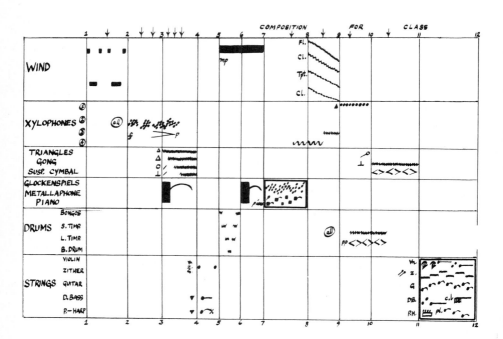

Young people should also have the opportunity to hear music by other composers, especially when it is relevant to their own work. I think we must always try to make the connection between children's compositions and the many different styles of music now accessible to us. Professional composers can't fail to be influenced by their musical culture and heritage, so why should it be any different for young composers at school? Music is a living tradition, and we must help young people to realise that they are part of it; that they are involved in a common enterprise.

After composing music for instruments of the same family, groups move on to compositions for a variety of instruments. The combination of instruments is carefully controlled by the teacher and the different effects available discussed with the classes:

Individual pupils are given the opportunity to explore and experiment with the wide range of timbres and textures produced by a class ensemble.

As soon as a pupil has begun to formulate his concept of a piece he is encouraged to try out his ideas *in sound* by directing his players with hand signals. The class are seated around the room in a semi-circle so that every player can respond to the conductor's gestures. From that point, with the teacher's help, a rough conducting score is made which helps to crystallize ideas and makes it easier for the composer to judge the overall shape of the piece.

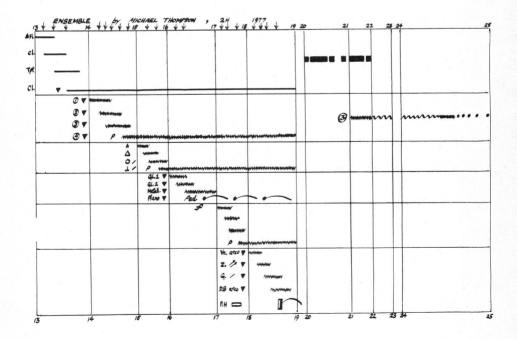

In year 1 Tom Gamble often makes use of indeterminate structures. Thus the individual composers are encouraged to design the general plan and direction of their pieces but leave the performers a certain amount of freedom in interpreting the way in which sounds may be produced. This enables the composers to hear a variety of possible solutions to the compositional problems they set themselves.

Years 2 and 3

2nd- and 3rd-year work develops in more complex ways ideas explored in year 1, and may also make greater use of images and stimuli from outside music itself (whereas the 1st-year work has tended to concentrate on coming to terms with the possibilities of the sound sources themselves: 'music = sound as sound'). At this stage class groups will also begin to respond in more varied ways to ideas suggested by the teacher. The traditional European forms (e.g. rondo) are introduced – always through practical work – and again the variety of response can often be striking, even with very simple assignments such as to compose a piece in a ternary structure.

Students' ideas about melody can be extended through experience of twelve-note composition:

> Some of this century's greatest music has used serial technique, and young people can be introduced to this idiom through practical work *before* listening to the music of Schoenberg, Webern and others . . . Every pupil in the class can be involved . . . Improvising on a given note-row, resulting in a set of variations . . . Pupils can go on to compose their own serial music, working in small groups . . .

Both classroom instruments (xylophones, glockenspiels, etc.) and orchestral instruments are used – as well as a variety of 'found object' sounds. The inclusion of orchestral instruments gives opportunity for those who are having lessons to make a particularly useful contribution by adding much needed new timbres to the more usual percussion sounds. Vocal sounds are also used a great deal and these will include not only singing but also speech, whispering, tongue-clicking and so on, producing interesting textures.

Years 4 and 5

The 4th- and 5th-year music syllabus offers a wider choice of topics or formal problems as bases for improvisation and composition. Not surprisingly rock music is a strong influence at this age but students' own compositions continue to reveal a lively interest in a variety of other possibilities; for example, the 'prepared' piano (and its links with the music of John Cage), and percussion ensembles reminiscent of the sound world of Harry Partch or a Balinese gamelan orchestra. The syllabus, constructed as it is around an extremely wide-ranging choice of music, starts with the students' own compositions and leads along many different musical paths.

Tom Gamble has made this kind of creative work the core of his music syllabus at Manland School because he believes that this is the surest path to musical understanding. By 'musical understanding' he means

> . . . the development of aural awareness and sensitivity; of musical imagination; and of the perception of form.

His principal objectives are, of course, musical:

> Creative work helps to develop an understanding of the basic concepts of music and it encourages a deeper response to all kinds of music.

But in addition, there are some general benefits:

> . . . it also aids the achievement of broader educational objectives: the growth of personality, the development of self-confidence, a respect for the work and ideas of others.

The importance of planning

We are apt to find courses built on step by step instruction attractive – key signatures, time signatures, clefs and so on – because it is relatively easy to see where the work is going. A sense of direction gives us confidence. The thought of trying to design a course on a more open-ended approach to the exploration of sounds, musical concepts or compositional processes is, for some, bewildering. Is it really possible to *plan* such work?

> How do you see a term or a year doing these things? As a new idea it'll be very exciting at first – but it seems to run out of steam after a few weeks.

If it does run out of steam it will probably be because we have not planned in sufficient detail. Good planning is the secret of this kind of teaching just as much as it is in a traditional type of course. The difference is that the plan must allow for changes in direction or alternative ways forward to cope with unexpected lines of exploration that may come from the pupils themselves. Such deviation is not only to be anticipated; it should, naturally, be encouraged. The important thing about a schedule is that it exists. We can always modify it once it is there; but without it we may easily drift, the work taking on an aimlessness which quickly leads to boredom. The teacher should have a secure idea of the general direction in which the course will go, so that students perceive a progression in what they are doing. And the planning should try to draw pupils in by ensuring that there is something that *everyone* can do. At the same time there must be sufficient substance to create the incentive to go on – and there must be musically satisfying assignments for the more able pupils:

. . . I try to approach every lesson – whether listening, playing, composing or whatever – thinking 'everybody must be doing something, giving to and getting from the lesson' – in other words, everyone must be involved.

Suggestions for a plan

An overall 'general policy' is the first step. This is the kind of thing we have outlined above. From there one can gather the various strands and arrange a series of 'frames'; projects or assignments which will provide helpful limitations to stimulate creative thinking. The teacher must be clear about each concept or process on which the work will be based, and should try to imagine the kind of sounds the class groups will produce, and where those results could lead. Look for opportunities to introduce works by professional composers which might be useful as follow-up material ('Here's a piece by another composer who has worked with the same idea: let's see what he does with it'). Details of the composer's life, dates and so on are not always relevant; concentrate instead on the way the composer has organised the sounds, and whenever possible involve the whole class in performances of music; preferably music which will link with the experimental and compositional assignments you have devised for earlier sessions. Having gathered your ideas and material, lay out a programme to cover a whole term, week by week (for example, the following scheme for a term's work using mostly vocal sounds). With some small differences in teaching style, this could be a first term (i.e. introducing this method of working to a year 1 class) *or* a term's work higher up the school with pupils who have already had some experience of working in this way but who have not previously worked with vocal sounds. It would, of course, be possible to spread this plan over more than one term.

Term 1 (12 weeks)

Aim: to provide experience of texture and timbre in music, and to do so with sound 'materials' which, as far as possible, are 'neutral' (i.e. not immediately associated with assumptions about cultural background). The scheme begins with familiarly expressive, but not conventionally 'musical' voice sounds and moves towards musical uses of these and similar sounds in the work of various composers – principally, but not exclusively, of our own time.

1 Start with voice sounds: everyday 'vocal gestures' and 'word substitutes' (Oh, Oo, Ah, Ugh – they are very expressive: we can convey quite a lot by using these sounds. How many different ones can you think of? What do they mean?) Groups make up sequences of 'vocal gestures'/small dramatic pieces. Build up an 'argument' using only one sound.

2 Sound-games (voice sounds and hand-claps only) – e.g. games from Trevor Wishart's *Sounds Fun* (Bk 1, Schools Council Publications; Bk 2 Universal Edition).

3 Groups make television advertisements in which the sounds of the words evoke the idea of the product (e.g. 'warm' well-rounded word-sounds for ideas of

warmth. Sharp, measured and strongly rhythmic word-sounds for ideas of time –
watches). Concrete poems – really a kind of music.

4 Explore word-sounds with the whole-class group: we can read fast, slow; high,
low; loud, soft (all qualities of musical sound). The interesting effect of
everyone reading aloud together. Forget the meanings of individual words:
listen to the total sound. Explore bits of the words – the hard letters only; the
's' and 'z' sounds; the vowels alone. Small groups make short pieces using these
resources of sound (suggest themes: 'an angry piece', 'a sleepy piece', 'a sinister/
mysterious piece').

5 Rehearse and perform a 'word-sound' piece, e.g. *Sound Patterns 3* by Bernard
Rands (in the series *Music for Young Players*, UE). This work, in graphic
notation which is very easy to understand and requires no previous knowledge
of notation, is conceived as part of a 'project for voices' which includes
experimental activities such as those suggested above for week 4.

6 Humming tone-clusters, tongue-clicking, finger-snap, hisses, shouts, etc., as
musical materials for group pieces. Begin to devise notations.

7 Groups complete the notations of the pieces they made last week. Swap
notations and recreate each other's pieces.
'Commission' one group to make a piece (and notate it) for next week.

8 Performance of the piece 'commissioned' last week. Discussion of techniques
involved.

9 Listen to use of the solo voice in selected sections of Schoenberg's *Pierrot
Lunaire* (e.g. 'Die Nacht'), and the choral textures in Ligeti's *Requiem*, David
Bedford's *Two Choruses* (DG 137004), Berio's *Visage* or the same composer's
A-Ronne (Decca Head 15). Alternative examples could be found in the music
of jazz singers (e.g. scat singing), in reggae (e.g. toasting) and *avant-garde* rock
singers. Draw attention to the variety of techniques possible between whispered
sounds, spoken sounds, half-speaking/half-singing (i.e. 'sprechstimme') and sung
sounds. 'Commission' two voice pieces for next week. These could be made by
individuals for the whole class to perform, or by very small groups (of two or
three pupils) or by two of the usual working groups (five or six pupils). Suggest
themes, e.g. 'Water Music', 'Fog', 'Star', '100 MPH'.

10 Composers (or one member of each composing group) direct their pieces.
Discuss. If there is time, rehearse and perform a piece on a theme similar to
that used by one of the groups (e.g. a simple 'atmospheric' piece using vocal
sounds or limited percussion sounds such as *Wave piece* by Brian Dennis (UE
16091) or *The evening draws in* by George Self (UE 15423)).

11 Establish the work so far, and the musical concepts upon which it has focussed,
by devoting the whole of this lesson to a 'concert' of selected pieces made by
the groups during weeks 1–10. No comments; just the music. Let it speak for
itself!

12 Choose an example of vocal/choral style different from the works mentioned
so far and explore it with the class. For example, an experiment with *sung lines
of melody* to form a freely moving texture. Conduct an improvisation with the
whole class, developing long 'unwinding' pentatonic melodies. (Everyone starts
on the same note – sung to Ah or Oo – sustaining it at first and then, each in
her/his own time, allowing it to develop into long lines of melody weaving and
interweaving freely with each other. Try to get the whole group to produce a
feeling of 'growth', everyone singing independently but with a similar sense of

direction to create a very gradual crescendo. Make the texture grow to a climax and then decrescendo to end quietly on another sustained note.) Repeat this several times until it is well controlled, then organise a small group of high voices to sing any well-known but suitable pentatonic tune, and introduce this tune above the interweaving texture at the climax point so that it is accompanied by the other voices.

Follow-up: draw the attention of the class to the similarity between what they have been doing and the opening chorus of Bach's *St Matthew Passion*; let them hear Bach's texture of interweaving voices and the way in which he places the hymn tune 'O Lamb of God most holy' like a crown on top of this choral texture.

We could follow this in Term 2 with a similar programme of group experiment, improvisation and composition but this time based on instrumental sounds (in the widest sense; i.e. 'found object' sounds as well as conventional classroom and/or orchestral instruments). It might be thought helpful to conclude Term 1 with work that would provide food for thought during the break. In that case something on the following lines might usefully replace week 12 of the programme suggested above:

12 Listen to parts of Penderecki's *Threnody: to the victims of Hiroshima* (VICS 1239). Compare this composer's exploration of instrumental timbres with the exploration of voice-sounds made this term. Begin to explore sounds of objects found in the room (cf. Trevor Wishart's *Found objects music* (UE 26911)). For next term: collect sounding objects – note variety of sounds.

Term 2 (12 weeks)

1 Explore the sound-objects which have been collected since last term. Group the sounds (How? high/low; material – glass/wood/metal; sustainable or non-sustainable?). Propose ideas for pieces – some atmospheric/impressionistic, others working from the sounds themselves and the various methods of sound production that can be discovered. Encourage *systematic* exploration of sound-sources.

Workshop: individuals and/or small groups. Limitations are often helpful, e.g. experiment with the metal sounds only and, having discovered precisely how many different sounds there are, make up a piece (perhaps called *Constructions in metal* – see John Cage's work of the same title; it is scored for bells, thundersheets, muted piano, various sizes of cowbell, Japanese temple gongs, motor-car brake drums, anvils, Turkish and Chinese cymbals, water gong, tam-tam, sleighbells, wind-bells). You might add a further limitation to the assignment (e.g. 'Use each sound discovered not more than two times in the whole piece.'). At the conclusion of the first session take stock of work in progress and point ways to possible developments of ideas (to be noted or remembered for the next session).

2 Continue workshop as last week. Develop ideas into definite 'pieces' and notate finished works (using whatever notational devices seem appropriate). Devote second half of this session to performance of pieces made.

3 Rehearse and perform David Bedford's *Whitefield Music 2* (*Music for Young Players*, UE 14650): each player has two instruments – one capable of sustained sounds (but there is no restriction implied by the word 'instrument').

4 Inventing and constructing instruments. You might begin by using junk materials to make instruments which are fairly straight imitations of existing ones. *The Musical Instrument Recipe Book* (Penguin Education) has some helpful suggestions. But try also to encourage experiment with materials to invent totally new instruments – unlike anything that already exists as musical instrument. Refer to the work of Harry Partch (the American composer who spent a lifetime creating new instruments and making music with them). For details of Partch and his music see Wilfrid Mellers, *Music in a New Found Land* (Barrie and Rockliff, 1964) and Partch's own book *Genesis of a Music* (Da Capo). There is also an excellent 'demonstration' recording of the instruments, and this is available with the Columbia set of Partch's *Delusion of the Fury* (M2/30576).

    Look too, at the work of Anna Lockwood a New Zealand composer who has concentrated on the sounds that can be made with glass objects (record: *The Glass World of Anna Lockwood,* Tangent Records TGS 104). Another helpful publication is *New/Rediscovered Musical Instruments* (Ed. David Toop, Quartz Publications, 208 Ladbroke Grove, London W10, 1974). See also Schools Council Secondary Music Project tape-slide programme *Materials and Instruments.*

5, 6 and 7   Continue making instruments and creating music with them. Improvisation sessions lead to more considered ideas which can be worked up into compositions. Notate/perform. Discussion of ideas – but not too much! Making music is more important than talking about it.

8 and 9   Modifications to existing instruments. Part of a composer's task is to reveal new sound possibilities in established instruments and to 'claim' new areas for expression. How often, in the history of musical instrument making, have new developments been initiated by composers in their need to extend the resources of music? (E.g. viols/violins, harpsichord/pianoforte, John Cage: the 'prepared' piano. It could be helpful to hear extracts from recordings of Cage's *Amores* and *Sonatas and Interludes* (Decca: Head 9). Rehearse and perform *Aquarelle* (prepared piano and 6 percussion players, by Brian Dennis (UE 14646)).

10 and 11   Using instruments made earlier in the term (and/or sound-sources collected for the first three sessions), explore various ways of organising sound-structures, such as:

Aleatory techniques (chance operations determining exactly the nature and timing of the sound events, for example, throwing dice – numbers are made to relate to specific musical functions: pitch/duration/loud-soft).

Indeterminate techniques ('open-form' organisations which offer a framework within which sounds are made with varying degrees of freedom. Something like a game of cards: there the rules provide the framework, and the general pattern and nature of what happens is known, though the precise development of the 'ideas' depends upon the 'performers'). See George Self *New Sounds in Class* (UE 14166) and *Make a New Sound* (UE 26909).

Number patterns as the basis of rhythmic construction (Perform *Crosswords* by Brian Dennis, UE 16044).

12 'Concert' of selected pieces made or rehearsed during the term.

This may well be the point where someone wants to ask 'Where does it all lead?' or 'What has this to do with music as we know it?'. Therefore, before going on to consider the possibilities for term 3, perhaps we should take stock of what it has been our aim to teach so far.

In both terms the priority has been the concepts of *timbre* and *texture*. This is not unreasonable since these are qualities most people notice first about music. This is doubtless because they are the most 'natural' of music's attributes, resembling the sound environment itself, with foreground and background sounds varying in density and quality minute by minute. By contrast, melody is the most artificial, 'un-natural' use of sounds. With the possible exception of bird-song it resembles nothing in nature. As starting topics that can give everyone points of reference they feel at home with, *timbre* and *texture* are particularly suitable. In addition to these qualities, the work in Terms 1 and 2 will have drawn attention to aspects of *rhythm*, *duration* and *pitch*. Some topics introduced in week 8 of Term 2 (e.g. the use of 'sets' of tones in 'prepared' piano music) could form useful jumping-off points for a more detailed look at the concept of *melody*. Above all, the assignments worked in these weeks should have revealed to all pupils the potential for *construction* in the medium of sound. Pupils will have taken their own decisions about how to put sounds together, and discussed between themselves and with the teacher a variety of possible solutions to structural problems. There is nothing high-flown about this. These things are fundamental in music. Whether we are beginners exploring the simplest of sound sources or advanced instrumentalists considering the interpretation of works in the classical repertoire, these same considerations will apply: How do *I/we* think this music should sound? How should it begin, go on, and finish? What possibilities are there from which I can select? Which procedures should I reject as unsuitable? And then – when the general outline of the work is settled – the detailed considerations: what use we should make of dynamics, speed changes, balance of fast music with slow music, and so on. These are all important musical and artistic points but, approached through assignments and topics of the general nature suggested above, they should offer something for everyone, not just the conventionally 'musical' players of orchestral instruments. At the same time, if there are instrumentalists in the group they should be encouraged to make as much use as possible of their talents and their skills.

So, where do we go from here? In Term 3 we could continue with similar projects and with some emphasis on twentieth-century music. Alternatively, we can use the work of the first two terms as an approach to more conventional musical material – if we have not taken this direction already (e.g. as was suggested for Term 1, week 12). By now the pupils will be used to basic notational possibilities. These could be developed to include precisely pitched sounds and rhythmic patterns. The earlier exploration of structures of sounds *in time* (recorded perhaps in proportional notation) can lead to more precise work on duration, pulse and metre. By the end of Term 2 there should be reasonably secure understanding of timbre and texture and this could lead to work on density with pitched sounds (e.g. simple harmony, using chords in various spacings and combinations). As before, it will probably be easiest for the class to work in groups at a variety of assignments, but we may also begin to move towards individual improvisations and compositions (perhaps by way of duos and trios). With this in mind, we can allow the 'workshop' activity to extend over a period of weeks, pupils choosing their own lines of experiment and exploration and following ideas through as far as they can. An emphasis on melody is a useful way of stimulating more *individual* exploration (i.e. as opposed to small-group activity). Thus, the third term's work could be organised in two broad areas (e.g. *melody* and *harmony*):

Term 3 (12 weeks)

1–6 *More advanced work on melody*   Refer back to Term 2 week 8 (i.e. the limitations of working with selected 'prepared' notes on the piano). Selecting materials is essential in any artistic work; it limits the scope of exploration and forces us to expand our ideas within a manageable framework. Melody implies structures of lines of pitched sounds and here the obvious limitations to adopt will be to make 'sets' of pitches; each series of tones having a particular character. So we can experiment with pentatonic patterns, modes (e.g. dorian, aeolian, phrygian, etc.), 12-note rows, major/minor diatonic scales, whole-tone scales, modes of limited transposition (e.g. scales which alternate tones and semitones). Groups and individuals make melodies within the 'frame' of specified note-sets, working always from the sounds (i.e. with a keyboard or glockenspiel or xylophone – these are most suitable because the note-sets are visible and easily understood).

Melody and timbre.   Are some melodies better suited to voice than instrument? What are the characteristics? What kind of melody suits the recorder? The violin? The trombone? (Use whatever instrumentalists are available in the group; encourage others to make what they think are suitable types of melody for these instruments to play. Listen to all melodies made and discuss them in relation to the instruments' characteristics).

General characteristics of melodies   Structures of short phrases or long phrases; repetition and extension; rhythmic/melodic 'figures'; 'jagged'/disjunct; 'smooth'/conjunct; putting two melodic lines together (i.e. simple counterpoint by trial and error with the sounds, not from 'rules'!); melodies that will work in canon.

Listen to recordings of as many different kinds of melody as possible (including pop/rock, blues, non-western musics and European 'art' music from plainsong to the present day). Wherever possible, link what is heard to melodies composed by pupils; discuss the similarities.

Staff notation is, of course, especially relevant to the recording of melodic compositions. There would be plenty of opportunities during this part of the course to teach and to make use of this knowledge. However, the emphasis should always be upon the sounds themselves not the notational signs. Melodies must be played and discussed from the instruments, and notated examples must not be divorced from the sounds. Pupils should be encouraged to make up melodies on instruments, to memorise them and (where necessary) to notate them from memory (but going back to the instrument to play the melody through as often as they wish). It is important to train the imagination *and* the musical memory through first-hand contact with sounds. No-one can learn to imagine sounds (i.e. to 'image' silently in his head) without substantial experience of actual sounds on a musical instrument. And as an essential part of the learning process the composer should play his/her own tunes because this direct contact with the source of the sounds is another aid to aural imagination.

If there is time during this first half of the term, another angle on melodic ideas would be to explore arrangements of existing tunes (e.g. the class learn a song then divide into small groups to work out a variety of ways of presenting the song; making simple percussion or hand-clapping accompaniments, and so on). This raises questions of interpretation; the possibility of giving a version of a well-known melody a special character or style which is the creative contribution of the performer.

7–12 Develop ideas about *texture* and *density* from the work of Terms 1 and 2.

Chords – any group of notes sounded simultaneously; the different effects possible by exploiting the characteristics of certain intervals (e.g. the 'open' sound of chords made entirely of 4ths and 5ths; or the poignant harmony of 'ladders' of 3rds); the intensity and tension of chords in which the notes are very close together (e.g. a cluster of minor 2nds) and the 'relaxed' effect of a very widely spaced chord. Encourage groups/individuals to work with instruments to make short chordal improvisations and compositions exploiting various different characteristics of intervals and spacing.

Primary triads: simple accompaniments to diatonic tunes (using guitar, chordal dulcimer, auto-harp, chord organ, chime-bar groups, etc.). Chordal accompaniments to songs (i.e. development of work on 'arrangement' started perhaps during the first half of term).

Although it is clear that the third term's work would need to include quite a lot of direct teaching of techniques and musical information, it will be most important to keep this in perspective, relating it always to the exploratory work of the pupils. The teacher's principal task is to draw upon the resources of ideas and imagination which the pupils themselves can bring to the work, skills and information providing the facility for the proper realisation of these ideas *as they arise*. A theory about how music works is of no use to someone who does not already 'understand' music or who is not motivated to want to do something musical. At the same time, we must not overlook the fact that skills are themselves often a stimulus to imagination. If the teacher is sensitive to the way in which pupils' ideas are stirring and developing, he can choose suitable moments to 'feed in' particular skills or aspects of technique which will help an embryo idea to grow. The balance between 'direction' and 'domination' is a fine one and calls for careful judgement on the teacher's part. Pupils must be given opportunity to learn to develop their own musical thinking through structures that grow organically from the first ideas. We should be wary of short-cuts which may appear to produce the desired effects speedily but which in reality work against genuine musical understanding. For example, it is tempting to present musical *form* as prefabricated structural models; lines of empty 'carriages' labelled A, B, C, D, each waiting to be filled and then hitched together to make a 'train'. Suggesting to pupils that they can create music by thinking up an 'A' idea and joining it to a second, unrelated 'B' idea may appear to be a good way of producing a musical continuity, but it does not help pupils to get to grips with the more valuable experience of deciding from the substance of a single musical idea how it shall go on in time. To develop that skill the material itself must be the starting point, because form is content not a pre-ordained pattern. This is important whatever the musical style we are using.*

Finally, it must again be said that the outline suggestions made above under the headings Term 1, Term 2 and Term 3 represent only one scheme of work out of literally scores of possibilities. The musical examples chosen for class or small group performance could be drawn from any number of different sources, using ethnic musics, 'popular' musics, and 'art' music both new and old. All music is relevant when it is made to live through the actuality of performance, and provided that it offers suitable starting points from which pupils themselves may explore musical concepts or structural devices; the style matters little. Obviously, it will be helpful if pupils can meet with a wide variety of styles, both European and otherwise.

The importance of motivation

The Project received this *cri de coeur* from a teacher:

> . . . somewhere I must be going wrong. Our children are not enthralled by experimenting with sound. They dismiss it as 'kid's stuff' . . . Classes of 32 uninterested children do not want to play games, but to take part in 'real' tunes and 'real' songs. They are happier singing traditional rounds rather than 'messing about' as they put it. Even with the supposed interest in 'pop' music I cannot get anyone to form a group. On the other hand we are overwhelmed with volunteers for the brass band and orchestra.
>
> You talk of the 90% who are left out – how do we draw them in? They do not want to participate . . .

---

* We can, for example, usefully examine the ways in which structural devices may stimulate musical invention (e.g. melody 'cells' in primitive musics and in Bartók; classical binary, ternary, rondo, sonata; 12-bar blues; medieval isorhythm, *color* and *talea* in the fourteenth century and in music by Peter Maxwell Davies). But the vital question is not 'What ideas can I pour into this form?' but 'What kind of structure will best develop my ideas?'

While one can sympathise with this statement and appreciate the honesty and good intentions behind it, reading between the lines it seems very possible that this teacher initiated the classroom work without a clear picture of what his musical objectives were, and without much conviction that the activities would really lead to musical understanding. We sometimes forget what powerful influences we are! If we really believe that what we are asking children to do is not 'real' or is 'messing about', that unspoken assumption will nevertheless communicate to them. We must be convinced about where the work is leading musically and teach it in the right spirit. The teacher we have quoted clearly has musical 'faith' in his brass band and orchestra, but it would be helpful to know just how 'overwhelming' was the demand to take part in those extra-curricular activities. Presumably it did not involve all that large a number because he goes on to admit that there is a substantial percentage of pupils he would like to 'draw in': those who 'do not want to participate'. Obviously he is anxious to succeed in class with this group; and he *has* tried. The disappointments seem to have arisen from a failure on the part of the teacher to be clear in his own mind about the musical values he was dealing with. There seems also to be a fundamental misunderstanding of working methods and syllabus content. For no-one has suggested that 'real' songs, 'real' tunes, rounds or indeed any specific styles or forms of music should deliberately be omitted. On the contrary, most of the published writing on this approach to music in education makes the point that *all* musical activity is relevant, and all music-making, whatever the musical style, is 'real'. What is irrelevant and manifestly 'unreal' is the so-called music-teaching in which theoretical concepts are taught without reference to musical sounds, or where emphasis is placed upon ways of 'explaining' music other than in terms of musical procedures (e.g. 'Listen to this record and write a description of the pictures that come into your mind'!). We might well regard these things as 'messing about', and it is hardly surprising that pupils become restless and bored by them. They know very well that music is not like that.

These are matters that must be sorted out at the start. The teacher should go into the classroom quite certain of the concepts he is aiming to teach through a carefully planned course. Then he may have more chance of success. As it is, the musical experience of a great many children in schools still gets no further than singing songs (which is an excellent thing to do but limited, even so) and a wall of mystery continues to surround the *cognoscenti*, the 'initiated' of the brass band and the orchestra. Clearly we must do all we can to remove that kind of barrier. As another teacher puts it:

> Breaking down the mystique that generally surrounds music (and which is encouraged by some teachers) is the key to good music teaching.

Of course our choice of material can be wrong but so can the way we present it. If our sights are firmly on what, in *music*, we are trying to teach, then it is up to us to work in ways suitable for our pupils to achieve understanding. But if we have only an imperfect idea of what we are aiming for, or if we are not ourselves wholly convinced about the approach we have adopted as a means through which these ideas can be taught, it will hardly be surprising if things go wrong.

Obviously, it is not enough simply to plan activities. We have also to motivate pupils, making points of contact to evoke responses and cause learning to take place across the whole ability range. We are unlikely to be successful if we cling to a view of 'musical' and 'non-musical' children to whom we offer 'real' music and 'games' respectively. In the end this is a matter of the teacher's attitude and the breadth of his musical understanding every bit as much as the material or the method he adopts. Whatever we do we must know that it is musically valid; and that doesn't have to mean 'musically complicated'. We should also bear in mind that children need time to find out about things for themselves. A comment by one of the Project teachers emphasises this:

> In the first year children need to experiment fully with the sound of voices and instruments . . . the sound must come before the sign . . .

Too strong an instructional bias at the start, with the teacher doing most of the work, will not encourage pupils to take seriously opportunities for self-directed exploration when they are offered. That is bound to arouse suspicion so that the teacher's lack of conviction about the 'free' work comes through. It is so easy to create the impression that the 'real' work is what the teacher *directs* and the experimental work is not serious music-making. But in schools where the pupils' own work is regarded as the key activity, the effect can often be very encouraging; as another teacher writes:

> It is marvellous to see girls who do not think of themselves as musical surprising themselves by their composing and playing.

Instrumental teaching and the general curriculum

It is strictly outside the scope of this book to deal in detail with extra-curricular ensembles (because the Project's brief was to look at music as a classroom subject). Nevertheless, it is impossible to divorce the orchestras, choirs, wind bands, military bands, jazz orchestras, pop and rock bands, early music groups, and so on from the classroom activity – which should, in any case, be the point from which everything else grows. Although membership of these groups will normally be selective, we should try as far as possible to offer a variety of musical opportunities and to make use of these instrumentalists in the classroom work (see also pp. 123–5).

   This is an area of school music which is waiting to be developed. The tendency is for those who play in the out of class ensembles not to contribute with their instrumental skills to class improvisation and composition. There are exceptions which serve as examples of what can be done. The Project's tape-slide programme *Music at Court*, shows how, at Madely Court School, Telford, skilled instrumentalists have been successfully integrated with the general class work. Peripatetic instrumental teachers could also be brought into the class activities, not specifically to teach instrumental skills but perhaps to help with aspects of interpretation. From this a valuable form of team teaching is developed. There are also a number of new possibilities for expanding the variety of musical experience in schools with pupils from ethnic minorities. A Music Adviser writes:

> . . . the most important musical contribution should come from the many different folk traditions represented . . . I am doing all I can to encourage the development and preservation of these and their use in the schools. I have been working on the background to reggae and would like to see a greater knowledge of the whole Jamaican background. This applies to most of the music of different cultures we have represented in this Borough. Ethnomusicology, if it is interpreted properly, can make a contribution to music education perhaps bigger than the one it is making at present.

Steel bands are now a feature of the music-making in some inner urban schools and, at Woodberry Down School in London, Piers Spencer has been able to make significant use of reggae styles (see Vulliamy and Lee, 1980).

   We have already commented on the 'unreality' of so much of what passes for music in class lessons. But there is no doubt about the reality of music-making in the majority of these extra-curricular ensembles. So many are of very high quality, that there should surely be some way in which we could capitalise on this work and let its influence feed back to enrich the general class work for the majority. We have hardly begun to explore the possibilities. For example, music-making in orchestras and bands generally draws young people from across the age range of three, four or more school 'years'. We accept this as one reason why, if these ensembles are to function at all, they must do so outside the timetable – which is built on stratified year-group assumptions. But schools which have a different organisation for music groups so that timetabled music 'classes' are drawn from across a given age range (e.g. 'vertically streamed'; say, years 1–3, years 4–5), make possible all manner of performance sessions, vocal and instrumental, with much greater musical significance than many an average music lesson in a 'normal' class arrangement could ever hope to generate. Not only is it then possible to encourage more youngsters to take up instruments or to enjoy using their voices, but there can be a great deal more scope for peripatetic teachers to work alongside the other music staff and to develop their instrumental teaching in the context of the educational philosophy of the department. At present, in most schools, however hard the music teacher works to increase the scope of the performance ensembles, that part of the programme will almost certainly have to be operated outside the normal class-lesson structure of the timetable, and therefore the majority of pupils will remain untouched by these lively musical opportunities.

Some teachers have made efforts to develop new forms of large ensemble which can involve singers and instrumentalists from the conventional orchestral background as well as guitarists, drummers, pianists, and vocalists from the jazz/pop/rock tradition. An example in this vein, from a school associated with the Project, is the choral and instrumental group founded by Tony Robins at the Sir Leo Schultz School, Hull. Such an ensemble would be ideal for 'vertically streamed' classes on the timetable. At present there is very little published material for such combinations but this would offer scope for student composition, as well as for arrangements and compositions by teachers.

The exercise of imagination, choice and preference is essential to musical experience, and while this is of course possible with very limited sound sources, the educational value of classroom work will clearly be enhanced by expanding the resources available so that more varied combinations of sounds can be used in improvisation groups, and in individual or group composition and performance. It is important to make extensive use of conventional instrumental resources wherever these are available.

Prejudice or misunderstanding

Prejudice is almost impossible to overcome simply by 'putting a case' in writing. It would be wrong to conceal the fact that, in the course of the Project, the response to some of our suggestions, or to our whole approach, has on occasion revealed a lack of sympathy with our aims and methods, which at times has verged on the impolite!

> Such exercises . . . have little relevance in a school where we place importance on musical literacy and on learning to appreciate and enjoy the standard works of established composers . . .

It might, nevertheless, be useful for such critics to review their own positions, even though the step they are being asked to take is a big one; for they are going to step onto territory which, as far as they are concerned, is unexplored. One teacher asks:

> Is fear an important factor? Even for experienced teachers to venture away from convention is difficult.

Books alone will not calm legitimate fear or remove well-rooted prejudice, but progress towards change may be helped if the critics can see and hear what others, who have made the step, actually are doing and saying in the course of their work.

A place for music and *Arrangements*, the Project's two films, and the tape-slide programmes are available through the regional centres (see pp. 235–6). These productions show teachers and pupils engaged in working along the lines advocated by the Project, and discussing their aims and achievements.

Nevertheless, it could be helpful here to clear away some unfortunate misunderstandings. To begin with, an idea we have already touched upon in the sections on planning and motivation: the belief that a curriculum taught on creative principles can be concerned only with twentieth century *avant-garde* music. This is simply not true. Any music from any period could be used. Indeed it is important that we should look at a variety of styles in order to observe the 'generality' of usage.

For example, all *melody* is at root an interest in pitch relationships and the expressive 'shapes' that can be created by lines of tones, disjunct or conjunct. But what makes the differences between a melody by Beethoven and one by Schoenberg? What is distinctive about so many of the Beatles' songs, and in what ways does more recent pop/rock melody differ? What are the features of Indian classical music, or the characteristics that would help us distinguish a tune by Mozart from one by Bach? What are the particular kinds of pitch relationships, intervals and melodic shapes that interested Debussy? What is the relationship between melody and words and melody and harmony in the blues? These are all features which we can examine and which we can try out for ourselves. Examples *could* be taken entirely from earlier periods. It would, nevertheless, be a pity to avoid all reference to music in our own time. Whatever we may think about the directions which twentieth-century music has taken, it is the product of the world in which we live and we should surely be prepared to keep our ears open to what composers today have to say? It is as much a mistake to ignore Cage or Messiaen or rock music as it would be to pretend that Machaut or Bach do not matter. Twentieth-century music has not 'thrown out the baby with the bathwater'. As in many other areas of our culture, the materials and modes of expression have been extended. That does not mean dispensing with what we had previously. There are now more ways of saying things, and what we are hearing in modern music is the 'more' that has been released for us to use and enjoy.

Another common misconception is that a creatively oriented course implies that pupils do nothing other than make up their own music. This is a very restricted view of creativity and one which overlooks the musical activity of performer and listener, both of whom must contribute

imaginatively if music is to 'happen' at all. These points are dealt with
more fully in Chapter 4, but for the moment it may be useful to remind
ourselves that the curriculum can profitably include opportunities for class
ensemble performance of existing music directed by the teacher (who can
thereby indicate his thoughts about interpretation) *and* performance in
which interpretative decisions are taken by the pupils. As with other forms
of creative ability, this work can often be done in small groups so that at
the end of a period of working (a single lesson or a series of lessons) the
groups can listen to each other and discuss points of style and
interpretation. Possibly this may seem a rather 'advanced' activity; but it is
not really so. Groups of school students can tackle relatively simple tasks
of interpretation (e.g. adding a simple percussion accompaniment to a
song) which can be worked in a variety of ways and in which the
performers will need to take their own decisions.

We have mentioned here briefly the major areas of misunderstanding,
but there are others – and it is sad to reflect that gifted musicians in
schools and teacher-training institutions may sometimes allow prejudice to
prevent music from making a bigger impact in education simply because
they are unable to concede that there is more in music than they
themselves have experienced, or that to engage the interest of a wider
audience it is frequently necessary to start with quite simple sound-making
activities and to lead on from there to the complexities of structure and
notation.

Progression

Uppermost in the minds of most of the teachers we spoke to was the
question of *progression* in a syllabus:

> One of the biggest let-downs for children has been, too frequently, a lack of
> *progression* . . . whilst many teachers understand what this means in terms of
> 'theory' or of 'technique', fewer have vision when it comes to composition.
> *Clear and progressive aims* [are essential] . . . all but the most gifted teacher
> need this type of musical O.S. Map.
> Many teachers still find great difficulty in planning their courses over three years,
> especially in relation to the proportion of time to be given to theoretical and
> practical work . . .
> [we need] . . . schemes of work showing development over a year or more . . .

Part of our dilemma may spring from being too strongly influenced by what
we see of other subjects. Education as a whole tends to stress the value of
verbalisation and clearly developed argument. Subjects which rely on a
steady intake of information, with relatively little time devoted to
interpreting or generating ideas, create a powerful model for the whole
curriculum. As a result the arts – which do not operate extensively upon

received information – have either to accept a lowly place in the subject hierarchy or try to bring themselves in line with the 'sequential information' view of a syllabus. Music has suffered more than other arts in this process because, unlike painting, sculpture, or ceramic art – all of which make direct use of their materials – music must wait for performance before it comes to life. For quite a lot of music this will mean first decoding the notation. Although notated music accounts for only a small part of world music, it does include the major masterpieces of our western heritage and therefore we understandably attach some importance to it. This has tempted some of us to emphasise the ancillary skills more than the substance of music itself – perhaps because notation, in spite of being intermediary and one stage removed from the real thing, provides that useful sequence of instruction which brings our subject into line with others (like mathematics) and gives us the academic confidence we need. But are we missing the point? Is this really the kind of progression most likely to foster understanding of an art?

Obviously, notation is important to some musicians – but not to all musicians. Are we tackling things the wrong way round, possibly for the sake of a ready-made syllabus? And could this be, in part at least, because 'Many teachers still find great difficulty in planning their courses . . .'? True, there is so much material from which to select; we cannot cover everything. Added to which we must satisfy both our musical inclinations and our educational commitments. But if we can at least begin with a clear picture of what we think we should be trying to do educationally, the rest should follow without too much difficulty.

For example, if we begin by acknowledging our commitment to all the pupils, then it is essential that the content of our music syllabus aims to meet majority needs. Secondly, since we are musicians and delight in what music offers, we should naturally wish music to be 'justified' in the school curriculum primarily for its artistic qualities. It follows that our ideas for classroom activities will emphasize the feeling, expressive, 'response' aspects of understanding rather more than evaluation based on factual information. The curriculum details then diversify a simple, all-embracing precept such as: 'educating aural perception so that all pupils can discover, through active involvement, how sounds can be used musically'. It is from here, of course, that we have to decide exactly how we shall build in a sense of progression, and what the nature of that progression will be.

As we have seen, it is relatively easy to organise a systematic progression from technical information and theoretical abstractions. But there is a danger that such matter becomes an end in itself. It is often a necessary back-up to musical experience, but musical insight is not the sum of an agreed series of theoretical points. The true rudiments of music are sensitivity to and delight in sound and its expressive qualities, and the *progression* we create must be within this mode of understanding and derived from musical experience itself. In this way musical insight is developed. As Jacques Maritain says in *Education at the Crossroads*,

> I purposely stress this element of *delight* in the grasping of beauty, for delight pertains to the very essence of beauty . . . unless we delight in and are moved by a work of art, we may thoroughly discuss and analyse it but we shall never understand it . . . (Maritain, 1943)

And in 1938 Marion Richardson wrote, in connection with an exhibition of children's art in County Hall in London:

> the artist discovers in the world around him (that is to say, in his raw materials) relationships, order, harmony – just as the musician finds these in the world of sound. This cannot be done by the conscious, scheming, planning mind. Art is not an effort of will but a gift of grace – the simplest and most natural thing in the world. Whenever people are sincere and free, art can spring up.

Obviously children must learn to 'work' their ideas and material and to build coherent and satisfying structures. But it would be misguided to organise a programme of analysis and information in the hope that these things will automatically synthesize in the pupils' minds.

It is clear that 'progress' in musical understanding involves something rather different from progress in subjects based primarily upon information. Continuing the train of thought from Marion Richardson, we might compare the continuity of class music work with the 'progress' made by a painter or a sculptor. A retrospective exhibition of his work would undoubtedly reveal progression but not necessarily a growing complexity or even evidence of the artist having acquired more theoretical knowledge than he had in his early years. Instead we would most likely notice the way in which the artist followed various lines of thought, responding afresh to stimuli, exploring new ways of working with his materials and developing techniques to meet new problems. Piaget wrote that education should help us to do *new* things, not just to mimic the past; it should make us adventurers and discoverers. And that is the essence of artistic working; exploring the potential of materials with imagination, skill and sensitivity, to reveal new meanings and relationships. Art yields insight and we make progress by continuing to look for new possibilities within our materials.

The key to progress in an art is the connection between exploration and construction (and in music 'construction' includes interpretation and performance of existing music). This is not a rule-directed process in which structures are made by applying formulae. The structure ('form') rests principally upon what we feel the materials can do. Therefore it is an essential first step to experiment with various possibilities (in music this will involve improvisation) so that not only do we discover the potential of the ideas but we are also able to assess the kind of techniques needed to control the medium and solve the 'problem'. Musical structures are made by making ideas 'go on' in time with appropriate balance of unity and variety to give coherence to the piece as a whole and maintain interest for the listener. A simple maxim to work by is that in music anything is possible so long as it doesn't bore the listeners! If ideas (which may be melodies, textures, chord sequence, rhythm patterns, etc.) wander or seem unconnected; or are insufficiently developed so that the piece is too short and doesn't seem to have much to say; or if they are over-developed so that it is far too long – the listener's attention will wander. There is no sovereign remedy for such miscalculations; no rule that can be applied to ensure success. The only thing to do is to go on working at more and more ideas, weighing carefully the results when they are presented to an audience and learning to assess new problems in the light of the earlier experience. This applies as much to interpretation and arrangement as it does to original composition. Each new work (or each fresh performance of a piece already known) should involve a re-thinking of the music in the light of experience gained.

In the classroom the teacher's task is to help pupils make the all-important evaluations of their work so that they are aware of the successes *and* the miscalculations. Obviously we should expect them to learn new techniques and acquire points of information that will assist them in further work, but the real progress will be measured by the extent to which they are able to use an increasing diversity of musical ideas with confidence. To this end we should emphasise the *structuring* process. Some teachers allow the exploratory, improvisation stage to go on too long; pupils lose their sense of purpose and quickly become bored.

If the work is based on musical concepts, we could reasonably expect an accumulative effect as the course proceeds, so that, for example, what is learned from discussing structures resulting from work on rhythm will carry over into work on melody. Although that part of the course dealing with melody will, in the main, look at various uses of sequential pitched sounds, there could be reference back to rhythmic structures and, by 'adding' pitch, these could now be used as starting points for melodic pieces.

Returning to our analogy with the working life of the professional artist and the way in which he makes 'progress'; apart from the stimulus of everyday things seen, heard or read about, he will to a large extent be influenced by what other artists have done and are doing. So he will make it his business to know what is going on in the world of art around him and to relate this to what he knows and can discover about art in earlier times. He does not *copy* the methods of earlier artists – because his business is to assert *new* ideas – but he will not ignore them. Exactly the same thing could be happening for young people in school, the teacher relating ideas generated and developed by pupils to the wider world of music past and present. We can learn from our colleagues in English teaching about these techniques. For example, David Holbrook in his book *Children's Writing* (Holbrook, 1967) – a book which, incidentally, should be read carefully by every school *music* teacher – has this to say:

> another important factor is the continual enrichment of the child's experience of literature. Sometimes I hear from enthusiastic young teachers who have gone crazy on creative work. They've kept the children at it for weeks: the pupils have suddenly 'gone off'. No wonder – they'd done nothing else! The poor little things were quite exhausted. The teacher had put nothing back. Creative work can't be all giving: and so children need to hear poems and stories read to them – and if it is possible, what the teacher reads should be *related to current themes in their work, and current interests shown in it.*
>
> Of course, this 'matching' needs to be done sensitively, governed by an understanding of the deeper implications of a child's work, not its mere explicit meaning. (p. 15)

For 'poems and stories read' we can, of course, substitute 'music played and sung'. Pupils' progress in understanding how music works, and what they can do with it, will grow with the realisation that their efforts are part of the continuing stream of human creative endeavour and that other composers have tried in similar ways to control the expressive medium of sound. Moreover, many of the things which prompt the imagination of musicians are universal themes with which mankind has grappled for centuries. It is obviously useful to know that composers in past generations have worked with these themes, and useful for us to hear their music and relate it, if possible, to the social context in which it first appeared. How do these same themes stand today in relation to present society? What differences will this (should this) make to *our* exploration of the same ideas? Historical perspective in music is valuable, particularly where it can be related to the present. But we should beware the temptation to use musical examples only as models to be copied. Again, David Holbrook:

> It is not mere vocabulary we wish to develop – but perception and the capacity to explore and organise experience, from inward sources, symbolically . . . This can be set off by outward stimuli: but the stimulus must be left to provoke a unique response from each child (since each child will bring to it a different capacity for perception, and a different need to symbolise) . . . (pp. 19, 20)

And he concludes by reminding us that an approach which seeks to force all children into the same pattern will only produce insincerity in their work.

Writing poetry is necessarily an individual activity. Music, on the other hand, has more obvious social connotations, and can be the outcome of either individual or group working (e.g. jazz and rock groups; Indian classical musicians; Balinese gamelan players – all of whom invent music in group composition). Either way, it is as true for the making of music as it is for poetry or any other art that whoever does it organises not only the materials, shaping them into controlled and coherent forms, but in a deep and subtle sense organises his/her own experience, making sense of thoughts and feelings by way of the medium of sound. (cf. Samuel Butler, *The Way of All Flesh*: 'Every man's work, whether it be literature or music or pictures or architecture or anything else, is always a portrait of himself'.) It is obviously extremely difficult for anyone (even the person most directly involved) to assess what kind of 'progress' this represents. It is, nevertheless, at the heart of musical experience and we gain nothing musically or educationally by scoffing at it or pretending it is unimportant because seemingly it cannot be tested and evaluated in exactly the same way as the acquisition of factual knowledge.

Music in the classroom cannot be separated from music outside the school, and our experiences in that wider world should remind us that there are forms of progress other than 'onwards and upwards'. Not everything in music can be calculated to 'work' on every occasion. Therefore we should not be too afraid of failure. It will not follow that, because we have acquired certain skills, we shall automatically find the best solutions to problems of expression and structure in composition or improvisation, or to problems of interpretation in performance. We are not concerned with systematic or scientific processes but with ways of working which encounter and deal with the unexpected *as the work goes on*. Some attempts will be unproductive and will have to be abandoned in favour of different lines of approach. But we should not regard this as wasted effort. In the arts nothing can happen by remote control. Every act of music-making calls for a constant and lively exercise of the imagination, but imagination is not an automatic pilot. We set ourselves problems and we use skill *and* sensitivity to solve them. It is important that students understand this: they are involved with a process of trial and error and there is bound to be the occasional cul-de-sac.

Naturally enough, for pupils in school, too much failure is depressing and discouraging. The teacher must be ready to help them over the most crucial difficulties. Nevertheless, for a proper understanding of how music works they should learn to encounter problems and find what they consider to be the best solutions. Teachers who are used to the directing role in music-making sometimes find this aspect of class music work difficult to cope with, and as a result they may take refuge in more conventionally progressive schemes of factual information.

We can look for progress in pupils' grasp of musical concepts. Also we can reasonably expect that, as far as the invention of music is concerned (and that includes arrangement as well as original composition), what begins as group improvisation will, for some at least, be developed over the years to a point where individuals are making compositions and arrangements for various combinations of voices and instruments in small groups, whole-class ensembles or the extra-curricular ensembles. Progress in such work can be evaluated, though not with the same instruments of assessment we would use for other disciplines (see pp. 174 *et seq.* and 215 *et seq.*). Further than this, we should hope to see pupils' interests in music of all kinds growing, and influencing the work they do in the classroom. Even among 'A' level music students regrettably few at present seem able to produce evidence of an expansion in musical interests that is the result of their own initiative; that is, exploration away from the paths laid down for them by the examination syllabus.

Ultimately progression in a music curriculum rests as much upon the attitude of the teacher as upon the things taught. Musicality cannot be judged simply by demonstrating factual knowledge. All over the world there are musicians of skill and insight who 'know' very little beyond their own ability to conjure out of the air expressive patterns of sound. In the end this is surely what we are all aiming for whether we approach it by way of naïve intuition or specialist instruction. A mixed-ability class of Secondary School pupils will almost certainly contain a wide spectrum of musical response. We shall be out of touch with reality if we try to channel it in a single direction. Our task is primarily to lay the right kinds of foundation and, as we have already observed, to educate aural perception so that pupils will be able to discover for themselves the significance of musical experience. No-one else can discover it for them, though we can try to identify the skills they need in relation to what they want to do. Progress thereafter depends upon our willingness to provide the right kind of help at the right moment.

In the Project's tape-slide programme *Music in Inner Urban Schools*, Alan Renshaw (Islington Green School, London) sums up his thoughts about where the music curriculum should lead and the kind of progression he expects in a comprehensive school:

> I feel that a teacher is a catalyst; a kind of reference book. And I think the key to successful teaching in any subject is to stimulate the young people to start thinking for themselves, and to use the experiences and the energies of the particular teacher to release their own potential.

A balanced curriculum

The Project has frequently been urged to provide not only guidelines but a detailed set curriculum: a 'balanced' curriculum. Without balance, it would seem, one is liable to 'go overboard'! Unfortunately there is considerable disagreement about exactly what is 'a balanced music curriculum'. For some there is a fear that essential things may be left out; a thorough course in musical theory, it is argued, will provide the best background. Others see skills such as literacy and instrumental techniques on one side of the scales with 'knowledge and appreciation of musical forms', all balanced against but never meeting with 'creative experiment'. Another group believes that methodology which emphasises practical creative music-making can only work at the expense of everything we once regarded as important. As we shall see, this view may arise from a misunderstanding of some recent developments. It is also partly the outcome of a tendency in many of us (born perhaps out of our musical training) to ignore the wealth of new musical experience which is now available. If a school course includes a high proportion of things not in the curriculum when we were students, there will undoubtedly be those who regard it as 'unbalanced'. Is it possible, then, for a 'balanced' curriculum to cope with change?

This is plainly an area of much heart-searching. Teachers' questions reveal uncertainty and a desire for guidance:

> Examples of various creative curriculum structures balanced with more traditional methods – must it be all or nothing?
>
> Does the subject require the acquisition of essential knowledge? If so, what?
>
> Does the subject require the acquisition of essential skills? If so, what?
>
> I felt there was little to be learned from it [a programme of creative experiment] . . . we place importance on musical literacy.
>
> What importance should be attached to:
>   literacy
>   singing
>   learning to sing
>   listening to music of established composers
>   improvisation and other creative work
>   instrumental techniques?
>
> Should the teacher attempt to offer a balanced diet by including all aspects of music, or trying to; or should he feel free to stress his own particular interests/strengths, perhaps to the exclusion of other matters?
>
> What is the relationship between 'creative/experimental techniques' . . . and literacy, traditional instrumental techniques, singing, music from the past, knowledge and appreciation of musical form?
>
> . . . emphasise the importance of a balanced diet in any musical curriculum . . . moderation in taking up new ideas is essential . . . new should not necessarily throw out all of the old . . .

At root the problem is 'How do we cover the ground?' Yet no-one could fail to be aware of the enormous explosion that has taken place in every field of knowledge. It would be impossible now to construct a school course – or even a university course – that covered every aspect of a single discipline. Of course, the teacher who asks if he should 'offer a balanced diet *including all aspects of music*', if pressed on that point, would no doubt wish to qualify it. 'All aspects' within an agreed frame of priorities, perhaps? But how do we define the priorities? And will they be the same for every school? Should we take it for granted that a course will be balanced if it concentrates upon European music alone? Can we really afford to ignore the vast range of world musics and the influences they have exerted upon our culture? We have commented above upon the growing number of schools with multi-ethnic intake. In those circumstances it would certainly be inappropriate for a course to imply by its content that the European tradition was more important than other musical traditions, many of them much older than our own.

We cannot do everything; we have to select. What we select will reflect our own enthusiasms, but it should also demonstrate our understanding of the musical interests and potential of our pupils. Music will never be a viable curriculum subject if its appeal is limited, and it will not become 'balanced' by concentrating upon topics and techniques meaningful only to the pupils having instrumental lessons. There would be little point in insisting that everyone learned to read staff notation unless we could be sure of providing opportunities for them all to use it. So often when 'literacy' is an objective in itself, the instrumentalists shine (for obvious reasons) and the others are quickly marked down as 'non-musicians'. So much for balance!

It is perhaps unwise to think of the music curriculum too definitely in terms of such things as 'singing', 'literacy', 'appreciation', 'creative work', etc. Balance is not achieved by seeing that all the recognised and accepted (or acceptable or fashionable) bits have been included, but rather by a unifying principle which will release musical potential in various directions and still ensure a general grasp of musical concepts.

Inevitably there will be some who will find this far too vague! One teacher urged us strongly to avoid 'idealistic phrases which are hardly practical'. But we cannot ignore the subjective core of music-making. Were it entirely a matter of objective facts it would never become music. Regrettably some people do try to teach music as though it were a science. Words are inadequate to describe what musicians feel but that does not mean that sensitivity is a myth. Creative thinking *is* practical. There is, for example, no division between 'creative experiment' and 'music from the past', as one of the teachers quoted on page 64 suggests, because 'music from the past', like any other music, is the result of creative enterprise and can only be understood in such terms. If we have had some experience, however humble, of taking decisions about how sounds can be put together to make music, we shall be in a better position to understand the composer's task. If we wish to, we can then begin to examine the various ways in which composers of different historical periods have worked on their own sound structures, and to explore (if possible through performance) the influences that produce differences in musical style.

It is unfortunate that some teachers appear to regard developments in music education over the past twenty years as an 'unbalancing' opposition to the valued and 'balanced' established curriculum. In fact, the so-called 'new' proposals are really nothing more than a re-affirmation of the art of music itself. If the established and 'traditional' curriculum seems to be threatened by the new approaches, this must be because the traditional methodology has avoided commitment to realistic musical experience for all but a minority of 'musical' pupils. That, it could be argued, is an indication of '*un*balance' in traditional practice.

A balanced curriculum is certainly desirable, and the conceptual approach could be the answer. For example, the concept of *melody* offers pupils the chance to sing, to improvise and compose melodies of their own, to listen to all kinds of melodies by other composers, and to learn about pitch notation so that they can write down their own tunes and play others on whatever instruments are available. In every case, these activities could be organised so that musical decisions would be taken by the pupils themselves and a variety of musical styles could be explored. Some of the work might be done in small groups, other assignments could be tackled individually. Several different things might happen simultaneously. At appropriate points, groups and individuals would share with one another the music they had been working on, and the teacher would discuss the results with the whole class. The work could be arranged so that all pupils would at some stage tackle all the assignments (singing, listening, playing from and writing notation, improvising and composing). Alternatively, planning could assign certain tasks to groups and individuals so that not everyone did everything. The breadth of experience would then come through the 'sharing' part of the session.

To achieve a balanced curriculum we must be sure that we are looking at the right things. The choice of this or that material for class use; whether to retain or abandon 'theory'; how much singing or listening to music on gramophone records we should include; whether we should use classroom instruments, orchestral instruments, guitars or kazoos – or whether we should abandon all these things and buy a synthesizer? These may appear to be the important practical issues, though they are in fact secondary matters. Any or all of them could find a place within a programme of lively musical experience which has something to offer to everyone. On the other hand, they can just as easily be channelled into a routine type of instruction that is ultimately unimaginative and unmusical because it ignores the responses, feelings and choices of the pupils themselves. The really crucial consideration is the overall musical and educational aim: that will provide the framework into which we can fit suitable activities.

Making it work: a matter of conviction

Understandably, many of us are inclined to think of curriculum content in terms of what 'works'. But it is no use grasping at straws of new things to *do* simply because the old stand-bys seem to have failed. For example, electronic sound sources and the range of possibilities in electro-acoustic music will certainly offer a new world of sound which may initially excite our pupils. But this will not 'work' any better than 'singing' or 'musical appreciation' if we are not ourselves utterly convinced about it as music, and about its value within the educational process. If we think of music principally as 'things to be taught' there can be no guarantee that anything, new or old, will 'work', since to regard music as little more than a body of information is to sidestep completely the question of what it is that music really does for us. There is no point whatsoever in abandoning anything simply for the sake of introducing a fashionably 'new' or 'modern' alternative, if we can already say with complete conviction that our programme offers genuine musical experience to all pupils. Electronic music is in no way superior to class singing or recorder-playing, nor is it 'better' than Bach. But if the content of the music curriculum is pitched in such a way that only a minority of pupils can respond to it with ideas of their own, then perhaps we should question our attitude to music as an education, and out of that questioning devise a more suitable approach so that music will be able to prove itself a real force in the curriculum.

Part 2 : Organisation

In the preceding discussion of curriculum content it was necessary, from time to time, to refer to classroom organisation. Content and organisation are virtually inseparable. Indeed, one experienced teacher and Music Adviser has suggested that there is something to be said for considering organisation before content:

HOW	then WHAT	and lastly WHY
(organisation, role of the teacher, etc.)	(content)	(philosophy)

and he goes on to say:

> As much help as possible should be given to *teaching techniques* including modes of organisation and operation of classroom activities . . . [which] . . . open up possibilities for content seen by many hitherto as unworkable.

This is perfectly true. Teachers have been known to dismiss suggestions for a new approach to class music on the grounds that they would find it impossible to organise, and attempts to introduce new material have sometimes failed because teachers assumed that methods suitable to one type of music-making would automatically be appropriate for every other kind of music activity. Teachers who introduce a 'workshop' approach in the classroom are sometimes worried about their own role; have they become superfluous? Should they see themselves primarily as technicians who are there to make sure the equipment is available, plugged in and working? What about their teaching/directing function? And problems can arise if a teacher's methods are noticeably different from those of his colleagues or from the general assumptions about method within that school.

These and other organisational questions affect not only *how* we teach music but to an important extent they also interact with decisions regarding *what* we shall or can teach in given circumstances. In this section we shall examine class-music organisation from a number of angles, and wherever possible attempt to answer specific questions that have been raised by teachers.

Image and influence: the Director of Music

One of the anomalies of the music teacher's position is the way in which he is often expected to be educator, conductor and impresario all rolled into one. This legacy from the Independent School tradition has been one of the most powerful influences upon the organisation of music in maintained secondary schools. Even the most forward-looking newly established comprehensive school may find it difficult to be entirely free from the pressure of that tradition. Today it is no doubt often a case of some having 'greatness thrust upon them' which could actually be a hindrance. But whatever the teacher himself may feel about being placed in this special category (did we ever have 'Directors' of French or Geography?), the existence of the title – so widely applied in schools – and the image that it projects, has had a strong influence upon class music teaching and upon teacher-training.

To begin with it determines the priorities for the teacher. He has been apppointed to 'direct music'; to organise the school orchestra, to put on concerts, to work primarily for the school's public image. Having to live up to this responsibility can sometimes affect attitude to general music class teaching. Hence the weakness of much that passes for music in the traditional curriculum such as talks to the whole class about standard repertoire works, followed up by dictated notes and interspersed with blocks of 'theory' teaching taken from a ready-made 'rudiments' syllabus to be tested at regular intervals. Not only is such a curriculum frequently the outcome of the 'Director of Music' emphasis but, because the teacher will need to convince himself that, notwithstanding his main commitment to the extra-curricular work, what he does in class *is* worthwhile, it automatically blocks any progress towards a pupil-centred method. Pupil-participation is likely to be no more than the occasional theory test of homework notes handed in for marking. A teacher who sees his job so strongly in terms of 'giving out': of directing, organising and instructing may find it difficult to accept that his pupils could be more musically, more creatively involved in these class lessons.

It would appear that some courses of teacher preparation give priority in their Music Method programmes to training the 'director' skills (orchestral and choral conducting) and, perhaps because time is short, are unable to give students adequate help in preparation for general music class teaching. It is not entirely clear whether this order of priority is a conscious choice on the part of the institutions concerned – because they feel that music education in schools should address itself primarily to minority interest extra-curricular music-making – or if it is simply a recognition of a state of affairs in the schools; a situation which, for better or worse, has to be 'serviced'. Either way, this is an example of organisational emphasis which conditions teaching method and, ultimately the content of the music curriculum.

We are not implying here that the preparation of music teachers should ignore conducting skills. Far from it; knowing how to direct ensembles is an important part of the teacher's professional equipment and will in any case be needed in class work. What is being questioned is the advisability of teacher-training placing emphasis upon certain techniques in such a way that the curriculum offered to the large mass of school pupils may be affected detrimentally. For in the last analysis it is the teacher's *attitude* that is being trained, and if we train directors, they will of course direct.

The music lesson as the core of school music activity

If we accept that a school teacher's basic obligation is to contribute to the education of all the pupils, then it is reasonable to see the classroom and the general music lessons as the point from which everything else will grow. An exciting programme of music-making in the classroom will stimulate interest in the extra-curricular activities which may easily increase in scope and diversity beyond the conventional school orchestra and choir. Here, for example, Grenville Hancox, a teacher closely involved with the Schools Council Project, describes the broad aims of his course at Madeley Court School (see tape-slide programme, *Music at Court*):

> What we do is to ensure that, from the beginning of their secondary school experience, the children are involved in making music together. We've arranged pieces so that, right from the start, if there are twenty-five people in a class,

twenty-five individuals will contribute to an overall effect . . . it's important that children should be able to express themselves through the use of an instrument . . . therefore they should have *some* working knowledge – not necessarily a great virtuoso degree of skill – on that instrument . . . they should know how to produce three chords, four chords, or how to blow a few notes . . . Then we use those skills to re-create music . . . folk songs . . . pop material . . . blues. And then . . .those two things coming together – the skills being acquired and the experience of re-creating other people's music – into creating their own music. But there is no formal instruction other than *the music staff going round from group to group in the room*, just helping the children on their particular project that they've got in tow at the time.

Grenville Hancox's lower school course sows seeds which grow into a wide variety of musical experience both inside and outside the classroom, aiming always to involve the majority of pupils. The classroom band is a central feature, working from musical arrangements with very flexible instrumentation to cater for whatever resources and players are in the room:

We have produced and put together a booklet called 'Music at Court' . . . a progressive and graded collection of pieces, of ideas, of improvisational pieces that go through the first three years . . .

Thus, while some pupils enter Secondary school having had previous instrumental experience (they may, for example, know a few guitar chords), others will be complete beginners. The 'Music at Court' arrangements take that into account. The first piece is a version of an Israeli folk-song. It is set in E minor. Those who know the E minor chord on the guitar can strum it throughout; beginners can join in plucking just the top and bottom strings. They can quickly be set to work to practise that in a steady 4-time pulse, and attention directed next to the players of xylophones. They will find notes E and B and be given a rhythm pattern to practise. Similarly, perhaps, with a pupil sitting at the piano. Descant recorders with, may be, an elementary clarinetist or trumpeter, can be encouraged to play the tune or – if they don't yet know enough of the notes – to make up an E and B ostinato. They can practise their part while a percussion group is set to work with a rhythm pattern based on the words of the song: '*Zum* gali gali gali, *Zum* gali ga-li'. The technique is for the teacher to move quickly from one group to another, setting each one a specific but simple task to practise. After not more than five or ten minutes, the group work is stopped and under the teacher's direction the class begins putting the piece together, perhaps starting with the strummed E minor chord and adding gradually, group by group, until the melody is finally played and sung above the accompaniment.

From such simple beginnings it is possible to move to more elaborate pieces in which there is also scope for the pupils themselves to have some say in 'how it should go' – in other words, to take decisions about interpretation. The important thing is that, with this pattern of organisation, everyone can be involved, whatever their current levels of attainment. Grenville Hancox has found that making class work the central feature of the course from the start has paid dividends in the variety of music-making that has developed among the older pupils:

> In the 4th and 5th years there is an 'open door': we're encouraging children to come in to carry on playing, making music, composing music together . . . From this there seems to come out an incredible amount of responsibility on the part of the pupils . . . Of the present 5th year group – a large one – 35/40 pupils – there is none that I wouldn't be able to send off to any part of this building to work by themselves for an hour and then come back and produce a piece.

Working initially in very difficult circumstances, and without purpose-built music facilities, the class work at Madeley was developed through small-group activities derived from the instrumental group organisation of the classroom band. As pupils moved up through the school and grew accustomed to working together independently of the teacher, it became more and more possible to deploy groups in odd corners, stair wells, and so on around the area allocated for music. The teacher could then move from group to group, offering advice and asking questions that would lead the work on. At a suitable point, or at a pre-arranged time, everyone could meet together in the main room to share the results of their group work. The vital thing is for the teacher to be there when he is needed, but not to inhibit:

> For children who haven't got natural ability it's a process of constant reinforcement and constant encouragement . . .

Although the class work is backed up by a well organised instrumental teaching programme –

> . . . there is ample opportunity after school, in break time, in dinner times for children to have lessons in woodwind, brass and so on . . . all children have the opportunity to extend their musical activities.

– the music curriculum is designed to encompass all levels of attainment; it is not geared solely to the high flyers:

> Some children develop at an incredible rate; others develop less quickly. But they all deserve, and all get, the same amount of encouragement . . .

As another teacher has written about working in this way:

> We should expect a wide range of standards and not be disappointed when no-one produces a masterpiece.

The Madeley Court School course had produced some outstanding musical work in the upper school, including a lively approach to examination opportunities in a Mode 3 CSE course run side by side with 'O' level. But perhaps the most impressive achievement is the way in which the class work, based on majority participation, has developed pupils' ability to take an interest in a variety of music at varying levels of accomplishment.

> . . . if it leads them on to showing the same degree of perception and sympathy that they show to their own compositions and other people's compositions here in school; if they can take that attitude and listen to other composers' music – classical composers, or Stockhausen, or baroque music – and apply the same sort of critical approach, then we may be on the way to achieving some progress . . .

Grenville Hancox is conscious of the gulf that exists between his priorities for music in school and the demands of most examining boards:

> . . . my internal battle is trying to do both: to ensure that there is the ability to be creative first and foremost, and to try to run alongside this the syllabus of university boards, which are totally unrelated to the work that we're doing . . . to try to match the two is very difficult . . .

Out of this dilemma and the determination not to sacrifice the 'music for the majority' approach, grew a Mode 3 CSE syllabus in which pupils could demonstrate

> . . . that, like pictorial artists, they're working in a medium they can *show* they understand . . . [There is] no requirement to show historical knowledge, but the chance to submit tapes of their own work, to submit instruments that they've made themselves, or anything to do with the actual creation of music rather than the 'biographical' side of it . . .

Breaking down the dividing line between 'the examination group' and general class music is clearly an important part of a programme such as this. At Belper High School in Derbyshire, Stephen Johns has developed a plan to deal with the needs of both groups (see tape-slide programme, *Creative Music Workshop, years 4–6*):

> I have my suspicions about 'O' level, like many teachers, but I'm not totally against it because I think a number of people get quite a lot out of it. What we try to do is to think of the middle and upper year as a *mainstream course* . . . we don't think about CSE and 'O' level: we just think, 'We're going to do music'. We have classes of about 20 – the largest about 26 – and they are mixed-ability classes: they contain pupils of the complete ability spectrum. What we try to do is to give them a mixture of creative music situations. For instance you may have some people who have a fairly lively imagination anyway, and who will be able to use this in making an interesting piece of music. Likewise you've got some people who've got a ready sense of what 'ordinary' music is about – the relationship of one chord to another comes easily to them – and they have a generally developed harmonic sense. So they would be encouraged to do pieces that develop that aspect.
>
> At the other end of the spectrum you've got a lot of people who are going to have trouble with any sort of creative work: they need the sense of achievement,

but they've got problems about actually co-ordinating their ideas. If you give them a fairly traditional piece to make up, something for instance involving chords and tunes, they're going to have problems. They need support in the simple matter of organising themselves and organising material and stirring their imaginations.

Stephen Johns' organisation of whole classes is also built around the small-group principle. The more able pupils will probably group themselves together and work at assignments independently, so that the teacher can give more of his attention to those needing most help. For the less able it may be a matter of showing them some simple guitar chord-shapes and encouraging them to work in pairs; one strumming the chords while the other, by a process of trial and error, invents a tune to go above the chordal accompaniment. To begin with, the melody is likely to follow the harmony fairly closely, but a little more independence and adventure can be developed by encouraging the player on the melody line to 'make a tune that does not always follow the chords but sometimes goes its own way'. Once the two players have been started, they will need to be left to explore their own ideas, but the teacher must visit them from time to time during the lesson to help them keep their work in focus. A nice sense of timing and balance is needed here. The teacher should help the pupils to avoid the kind of meandering which would ultimately cancel out their effort and produce nothing of real substance. At the same time he must encourage them to explore in order to get the ideas flowing:

> You won't let the ideas flow unless you churn out a lot of rubbish as well . . .

At the heart of any creative activity there are decisions to be taken. Even with the simplest material it is a process of selection and rejection. That takes time; it also implies a need for work spaces – practice rooms, corridors, vestibules, cloakroom spaces, and so on – where pupils can go in groups of anything from two to six to work out their ideas. This is not always possible and groups may have to work together in a school hall or a large classroom:

> You're going to have lots of separate people doing separate things within one class, and we try to organise it so that it isn't too chaotic. You can do it with, say, two or three main streams of work going on – somebody doing some work with tape recorders, somebody listening to music, some making up pieces. *Group work is the essential factor.*

And when it comes to certain purely factual elements of 'O' level study, Stephen Johns has a simple answer:

> We reckon that the people doing 'O' level ought to spend half their time on mainstream work and half their time on 'O' level work. But a lot of 'O' level consists in knowing your stuff about a Mozart symphony so the stuff to be known can be dealt with *on a worksheet and a tape.*

All this obviously calls for very detailed planning: worksheets and tapes won't prepare themselves! But Stephen Johns is clear about his priorities (and therefore about the type of organisation that is needed to make them work): the course must be able to cope with the entire ability range and it must be based on creative principles:

> . . . the first simple value is that there is something very important in doing something yourself . . . [i.e. for the pupil]. But more than that, I think there's a payoff because if you involve yourself in exploring music, you become much more aware of what music is and what it's about. And in addition to that, I think you become much more aware of a new set of possibilities; you're on a road to new things rather than constantly going over a series of techniques. You've opened doors that could lead you anywhere.

Keith Sedgebeer (Finham Park School, Coventry) is another teacher who has found worthwhile and sometimes unexpected benefits arising from class work that brings 'examination' and 'non-examination' pupils together (see tape-slide programme *Creative Music Workshop, years 4–6*):

> We offer an 'A' level course and two General Studies courses at VIth form level . . . We find that the so-called non-musicians (in that they are not Grade VIII pianists or Grade VIII horn players) mix together very happily with the specialist musicians. The specialist musicians are able to show the 'non-musicians' certain possibilities; the 'non-musicians', however, very often have fewer preconceived ideas about music, and are able quite often to throw light in a different way on a given topic.

For this group a general music course was organised concentrating upon techniques and stylistic elements in the work of several twentieth-century composers, notably Penderecki, Berio, Stockhausen, Messiaen and Boulez. Together the students worked at improvisations based on some of the stylistic trends observed, and developed their ideas into a joint composition which also involved work with sound transformation by means of tape-recorders.

Finham Park School has a very healthy out-of-class music programme: a large orchestra and other 'traditional' ensembles. But the musical energy is generated first in the class work.

For these teachers (and others who work in this way) decisions about method and the organisation are the outcome of a determination to make music available to everyone. The curriculum content follows and brings with it detailed organisational problems which have to be solved. In the end it comes down to clear planning: 'If I do this, what will happen? What shall I need to do as a result of that?' And so on.

Small-group 'workshops'

> . . . novel methods of organisation open up possibilities for content seen by many hitherto as unworkable.

Even so, taking the plunge is never easy:

> How do I begin to involve so many children in one mixed-ability group in one session?

Having asked that question, perhaps the next thing to ask ourselves is 'What would I expect a mixed-ability group to produce?' To which the answer must surely be 'Lots of different thing, or the same thing at different levels of attainment'. One way or another this suggests an organisation that allows individuals or groups to work at their own pace. The word 'involve', in the original question, is a key factor. This teacher clearly sees the need to ensure that there is something everyone *can* do. Projects and assignments are often pitched at too high a level so that the most able get through the work quickly but others are left mystified (or bored).

As we have already seen, one answer is the *classroom band*: individuals and small groups being set to practise parts that are directly related to their technical ability. That is to say, we begin where they – the pupils – are, and we start with arrangements which use only what they can do (open strings; first position; descant recorder left hand only; drum rhythms which can be quickly memorized; etc. together with more advanced parts for those who have had some previous ensemble experience). Pieces tackled in this way should be arranged so that only a small amount of practice time is needed on the separate parts (7–10 minutes maximum) and the whole group can quickly be gathered to start putting the piece together. If too much time is spent on the first stage the musical impetus will be lost. It is important to generate interest quickly in those features which are central to a musical experience – in the case of a band this is the excitement of *ensemble*; of contributing to the perfection of the whole piece. We should keep that in mind throughout, and aim to leave the class at the end with a feeling of achievement through ensemble playing.

From beginnings like this we can move on to small group arrangements in which several groups of five or six pupils each work at pieces allocated to them: spending now rather more time on rehearsal; taking decisions about interpretation wherever possible; the teacher advising group by group as necessary, and all the groups performing to each other at the end of the lesson period or at certain points during the term. This can, of course, include voices as well as instruments. The teacher will probably find it necessary to make arrangements of his own, at least to start with, but there are a number of useful publications available.

Another possibility (which could grow out of or run alongside the classroom band ideas) might be some form of experimental activity leading to improvisation and group composition. Here the most satisfactory solution is generally to choose one topic which can be worked on in various ways, simple and complex. The basis of the idea is explained to the whole class in the first few minutes of the lesson. This might include a brief demonstration of some of the possibilities but it should not be so developed that it leaves no real opportunity for the pupils' own experiment. A suitable topic might be a very simple technical idea, such as *long sounds and short sounds* (and the corresponding long and short silences). The teacher could start by drawing attention to the way in which some sound sources (e.g. blocks of wood, struck with beaters) will produce sounds which are 'sharp' and which cut off almost as soon as the sound is made. Others, (e.g. glass or pottery or suspended metal, struck) produce sounds which will go on ringing if we let them. [See also George Self, *New Sounds in Class*, London, Universal Edition 1967 (pp. 11–15) for a systematic exploration of sustaining and non-sustaining sound sources.]

This brief introduction could lead straight into a general exploration of sound sources by the whole class, to discover for themselves, in a specified time – say 3–5 minutes – as many different short sounds and as many different 'long' (i.e. self-sustaining) sounds as possible from any objects in the room. Conventional musical instruments could be included if necessary. A further possibility might be added before the experiment begins: can we discover any sounds that do not automatically sustain themselves but can be *made* to sustain – i.e. made into a continuous tone? A general assignment such as this can immediately involve everyone and includes something that even the least able can do. The more perceptive pupils (or perhaps those having violin lessons!) will quickly think of ways of making certain things sustain their sound (e.g. with a violin bow). Others may suggest fast repetition, and although this is not precisely what we are seeking it does offer a good opportunity to discuss the difference between repetition of note, fast or slow, and a continuously sustained sound; plus, of course, the difference between sounds that sustain themselves and decay and those that *we* sustain and maintain at a steady amplitude.

As we have suggested, this general exploration should be followed by a short discussion in which pupils can demonstrate their discoveries. From there, either the teacher can suggest various assignments from which pupils can choose, *or* he can assign specific tasks to groups and/or individuals. Timing is important. The class (if it is to work in small groups) must be divided up quickly and must know where the work spaces are. Self-selecting groups are generally most satisfactory and that requires no more than the instruction 'Get yourselves into groups of about five' (or whatever is the most suitable division). Five is a good number for this kind of work: there are enough hands or voices to make sounds but not too many. Several different ideas will no doubt come up, but again a group of five is not too large for discussion and agreement. Six will generally work satisfactorily – so that a class of thirty might divide into six groups of five, or five groups of six depending upon the availability of work spaces. Seven or more in a group is not normally very satisfactory, although it will depend, of course, upon what they are being asked to do.

When the groups have been formed, the teacher can give each a different task (taking account of the make-up of the groups and the ability range represented in each), decide where each shall work and what equipment if any they can/should use, and then let them get started. If necessary, the various assignments could be written out on workcards, one for each group. Alternatively, a single assignment could be given to all groups (divide the class first and then, when they know their working groups and spaces, tell them what they are to do). In this case, we would expect different interpretation of the ideas, and different levels of realisation. A topic such as 'long sounds and short sounds' will provide many paths for exploration leading to structuring pieces and learning about durations, the importance of silence as well as sound, timbres, dynamics, pitch, elementary notations, and so on. Detailed suggestions for group and class activities on this and similar topics will be found in several of the books listed on pages 245–7. Here we must be concerned primarily with questions of organisation.

What can we do about the noise?

The first thing that worries most people when they begin this kind of work is the noise it makes. This is obviously unavoidable. We did hear of a student who, on a school practice, was given a 'music' class in the school hall where there was already a mathematics lesson going on in the gallery and a drama lesson behind closed curtains on the stage. The student was told that she could do whatever she liked in 'music' so long as it didn't make a noise! No doubt there are experienced music teachers who sometimes wish theirs was a silent art; the temptation then to take refuge in dictating notes about composers can be strong. But if school music teaching is to get anywhere we must face the simple fact that music makes a noise. We must press hard for the right kind of accommodation which includes facilities for dividing a class into small groups working independently of each other – and indeed places where individuals can work alone. On the other hand, if we postpone all attempts to develop the music curriculum until a time when we have ideal facilities, it is very clear we may never get started at all. Perhaps the simplest thing we can do is to take the advice of the teacher who wrote: 'Learn to develop a thick skin!'

Be that as it may, there *are* other things we can do and for the most part these involve quite a lot of forethought, as many people have testified, for example:

Good preparation is essential . . .

Good classroom organisation . . . planning and position of groups, instruments, etc., and rotation of activities to keep the noise level and group interference to a minimum.

Classroom organisation needs to be of prime importance to economise on effort, to ensure discipline is firm. Unwarranted chaos, due to bad organisation, leads either to the pupils' control of the teacher or to a rigid 'military' approach not in the least creative!

Working creatively with sounds demands enormous concentration from teachers and pupils *and* the ability to organise

There is no doubt that music is a difficult subject to teach in class, and it may seem a lot easier to teach it as though it were history. Yet there are some quite simple strategies we can adopt for practical music-making, and need to adopt, not only for our own sakes but more particularly for the sake of our pupils and the development of their musical sensitivity. For it is ironical to talk of developing aural perception and musical awareness in a single room where there is so much noise that no-one can hear clearly what he or she is doing.

To start with we can try to secure the use of suitable spaces around our music room. Probably the best way to approach this is by demonstrating that some activities can be successful (or moderately so) with everyone working in the same room. With a little success to show for our efforts we shall be more likely to persuade those who have to be persuaded that some modest expansion of space could achieve even better results. Unsupported demands for extra accommodation have a habit of falling on deaf ears. This is the old story of 'nothing succeeds like success'. On that basis we have to begin somewhere and with a strategy that is capable of being developed. Thus, our first small-group projects may have to be on a limited scale but they will, nevertheless, establish the idea of group-work which can be expanded as opportunity arises.

For example, during a lesson which is primarily given over to working with the class as a whole, we can begin discussion of a topic to be developed into a group improvisation or composition and invite four or five individuals to demonstrate the kinds of sounds they think appropriate. This small group can be built up in approximately five minutes or so and, with comments from the teacher and other class members, can begin to develop ideas into an improvisation together. At this point the teacher can stop the work and suggest that the small-group meets again later (say, during break or towards the end of lunch-time) when – with the teacher's encouragement – they will be able to complete their work on the idea begun in class. The lesson then proceeds as before with the whole class (singing, instrumental work, listening, or whatever). The small-group meets with the teacher as arranged to complete the piece, and at the next music lesson they play their piece to the rest of the class. Its content and structure are discussed so that everyone knows how it was made, and the teacher then develops another idea with a different group of four or five pupils. This second piece can be performed the following week. And so on, for a number of weeks until instead of a normal class lesson, a whole period might be devoted to 'performing the pieces we have made during the first part of the term'. On that occasion allow a few minutes for the groups to get the equipment they need, to organise themselves in suitable places around the room and briefly to rehearse – to remind themselves of how the pieces go; then have a concert.

This arrangement avoids the excessive noise of several groups having to work together in the same room but it has obvious limitations, not least in the time in which it takes to build up ideas. This might be a useful point to appeal for some additional small spaces so that the work could grow and whole lessons be given to creative activities along these lines. Spaces used need to be reasonably near to the main music room so that the class can meet all together for the start of the lesson and the teacher's introduction, can divide up quickly and get to work without too far to go, can be easily within range for the teacher to move around the groups, and can be quickly gathered together for a final 'sharing' of work done. It is generally possible to find four or five such spaces at not too great a distance and with one group remaining in the music room a total of five or six groups becomes a possibility.

If the work *has* to be done in one room it is possible provided that the room is reasonably large. Results from working in these conditions are not generally as disastrous as may be supposed. A school hall is particularly suitable because groups can be placed some distance from each other but all are within sight of the teacher who can then easily see where and when help is most needed. There will be a tendency for the noise level to rise as the work goes on. This can be controlled by timing the group work carefully and interspersing 'report back' interludes. After the teacher's introduction (3–5 minutes at most), the class divides into groups and starts work. The teacher can now go quickly round all groups to check with each that they have understood what they have to do, have got some ideas to work on, and so on. It is important at this stage not to spend too much time with any one group. Let the work proceed for a few minutes and then stop the whole class. Ask some (not all) groups to perform what they have done so far. Comment on this work in progress, calling attention to the strengths and weaknesses and inviting discussion with the rest of the class ('Have they perhaps got too many ideas there? Do you think they would find it easier to develop this piece if they concentrated on one idea? Which would you choose?' – then to the group who have 'shown' their work: 'Which do *you* think is the best idea to develop? How do you see the piece ending? Loud, soft? Dying away?' And so on. Let these comments and questions be purposeful and specific. Avoid vague general appeals to the rest of the class such as 'What did you all think of that?').

After a few minutes of this kind of 'reporting back', set the groups to work again. This time spend a little longer with each group and, by asking questions rather than directing operations, help them to see how their ideas may be developed and how the piece can be given overall 'shape'. It is not essential to get to all groups again before the next 'report back' but we must try to notice which groups are making good progress on their own (and so can be left to work without our help) and which are in difficulties and need more encouragement. Insert further 'report' interludes on work in progress as time will allow. These short periods of coming together are vital because they are points at which the teacher can use the work of one group for the benefit of the whole class. Attention can be drawn to general questions of structure and process. It also helps the groups whose work is discussed to focus more clearly upon their ideas and to avoid wandering away from the principal lines of development. Young people generally find it a lot easier to invent ideas than to develop them. The occasional general class discussion is valuable because it can highlight features that are most suitable for extended working. In other words, it assists with that important selection/rejection process which is the background to all creative thinking. In addition, these productive interruptions help to keep the sound levels down because when the groups return to work they will normally do so at a lower level than that at which they left off.

When all groups have completed their work, everyone meets together to listen to the finished pieces. Again, this is a point at which the teacher should have positive comments to make, drawing upon the resources of his own experience and musical sensitivity. Try not to leave it at simply 'Yes, that's good' or 'Thank you, I liked that piece'. Whilst we must properly respect what is offered, we should beware of giving the impression that it is no more than a question of likes and dislikes. We shall want pupils to understand how music grows from a conscious organic development of ideas, and to an important extent our *organisation* of sessions like this will demonstrate the care that is needed in working with sounds. A teacher writes:

> Children need to be shown that music demands more self-control than many other subjects . . .

Motivation and control

There is no doubt that, from time to time, 'creative music-making' has got itself into disrepute by being badly organised. Teachers have not planned clearly enough, nor thought through beforehand the kind of results they would expect to see coming from the work. There has been little in the way of constructive comment on pupils' music, and little or no follow-up (e.g. reference to other composers' work, or class performances of music linked to the topics set for class groups' creative exploration). In consequence, the lessons have often lacked direction and purpose. Worse still is the prevailing misconception that 'creative' work means only improvisation, and implies leaving the pupils more or less to their own devices to play with instruments and 'see what turns up'. Nothing could be more dangerous. Given that sort of 'opportunity' they will most certainly create – in a sense which none of us would wish to encourage.

Part of the problem would seem to be teachers' lack of experience of *making* in music themselves. Even where a teacher's training has emphasised performance, more often than not there has been hardly any opportunity to explore questions of style and interpretation and to learn to take decisions in such matters. In such a course, room to find out what it means to generate and develop our own ideas is usually very limited, so that when we come to work with children we have no first-hand experience of our own on which to draw and on which to base classroom activities. If that kind of experience has been missing from our training it is imperative that we try to fill the gap through attendance at in-service courses or locally organised meetings of teachers. Wardens of teachers' centres will normally be able to help with the arrangements for such meetings. But avoid mere 'talk' occasions; instead arrange practical sessions as often as possible at which teachers can try activities they hope to introduce in school.

There is evidence that some teachers may be inclined to reject small-group division of a class after one attempt because discipline problems have arisen. This is a pity because, as we have seen in the examples quoted above, it can be a very productive way of working. Indeed, as a method of organising class work it has many advantages over the normal whole-class arrangement, especially with a mixed ability group. Pupils working at a variety of tasks suited to the different abilities represented are more likely to become involved with what they are doing, and so take the music lesson seriously. The whole-class arrangement may appear to give the teacher more control but it cannot deal so easily with the pupils who are out of their depth and bored. Discipline problems often arise from one pupil whose open rudeness to the teacher amuses the less bold spirits in the class and gives them confidence to develop general unruliness. This is less likely to happen if the class is working in self-selecting small groups.

Questions such as the two following are understandable. But real as the problems are (and have we not all experienced such dilemmas?), they must be related to lesson content and the kind of organisation needed to carry through specific assignments:

Is there a reliable way to communicate with belligerent children in a free situation where thirty plus others require the teacher's attention?

How do you deal with naughty children without permanently antagonising them?

'A *free* situation' presumably means a 'workshop' arrangement. But how 'free' does that have to be? It must certainly not be so haphazard that it is out of the teacher's control. The teacher must establish, right from the start, ways of proceeding that are understood by everyone, and which it is clear will apply to all the work done in this way. Preliminary organisation of instruments, work spaces, and materials (e.g. workcards) is essential. There used to be an old maxim which many of us learned in the days of the junior school percussion band: 'Do the talking first; *then* give out the instruments!' It still hold good. It is unrealistic to begin by giving out instruments and then expecting children to sit quietly while we explain what we want them to do. Later, when they have had some experience of these 'workshop' methods, that may become possible – indeed it must, because there will certainly be occasions when we shall want a class to come in and go straight to waiting instruments. But not in the first lesson; nor the second! So these aspects of organisation need careful thought beforehand. Where will the instruments be? Does the teacher get them out, or are they fetched by groups (or one member of each group)? Such considerations may seem very obvious but it is surprising how often they are the points at which an otherwise well-organised 'workshop' disintegrates.

Obviously there are disciplinary actions which anyone can take with 'naughty children' but the teacher who raises this question above is obviously well aware of the further difficulties that can ensue. This is a particularly important point in relation to a subject such as music. Success is very much dependent upon the right kind of relationship between teacher and pupil. A too heavy-handed and 'directing' manner on the teacher's part will crush the very sparks of individuality and imagination we set out to encourage. At the same time, just a few uncooperative pupils can make life very difficult. In the end, wildly idealistic though it must sound to teachers struggling with large classes, we are back to the business of *involvement*. In music, though, we have at least one distinct advantage over other subjects when it comes to mixed-ability groups. A French irregular verb remains an irregular verb, to be learned or not learned in the same way by everyone. But a concept such as 'melody' can be explored by each pupil if necessary working at his/her own level and could produce musically worthwhile results across the whole range; anything from 'primitive' repeated two-note cells to binary and ternary structures with strong harmonic implications or passionate Schoenbergian twelve-note melodies.

Ultimately involvement must be the answer, and our professional training should have done something to help us there. If it has not, then this is presumably another instance in which we should look to in-service courses for assistance, and to the opportunities – whenever they are presented – of discussing these issues with other teachers. It is primarily a matter of practical experience, and no amount of words in books can really help. What a book may do is remind us of a few basic points to keep in mind:

> 'Organise' the discipline by careful planning and by ensuring as far as possible the suitability of the material for *all* pupils in the group.
>
> Make sure that the material and methods you decide to use are such that you are thoroughly convinced yourself about their value musically and educationally. Lack of conviction on the teacher's part will communicate to the pupils.

Poor discipline almost always arises from boredom when pupils cannot see the relevance of what they are doing and cannot feel involved. The answer lies therefore in the kind of curriculum we evolve, the relevance of the material or the ways in which it can be seen to be relevant, and the sense of progression and purpose that we are able to generate. This may mean that we have to broaden our own view of music and possibly its relationship with other arts. The development of 'faculties' of creative arts in some schools has been a help to some teachers of music, as the following comment shows:

> In this school music was under an 'arts' umbrella so that projects were discussed regularly, and very often painting, pottery, needlework, woodwork, etc. could be incorporated. About twice a term a whole year would meet together and hold a display/demonstration of work done.

To others, however, this kind of thing may appear to be selling music short (see pp. 240–2). Clearly music does have an integrity of its own which must not be sacrificed or watered down, but related arts projects can have their uses and be a way into a 'workshop' method which can then be taken on into separate music activities.

How long should we work at a topic?

It may be necessary to plan entirely within a framework of single lesson periods, setting a new topic each week or producing a new arrangement for the class band. On the other hand, if it is possible to organise the class work as an on-going 'workshop', groups and individuals can proceed in their own way and at a pace appropriate to the topics chosen. At the start of each 'lesson' pupils would pick up the threads of what they had been working on and continue until they had completed the assignment – which might be a composition or an arrangement for the small group working together (and eventually to be performed by them to the rest of the class), or a composition or arrangement made by one member of the class to be rehearsed and performed, under the composer's/arranger's direction, by the whole class ensemble. Work on assignments would be completed at different times and it would be necessary to have further material prepared, either leading on from the previous topic or opening up something totally new. Sessions devoted to the performance of pupils' work might lead to performance of other composers' music on related themes or to listening sessions prior to everyone starting work on new topics. The model here is, of course, the organisation normally adopted by craft teachers. In metalwork, for example, a pupil will continue work week by week until what he is making is completed, but there will also be occasional whole-class sessions in which techniques are demonstrated and ideas discussed by everyone together.

In music pupils should be able to pursue ideas long enough to develop them as far as they can, but if an idea is proving totally unproductive, or the imaginative possibilities seem to be exhausted, there will be no value in taking it on to the point of boredom. This requires careful judgement on the part of the teacher. Sometimes encouragement to go on just a little further will be enough to reach a point where the whole thing unexpectedly develops and a workable structure becomes apparent. On the other hand, to continue with an idea that seems hopeless can be dispiriting and may make it difficult for pupils even to begin to work on a new topic. In this, the teacher's own experience of developing musical material will be important. If he can see potential in an initial idea, then he must ask the kind of questions that will lead the work on to a productive point.

It is possible to work almost any assignment within a single 35-minute or 40-minute period, but then we must recognise the limitations of time and not expect anything very extensive to come out of the small-group working. Having said that, there are clearly occasions when it is helpful, and indeed productive, to ask pupils to produce something in a very short space of time, e.g. two or three minutes. Given longer they may simply go round in circles and find difficulty in focussing upon the really significant features of their musical ideas. A useful compromise between the on-going workshop and the 'new-topic-each-week' arrangement might be to plan the course in three-week blocks. The first week would contain a 'lead' lesson in which the teacher demonstrated possibilities and discussed ideas with the whole class. This would conclude with the organising of groups and the allocation of assignments. Group work would occupy the next week's session(s) entirely, and the third week would be a 'plenary' session in which compositions/arrangements were performed and discussed. If a class had only one music lesson each week this plan could be extended to a four week pattern, the two middle weeks being given over entirely to group and individual work (see description of work with lower school classes in the two tape-slide programmes *Music at Notley High School, Part 1* and *Starting Points*).

Organisation and equipment

We have already referred to the difficulties that can arise if instruments are given out at the wrong moment, but the problem can go much deeper. On the one hand we need varied and interesting sound sources to give pupils plenty of expressive scope, and in some instances we shall need specialised equipment if we are to tackle certain kinds of music at all – for example, pop and rock music is hardly a reality without the appropriate electric instruments, though some aspects are just about possible using classroom xylophones and glockenspiels (see Vulliamy & Lee 1980, pp. 74–96). On the other hand, distributing a large number of instruments (especially if they are the kind that have removable bars and use beaters) or checking the functioning of a lot of electrical apparatus can cause considerable delay in a lesson, so that the impetus is lost. Too much equipment can be a hindrance, particularly in the early stages of first-year class work. There is an added danger with electronic sound sources (e.g. synthesizers) that the equipment will become an end in itself, and the pupils more ready to be fascinated by knobs, dials and switches than by the sounds produced. Obviously, that doesn't have to be the case. There is a great deal of productive music-making to be done with such equipment but, as an introduction to electronic music, it could be more profitable to encourage pupils to bring into school the cassette tape-recorders, reel-to-reel tape-recorders, portable radios, electric guitars and many other pieces of 'simple' electronic sound equipment that so many of them possess, and to show them how such things can be used to create new and interesting ways of listening to sounds. Basic tape manipulation and editing is perhaps the best way into this new sound world. The synthesizer can come later.

It is essential to plan the use of equipment in relation to our aims for particular aspects of a course. For example, if it is our intention at the start to draw attention to ways in which sounds can be put together to make interesting structures, and if this is something a class has not done before, we should focus upon the *structuring* process. In which case, we can use a sound source that is at once the simplest and yet one of the most subtle – the human voice. There need be no delay between the teacher's introduction and the start of class and group experiment. Moreover, unlike a xylophone or a cymbal, where we must first discover how best to make the sound – where to strike it, what kind of beater to use, and so on – the voice with all its subtlety of inflexion, is already well-known to us. We can made it do all manner of expressive things in speech sounds, whispered sounds and sung sounds. (See the notes on performance for Bernard Rands, *Sound Patterns 3 – a project for voices*, Universal Edition 15348, and the suggestions for Term 1, week 4 on p. 45 above). Once the structuring process has been understood through the use of vocal sounds, it will be a lot easier to approach instrumental sounds, and the occasional delays as things are organised will be more readily accepted because the nature of the activity to follow will be understood.

As a general principle, it is probably better to begin work in improvisation, composition, or arrangement with limited resources (see Appendix I, Tom Gamble's syllabus). The underlying principles of structure, 'working' motifs and developing ideas should be firmly understood before getting into areas of wider choice. Even when we are using very 'simple' means (e.g. vocal sounds) we should try to reveal the unexpected qualities and to generate interest and excitement with the potential of these sounds.

It can ease some of the organisational problems if the equipment needed for a particular session is brought out of the store before a class arrives. It is then a question of where the equipment should be placed. With more advanced groups it should be possible to have instruments (especially the larger instruments: gongs, large drums, chord organ, etc.) in place so that the players can be directed straight to them. In the earlier stages it is perhaps better to have the equipment in a block near the teacher. From there it can be distributed when the appropriate moment comes, or it may be seen as a resource from which pupils would be invited to select what they thought appropriate to the tasks set (e.g. in the preliminary talk between teacher and class, we might invite suggestions: 'Which instrument – from among those we have here – would you think best for this idea?' Then hand out whatever is suggested and invite the pupils to demonstrate how they would use it for the idea being developed. 'Could we add anything to that? . . . yes, show me . . .' And so on, gradually building up a suitable ensemble).

Again, limiting the range of instruments available can help a group to concentrate upon certain aspects (e.g. provide only drums and tambours so that the emphasis will be upon rhythmic structures as an 'answer' to a specific problem; provide only glockenspiels so that the work will be directed primarily towards melody; or cymbals, gongs and triangle to promote structures that are mainly timbral).

Making changes

We have already remarked on the way in which one aspect of curriculum design interacts with another. This is particularly pertinent in those instances when teachers may decide to make radical changes of method.

Change requires careful thought. There could be a case for a complete turn-about; a total revision of everything we do. On the other hand, it may be wiser to make it a very gradual process (e.g. the method suggested on pp. 79–80 by which small-group activities can be introduced over a period of several weeks). It is often assumed that any proposal for a new approach automatically implies the rejection of everything we have done before. In consequence, some teachers try to make 'all-or-nothing' changes only to find that, apart from throwing pupils into confusion, they (the teachers) do not give themselves time to digest the principles and implications behind the new approach. Inevitably things go wrong.

It is important to consider the effects of proposed changes in relation to the rest of the school curriculum. In certain circumstances a music course based on the most impeccable educational and artistic reasoning will fail with the pupils if it is introduced too suddenly, without tact and in the face of an overall school philosophy that sees the general aims of education differently. Some critics of recent proposals for music curriculum development have been quick to point out that the older and well-tried methods unquestionably work in their schools and that their pupils find the newer approaches 'silly'. Investigation usually reveals that in these cases success has been measured principally in terms of class discipline applied to a fairly limited topic. The method is instructional rather than active, based mainly on information and theory exercises; where it is active (e.g. singing), it is normally teacher-directed. It is successful because it fits into the norm of that school. Anything different – even though it might obviously be more musical – would be out of step with the accepted pattern.

By their nature the arts demand a different method of teaching from other subjects. But if the majority of teachers in a school employ a strongly conventional 'academic' approach, teachers in the arts need to be very sure of their ground, their curriculum content and methodology, if they intend to move in a different direction. As one teacher in this situation has remarked:

> The pupils have come to expect or have been brought up to expect exactly the kind of things they are given – they expect to be taught skills, music history, to listen to records, to take notes, to be disciplined, and above all *to be led*. They expect the educational path to be clearly and securely defined, and they have no real idea of their own capacity to shape it, to bring something new or individual to it: their education is basically a received rather than a discovered one. Even in music the system relies heavily on the pupils' readiness to respond in the expected way, to fit in with the plan . . .

It is, of course, impossible to say categorically that, in such a school, a new approach would fail simply because in organisation and policy it was different from other subjects. A teacher with a lively and compelling personality might easily capture the imagination and enthusiasm of pupils and be able to give the class work a new impetus with plentiful opportunity for the staff to take their own musical decisions. Nevertheless, an inexperienced teacher might be well advised to approach with caution and not to try to change things overnight.

The influence of a prevailing 'method' policy in a school is bound to be strong but what has been said above should not be taken as advocating the retention of a frankly unmusical approach just because that is what the school would seem to expect. It would be difficult to defend continuing with a method that totally ignored the subjective elements in musical experience for no other reason than that to do so appeared to secure good classroom discipline and fulfilled the normal expectations. Whatever the circumstances, our job is to educate through music and it is up to us to find the most appropriate way of using the *reality* of musical experience as a means of education. We may find that we have to walk a tight-rope between what we believe is right in music education and the general policies of the school which we must not treat in too cavalier a manner. Gradual changes might include the introduction of a larger element of practical music-making in class, to begin with directed by the teacher – the whole class working as a single unit. In time individual pupils could be allowed to take over some of the ensemble direction or organise a class improvisation. In this way we might work gradually towards a method based on small-group rather than whole-class activity.

Part 3 : Education through music

No-one who has ever tried to arouse enthusiasm for music among secondary school pupils will deny the importance of knowing, first and foremost, what you are going to do in the classroom and how you are going to do it. But having got through the first lesson the next one lies ahead, *and* the one after that; and so on, week by week, term by term. Not surprisingly, it is easy enough to feel that, however well we got through to begin with, before long we shall find ourselves running out of steam. Apart from anything else the day-to-day pressures of this work are enormous and there is little time to be thinking out fresh approaches, researching new material, or considering *why* we do what we do. But as we have seen in the foregoing pages, whenever we do pause to consider lesson content or method, it is virtually impossible to avoid the question, 'Why teach music in school anyway?' An answer to that question could be the first step towards solving problems of continuity and progress in our classroom music-making.

Of course, we can try to put the question aside, and concentrate upon the more obviously important (because they are immediate) issues: keeping track of the xylophone beaters; ordering the band parts of 'Oliver' and checking that the record player has been repaired. The job is there to be done and we must get on with it. It is well-known that the successful music teacher is the one with seemingly unlimited energy; always on the go, drumming up support for choirs and bands, rehearsing at every spare moment of the day:

> Music must depend for its success on the attitude of the Head, staffing, and *enthusiasm of individual teachers* . . .

That is very true, but we are also involved with something that goes beyond enthusiasm and energy, important though these things are. The profession of teaching demands not only enthusiasm and expertise within one's subject but also a deep commitment to the entire process of education and to what it is that we are doing for children and young people. It is this, and the consequent philosophy, which will determine what we do and will sustain the curriculum teaching which is at the core of our responsibility. Without that conviction there are dangers for any teacher, but the music teacher is particularly vulnerable. For if the music teacher is not completely convinced about his role in general education, it is all too easy for him to divert his main energies to the extra-curricular activities. It is then that the class music work either becomes a chore to be got through, or a nightmare of wondering how to maintain pupils' interest. Before long the law of diminishing returns begins to operate and music as a 'curriculum' subject becomes geared more and more towards the minority 'examination' group.

That this has so often been the pattern of music in schools is evidence of our failure to define a satisfactory curriculum rationale for the subject. By contrast, where music has been seen to flourish in the curriculum and to have something to offer to the majority of pupils it is almost always because the teacher concerned has started from a firm conviction that he has an educational as well as a musical duty. It matters little whether this is expressed in a curriculum of predominantly instrumental activities, or of choirs, or rock bands or improvisation and composition, so long as the activity can involve pupils right across the ability range in music-making that is meaningful to them because it is not simply imposed upon them but offers some degree of choice.

In the previous section we examined the kind of classroom organisation which Grenville Hancox adopted to make his curriculum work. Let us look now at the thinking which underpins that organisation:

My philosophy of music teaching is based upon the experiences I was forced to suffer. My own musical education was to be part of a regime that fostered an élite; a small group of children in a grammar school but where music was very much the poor relation. I was fortunate in having musical parents and they encouraged me. The school did nothing for me except to try to put me off music – and it didn't succeed! The system consisted of a basic recipe of musical biographical details being churned out, and we were required to regurgitate them. You were a 'good musician' if, at the end of term, you got 70% . . . very few people had the chance of playing instruments. There were no classroom instruments.

As my education went on the situation got worse, and so by the time we got to university the numbers of people involved in music-making were very small. And when I got into teacher-training department my training consisted of being instructed how to teach children to write primary triads in C major – or something like that!

And so I was determined that, if I had the chance to teach, I should try to do everything in my power to involve everybody in making music – not just to look after the small band who will be able to look after themselves anyway, but to make everybody conscious of music-making socially, creatively, re-creatively, and so on. That's basically the reason I work as I do.

Reaction of this kind to a 'traditional' school music course highlights the rather spiritless nature of such courses where they are directed mainly towards 'the small band who will be able to look after themselves anyway'. For those who are not fortunate enough to have musical opportunities outside school, the 'traditional' course may offer very little musically or educationally. Yet a few moments' reflection could set it on a more productive path. Artistic expression ultimately depends more upon individual judgement, born out of experience, than it does upon the accumulation of facts. This could be a good basis on which to begin to formulate new principles for music in schools.

We educate through music. Our commitment is to education and not merely to music training. Naturally, the two things go hand in hand: educational principles are worthless without the means of carrying them through, and in our case those means are musical. But the balance must be right. The elements of the music course; the activities and the projects we design, will only have educational significance in terms of a *school* curriculum if in principle they can be offered to everyone. Out of such a curriculum can grow a wide range of exciting music making within the scope of the time-table, extending to support the extra-curricular ensembles *and* the specialised work of those who are going on to music courses in Higher Education.

Music, unlike words, is not tied to precise meanings. It is therefore capable of almost limitless interpretation and re-interpretation. Thus it is ideally suited as a medium through which young people can develop skills of judgement and expression. This is not the same thing as *self*-expression, which is by and large an indulgent and inward-looking process, but rather an understanding of ways in which structure develops the inherent expressiveness of musical ideas in many different styles, creating coherent forms to reveal unexpected relationships of pitches, rhythms and timbres. Such understanding comes principally through first-hand experience of working in the medium of sound. And it is *that* – a symbolic seeking after order and integration – which is educative.

4 Creativity and the music curriculum

It will be evident from all that has been said in the previous chapters that the concept of music as a creative art – and therefore as an area of what might be called 'special' creativity within the curriculum – is absolutely central to the Project's thinking. Yet in recent developments of school music there can be few things that have given rise to as much strong feeling and such widespread misunderstanding as the idea of 'creative' music-making. For advocating the principle of music as a creative art the Project has been called 'partisan' and has been accused of promoting a restricted view. Yet the aim has been quite clearly to *enlarge* the scope of music in the classroom, to include many activities which were hitherto excluded, and to develop an all-embracing principle which can include virtually any 'method' and any content so long as pupils are actively involved with music which they have a chance to 'make their own'. Such a principle is encompassed by the belief that *all* musical activity – listening, composing and performing – is essentially creative. It is this point which the present chapter seeks to examine in greater detail.

Definitions and vocabulary

First let us explore some definitions and vocabulary for creativity and originality:

CREATIVE

Having the quality of creating; of or pertaining to creation; originative; productive of.

Unimitative, *inventive*, original, not derivative, *first-hand*, *individual*, personal, independent, imaginative, lively, idea'd, ingenious, resourceful.

Create: to produce, give rise to, to cause; to make; form or constitute.

ORIGINAL

Produced by or proceeding from some thing or person directly; underived, *independent*, *first-hand*; such as has not been done or produced before; novel or *fresh in character* or style; (of a person): capable of original ideas or actions, *inventive*, *creative*.

CREATIVE	ORIGINAL
Create: 'To make a fuss or a to-do' (slang or vulgar! O.E.D.)	Originate, initiate, launch, invent, discover, introduce, usher in, start up, switch on, set going, lead off, pioneer, broach, set the ball rolling, take the plunge, spark off.
An original production of human intelligence or power.	
Creator: One who gives origin to.	
Creation: The action of making, forming, producing or bringing into existence.	*Originate*: To give origin to, cause to arise or begin, initiate.

Creativity is 'the process of change, of development, of evolution in the organisation of subjective life.' (Ghiselin, 1952, p. 12)

Creativity has been defined, simply and concisely, as 'the ability to bring something new into existence' . . . Fortunately, it does not have to imply that the 'something new' need be new to everyone, or, indeed, new to anyone else save the person who creates it. The child who links together in his mind two ideas which have hitherto been separated, and who produces a third as a result of the fusion, may find, disappointingly, that he has not been as original as he had supposed when his teacher points out that someone else had the same idea before him. None the less, he has been creative in that he has produced for himself something which is new to *him* . . . (Storr, 1972, p. 11)

The Creative Arts

None of the arts has a monopoly of creativity. Indeed, whatever complex theories there may be about creative genius and originality, at root creativity would seem to have quite a lot to do with those simple everyday faculties which enable us to get through life: taking decisions and acting upon them; making judgements; putting two and two together and reaching a conclusion about what to do in unfamiliar or unexpected circumstances. Its characteristic is that we make inward, imaginative models from which we can extrapolate. The models are based upon aspects of our experience but are, of course, applied beyond the boundaries of that experience to determine new possibilities. Clearly it is (or it should be) a function of education to encourage and develop such lateral thinking.

Music, poetry, dance, drama, painting and sculpture may not have a monopoly of creativity, but these and similar pursuits *are* spoken of as 'creative arts', and we can therefore assume that creativity is of prime importance to anyone who is in any way involved with the arts. That is to say, the processes of art-making and art-understanding develop ideas principally through imagination and fantasy rather than measurement and calculation. Every conscious involvement with music in performing, composing *and* in listening is the result of an independent imaginative response. It cannot be quantified or reproduced exactly a second time. It is personal and individual. No matter how much we analyse the mechanics of a piece of music, or pay attention to what other people tell us about it, music will not 'happen' for us unless we ourselves enter into the particular sound world it inhabits.

Music demands action. It cannot properly be apprehended by passive contemplation. It calls for commitment; for choice, preference, and decision. When we perform music or listen to it we re-*make* it within our imagination, relating it to other imaginative and emotional experiences. This is a creative process, and never more so than where unfamiliar music is concerned. *Then* we need all the qualities of the pioneer and the discoverer, the courage to take the plunge and let things start up in the imagination – all attributes of originative and creative thinking.

This is not to say that every experience of music must be deeply moving and intense! But for it to matter at all there must surely be some degree of delight; of enjoyment and sensory pleasure. Even were we to suggest that music were no more than a relaxation and entertainment – a kind of decoration to living – our lives would still be enriched by it.

Yet the arts do more than entertain. Because artists present us with highly personalised, subjective views of the world and life, they challenge us to look at familiar things in a new light, and to consider afresh our own situation, our reactions to where we are, to the things that happen to us and to others around us, to the things we see and hear. The arts open doors on an inner world of fears, fantasies and joys; a world we all have to come to terms with. Thus the arts engage with what is central in the human condition, and are manifestly both humanising and educative.

Each age has its own ways of using the inherent expressiveness of materials, and so style in poetry, painting, music and dance reflect the undercurrents of thought that we would call the spirit of an age. The artist cannot create 'out of thin air'. He is an interpreter of experience, drawing ideas from the cultural and physical background:

> The opening up of . . . new realms of feeling has always been the artist's chief mission. A great deal of our world would lack all emotional significance if it were not for his work. As recently as the eighteenth century, mountain scenery was felt to exhibit nothing except a formless and alarming confusion. Winckelmann, the discoverer of Greek art, could not bear to look out of the windows of his carriage when he crossed the Alps into Italy, around 1760. He found the jumbled granite masses of the St Gotthard so frightful that he pulled down the blinds and sat back to await the smooth outlines of the Italian countryside. A century later, Ruskin was seeking out the mountains of Chamonix as a refuge from an industrial world that made no kind of aesthetic sense. Ships, bridges, iron constructions – the new artistic potentialities of his period, in short – these were the things Ruskin pulled down the blinds on. Right now there are great areas of our experience which are still waiting to be claimed by feeling. Thus we are no longer limited to seeing objects from the distances normal for earth-bound animals. The bird's-eye view has opened up to us whole new aspects of the world. Such new modes of perception carry with them new feelings which the artist must formulate. (Siegfried Giedion, *Space, Time and Architecture: the Growth of a New Tradition*, Cambridge, Mass. 1967 5th edn p. 431).

Any worthwhile attempt to understand our present culture or the culture of past generations must include the work of artists. But how do we *understand* art? The creative process fuses emotion and intellect: the artist working on his inner world, responding to feeling, but at the same time striving to make those feelings coherent through structure and form. He is guided by intuition and inventiveness, by acquired skills, by imagination and a sensitivity to the materials, and by a knowledge of what others have done in the same field. It is a complex process of selection and rejection, of informed guesswork in which the artist juggles with ideas and formal possibilities, follows leads and takes decisions. In the end it is artistic judgement that counts. It is not a mechanical process and there are no rules other than the rule of a sensitive ear, eye or whatever sense is being used. Only the artist can take the ultimate decision and declare the work finished. For better or worse, the shapes and forms he sanctions at that stage will be the means by which the work must be received. If we view it, read it, touch it or hear it (whichever mode is appropriate to the material), we must assume that the artist believes we can and should understand his work in its own terms. So, whatever the subject matter – abstract or representational – a painting is understood primarily as an experience of two-dimensional colour–space forms, and a piece of music as an experience of audible sound-patterns happening in time. It would be as misguided to expect the music to communicate like discursive prose as it would to demand of a painting the objectivity of a photograph: 'Music creates its forms and materials wholly out of itself' (Révész, 1953). The *meaning* is to be found in the artist's use of the materials and forms, and in our experience of what is thus presented – which will be different for each one of us. Therein lies *our* creative response, our understanding of what the artist has made.

It is tempting to try to make sense of a work of art by comparing it with other pieces of painting, poetry, sculpture or music that we know, or by evaluating it against the observable 'real' world. This cannot succeed because art is the product of subjective experience, and each work presents us with the artist's view of the world transmuted by imagination. Since 'The opening up of . . . new realms of feeling has always been part of the artist's chief mission', we may well be presented with an unfamiliar view. That is all part of the adventure of the arts. It is the individuality in creation and interpretation which makes this such a distinctive activity – and, incidentally, suggests a particularly significant role for the arts in education. For, as a way of thinking, we have here something which is not regulated by formulae or by any kind of 'agreed' knowledge. Educationally it is an essential area; one that offers particular opportunities for the development of initiative and inventiveness. What the arts contribute to education must to some extent overlap with what is offered in other

We do not 'understand' the sculpture in terms of anatomical facts, but rather in terms of the medium itself (bronze) and the variety of forms and shapes upon which the artist has focussed. He draws our attention to these forms and the relationships between them; and between them and his ways of working the material. His is not giving us a lesson in anatomy. Moreover we cannot 'understand' his work through a photograph. It is a 3-dimensional expression and it has to be experienced 3-dimensionally *in space*.

subject areas, and it would be pointless to indulge in too much special pleading because, in any case, we need to work for a proper integration of the curriculum in all its facets. At the same time it would be foolish to overlook the essential characteristics of the various subject areas. The arts are unique in their emphasis upon the primacy of personal and imaginative interpretation of information received directly through the senses.

Art must have substance. It is a coming together of feelings, thought and materials. If this applies to invention it also applies (in the performing arts) to interpretation – and to understanding; the receiver of art cannot be left outside the process. One of the strongest ways of coming to understand what it is that artists do, is to do it ourselves! Our first efforts may be very humble indeed, but that does not matter; even the most gifted artists have to begin somewhere. And they begin with the essential experience of the art, not with abstracted theories. For example, dance is 'about' the expressive potential of bodily movement in space and time. Understanding dance starts with some awareness of those elements – not with a formal analysis of effort qualities, though such things may become important later on. Poetry and literature and drama are 'about' the expressive potential of language images and gesture – not just texts for study. The visual arts are 'about' shape, colour, texture and form in two- and three-dimensional space. Music is a way of listening to sounds in time and its first principles are the expressive possibilities of its raw materials as they can be perceived through attentive listening. Obviously there is more to it than that, but these are the rudiments, and without understanding at that level there is surely little point in attempting more advanced study. In school, too often we take that first stage for granted. We either assume there is creative understanding, or we may ignore it in the belief that the arts can be understood by other means.

Creativity obviously has to do with originating and inventing, but it can be – and should be – applied more widely. Even the slang use of 'create' meaning, according to the Oxford English Dictionary, 'To make a fuss or a to-do', seems to imply strongly held feelings on the part of some*one*. The element of personal decision and commitment is undoubtedly there! Whenever music sounds it is imbued with this quality of *commitment*. Even the most obviously derivative music-making would be impossible without a modicum of originality and a personal viewpoint. Everything else we relate to music; analysis, acoustics, historical studies and so on, supports the creative involvement, which is ultimately what matters.

Improvisation and composition

For most people creativity in music probably means the act of composing. Unfortunately, relatively few school music teachers have had any serious compositional training. Most music courses in conservatoires and Colleges of Higher Education tend to emphasise instrumental performance, and the majority of university music courses are still heavily biased towards musicology. Students intending to teach are normally assessed primarily on their performing skills and their ability to write *about* music. Opportunities to invent and develop musical ideas are rarely given, except within very narrow stylistic limits.

Yet many teachers who have come through this kind of training would nevertheless like to encourage 'creative activities', in the form of improvisation and composition, in the classroom. For them the problem is knowing where to begin. There are major differences of approach between, say, studying the violin and studying composition. A music college student whose first study is violin expects to find himself in the role of apprentice. His teacher is the Master Craftsman whose task it is to pass on the inherited wisdom of musicianship and, above all, the skill which he has himself acquired by arduous technical practice. Although there are several 'schools' of violin-playing this is nevertheless not something about which we should expect the student to have many ideas of his own. Of course, a major part of the work will be the study of interpretation and style, and in this respect, as well as in other ways, the process is surely a creative one. It rests nevertheless primarily on the acquisition of a strong technique which is based almost entirely upon other people's thoughts about violin-playing.

Composition also involves the acquisition of a secure technique, but by contrast with the way in which instrumental skills are taught, the teacher of composition *must* expect his students to come with ideas of their own. Craftsmanship in musical composition involves much more than the ability to work within the frame of established models. Even at the start it must draw upon and develop a student's powers of invention: the teacher is hardly in a position to make any worthwhile comment until the student does produce ideas – in sounds or on paper.

Points of interpretation apart, the process by which we acquire instrumental skills is largely a convergent one. On the other hand, the process by which we develop as composers is, in the main, divergent. Anyone who has been through a music course in higher education and has concentrated particularly upon instrumental performance is likely to find the former process easier to understand than the latter. In addition, it would be natural enough to assume that what applies in learning to play the violin also applies in learning to compose; is that not also basically a 'rule-directed' process? * In which case, how could school pupils possibly start to compose before they have first mastered the rules? But which rules? It is certainly useful to examine the variety of ways in which composers have solved problems of balance and structure in harmonic and contrapuntal music, but so much depends upon *how* these things are studied. They can be a springboard for original work which tries out a number of possibilities and returns to examine similar 'problems' and their solutions in the music of established composers, past or present. Alternatively, facets of technique and usage can be extracted from 'established' music and treated negatively as restrictions to be learned and obeyed more or less for their own sake. Regrettably, the heavy-hand of that kind of academicism has too often prevailed. One is reminded of Peter

---

* A point which could seem to be confirmed for those who, although not regarding themselves as composers, have studied orchestration and arrangement – often presented as aspects of composition. Here well-established procedures are sometimes taught as 'rules'.

Ustinov, quoting – in his autobiography – from one of his own school reports: 'He has great originality which must be suppressed at all costs'! Education should teach us how to learn, and nowhere is this more obviously true than in learning to develop our powers of invention. Copying what someone else has done in order to see how he solved a particular problem will undoubtedly be useful, but we cannot make 'rules' for composition out of such a practice and in the end it does very little to help us generate our own ideas. Composition is the art of developing structures through which ideas are expanded and which reveal the inherent expression in those ideas. Only the ideas themselves will indicate the paths to be explored. The techniques we shall need in the first instance are those which help us to estimate the potential of the ideas. We acquire such skills by first-hand experience of working with sounds.

Composition begins, then, with improvisation. All sounds, individually and in combination, have characteristic features which can indicate their potential for development. The invention of musical ideas is less of a problem than making the ideas go on in time. Imposed rules can help us very little here since our ability to make something musically interesting grow from a given starting point is fundamentally a question of sensitivity to the material. Others would, doubtless, treat it in very different ways, but that doesn't make their 'solutions' any better or worse than ours. The wonderful thing about music is not the extent of conformity but the truly amazing diversity which is possible, even within the scope of relatively simple ideas – melodic fragments and rhythmic or timbral patterns.

Beginning to improvise

Before dealing with structural possibilities it could be useful to consider the characteristics of various sounds and sound-combinations. For this purpose we could use a device such as the set of cards called *Colour-Shape-Sound*, devised by Roy Cooper and designed by Paul Johnson (examples on p. 101).

This kit of one hundred cards exploits the relationships we seem to be able to make between shapes or colours and sounds. There is no logical reason why we should associate these things, though the phenomenon of synaesthesia is well known and many people undoubtedly do 'see' colour when they hear music, and would associate certain colours with specific musical ideas, instrumentation, keys, etc. The experience of colour and music, although widespread, is certainly not universal. neither is it especially applicable to musicians, and it is not, in itself, an indicator of 'musicality'. Even so, most of us, faced with card 1, and asked to make the kind of sound suggested to us by what we see, would probably produce fast, light, point-sounds. On the other hand, asked to do the same with card 2, we should probably make a simple, rich, loud low-pitched sound – the opposite of card 3.

red   yellow   blue

1

2

3

4

5

6

Card 4 would be likely to suggest fairly loud 'smooth' sounds, continuously sliding up and down, whereas card 5 would probably produce a single very loud, bright and 'bursting' sound.

Similarly, a figure such as card 6 suggests a combination of sounds; one a 'curving' glissando getting louder or quieter (or higher or lower) – depending on which way you 'read' it – interrupted (though without its progress being impeded) by another smaller (louder) sound 'event'. Something like this, perhaps:

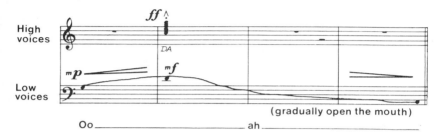

Each card suggests a complete sound idea, and each has its own very definite characteristics. Having responded to the stimulus of the cards and confirmed the sound ideas, we could put the cards aside and play with each idea in turn, extending it in various ways; making changes of pitch, duration, timbre and dynamics. Then, by choosing two or three of these sound ideas, we could begin to improvise with them, building up structures by exploiting the unifying or contrasting characteristics we have discovered in the first stage of experiment. This will probably be easier with a *group* of instruments or voices (about five at maximum) because that will give greater scope for combining sounds simultaneously and so varying the texture.

In defining the sound-ideas with which to start, we can take into account as much or as little of the visual stimulus as we like, but the 'direction' of the shapes and the colours can also provide a stimulus for sound characteristics. For example, the red triangle in card 6 is clearly 'stronger' than the curving band of yellow, but how should we interpret this extra 'strength'? Is it a question of amplitude, pitch, dynamic, or what? There is considerable scope for imagination in even a limited graphic stimulus.

No one decision will be the 'right' answer, though in discussion it is inevitable that some interpretations will seem more satisfactory than others. The important thing is, of course, not the 'rightness' of our interpretation of the original stimulus but what we can do with the *sound* idea to develop it and make it grow musically (without losing its essential characteristics) through improvisation. From there we can work over the improvisation again and again until the order of events and their development becomes established in an overall design which starts, goes on and finishes with clear definition and which we can remember with accuracy and if necessary repeat. This is composition. Having begun with simple sound ideas, unrelated to one another, we have drawn out the potential relationships and worked upon them building up a piece by trying one approach or another, rejecting things which do not 'fit', developing unifying ideas, and so on. The whole process demands a lively awareness of the sounds themselves and the courage to take decisions and abide by them. In the end, only those who have made such a piece can say whether they feel it is complete or not. But a teacher can advise, guiding the players as they explore a variety of ideas and juggle with several possibilities. It is the sound-ideas themselves which will dictate the final 'form' – the structure that reveals musically interesting relationships between the sounds and which (hopefully) holds the attention of the listeners.

In many ways musical composition has an affinity with sculpture. The sculptor must quite literally develop a *feel* for his materials. The potential of stone will be different from that of wood. A range of stones and woods of different hardness will suggest various possibilities. The sculptor, taking a block of his selected material, 'sees' the potential developments within the material. Similarly, in working with sound ideas, we can learn to respond to the ideas themselves, following lines of development which the sounds themselves suggest. Ultimately, the pieces of music which we make from the sounds reveal the expressive potential that was always present. Just as what the sculptor finally reveals was, in a sense, always present within the block of stone or wood.

Musical meaning

Perhaps the most valuable characteristic of music is that it is non-verbal. Unlike words or visual images it cannot describe. Far from being a disadvantage, this is the strength of musical sound. It lacks the definition of verbal expression but for this very reason it can 'mean' different things to different people. Musical sound is susceptible to individual interpretation and exploration even at technically very simple levels. So long as we are able to make sounds and control them, our imagination and inventiveness can engage with the medium in improvisation and composition. Other musical knowledge may help us but it is certainly not a prerequisite of such work. Composition is concerned first and foremost with ideas in *sound*. Students' work in the classroom should start from there.

Music is probably the most flexible medium in the aesthetic area of education; it can appear to 'mean' almost anything we choose. The implications of this are not always fully appreciated by teachers, especially in relation to classroom improvisation projects. Emphasis upon visual and literary stimuli can suggest that music is merely another way of saying something that could have been said equally well in words or pictures. Pupils may gather from this that music is little more than a translation of other art forms. The position is certainly not made any clearer by the fact that, throughout history, composers have themselves made considerable use of literary and visual links. In many instances such links go no further than a title, but in the case of 'programme' music there is a clear assumption that music can 'portray' specific ideas and events, things seen, experienced or heard about in the 'real' world. Programme music has a long and honourable history, but in spite of this it remains true that music is not a substitute for words or visual documentation. There is no way in which, from the music alone, we could agree upon a literary interpretation of Dukas' *The Sorcerer's Apprentice*. We must first know the story which the composer had in mind. Mendelssohn's *Fingal's Cave* would be meaningless as a 'description' of a geographical location had the composer not revealed it in the title. Of course it would be possible to say that the 'wavelet' figure in the lower strings is 'water-like' because we have heard other 'water' sounds in music and have them as points of reference. Indeed real water does make a bubbling and falling sound in some circumstances. But, such references apart, there is nothing in the sound structures of the *Hebrides Overture* that will itself independently suggest either water or the location of the title.

All sounds are evocative; usually, when we hear a sound we want to know what it is. If we are unable to tell what it is immediately we may start to guess what it might be. So, imagination begins to work. Music certainly makes effects in sound, but that is not the same thing as sound effects. Sound effects relate to the 'real', external world. Even if we cannot see the source of the sounds, they suggest that whatever it is could be visible or tangible. Musical effects, on the other hand, spring from the inner world of the composer's imagination. Events from the physical world may stimulate sound ideas, but in the end the sounds represent an experience which is subjective rather than objective. In school we may sometimes find it convenient to use visual or literary stimuli as starting points for musical experiment, but we should try to avoid giving the impression that music is simply a 'translation' from words to instrumental sounds. Listening to a piece of music is not a guessing game in which, if we don't know the title, we have to find out what it is about. If the composer has given it a title which links it to something in the physical world, or in visual art or poetry, drama or literature, that title may help us, when we experience the music, to relate our own feelings *about the title* to what we hear. But it is not music's prime function to elaborate on literary images. A symphonic poem with a 'programme' is not necessarily easier to understand than a Mozart symphony. Ultimately 'understanding' in music relates to the sound ideas, not to their associations. Mendelssohn was certainly under no illusions about music's independence from words and verbal description:

> People usually complain that music is ambiguous, that their ideas on the subject always seem so vague, whereas everyone understands words; with me it is exactly the reverse; not merely with regard to entire sentences, but also as to individual words; these too, seem to me so ambiguous, so vague, so unintelligible when compared with genuine music, which fills the soul with a thousand things better than words. What the music I love expresses to me, is not thought too *indefinite* to be put into words, but, on the contrary, too, definite.

Music is music, and one way in which we can begin to break away from the literary ties is to start evolving our own *sound* ideas, independently of literary, poetic, dramatic or visual associations. These ideas can be developed through improvisation, not for what they 'portray' (in sound-effect terms) but for the purely musical potential each possesses. This is part of the purpose of the *Colour-Shape-Sound* cards by Roy Cooper and Paul Johnson. Some of the shapes may suggest familiar objects – and a certain amount of fun could justifiably be had making music around such ideas. But the cards are especially useful in suggesting characteristic sounds which are interesting in themselves and are not related to other visible forms.

Literary stimulus

Teachers sometimes take poems as starting points for music. The poem is read and the images are discussed with the class. Pupils then make up pieces of music based upon the images in the poem. There is nothing wrong with this idea (it is after all exactly what Dukas was doing with *The Sorcerer's Apprentice*). But it is a very difficult assignment if we are aiming to produce an effective and whole piece of music. The tendency is for the children making the music to take the first image in the poem and 'translate' that into sound ideas; then to take the next image and 'translate' that, and so on. But a piece of music needs a unity of its own that arises from the musical ideas rather than from the parts of an external stimulus. Generally speaking a poet has one central thought around which the images of the poem revolve. The art of poetry is to compress experience into poetic language and images and it is in this that it differs from prose description. If, in discussion with the class, we can determine what is the central motivation of the poem, it will probably be better to take that as stimulus for music and, having devised a suitable sound idea to work upon, through improvisation and then through more considered structural repetition to create a whole piece of music which has its own internal logic and unity. It is essential that a piece of music can be 'read' as a

Holes

One day
My mother yawned, her
Mouth an out and outstretched
Hole.
Keeping my feet firmly on the ground,
I peered in.
Almost fell, in.

Look, said the clown,
Your nose has two holes in it.
For every word mouth speaks,
Nose utters two,
Siamese sniffs and snores.

He talks and talks,
Building a wall of words.
I take my muted trumpet
And silently blow, blow, blow
Out, through his word-wall.
Still, my, head, nods,
Politely, thinking miles away.
And still he talks and talks,
Certain-sure that I'm still, still,
Inside his Jericho, ericho, ericho, ericho.

Justin St John

Dots or holes?

whole, and to this end we should avoid anything that merely strings together a number of separate and undeveloped sound ideas.

A purely musical concept can be difficult for some young people to grasp; they seem to need the narrative or visual images in the background. Poetry, pictures or stories may appear to be good starting points for generating musical ideas, though they are in fact rather deceptive stimuli. They provide ready-made images – something to hang on to – but they do nothing to encourage us to 'work' our sound ideas, developing the potential in the sounds themselves for *musical* reasons. This is why we also need plenty of experience of working with musical materials independently of literary associations.

Surrealism: developing ideas beyond reality

Similar problems exist for most of us in the interpretation and appreciation of abstract visual forms. We want to make them 'mean' something, and so we relate them to familiar objects. For example, a pattern of large black circles may fail to excite us or mean anything to us unless we see them as holes. This may not be primarily what the artist intended, but one way into his imaginative world might be to allow ourselves to think of these dots as holes and to extend *our* imagination almost literally *through* them (see p. 106). This is the technique of surrealism: to take something familiar and 'bend' it. Thus through paintings such as René Magritte's tuba on fire or boot which has sprouted toes (see p. 106), we are reminded that things are not always what they seem, and that in addition to the external 'reality' there *is* an inner-world of the imagination. There has been a long tradition of surrealism in films – particularly in films for children. In a classic children's film such as *The Wizard of Oz* we are presented not only with the simpler forms of anthropomorphism (e.g. as the scarecrow comes to life) but also the more subtle transformations when, for example, in a dark and sinister forest, twisted branches of trees become the tentacle-like arms of frightening and semi-human creatures. This technique is the basis of almost everything Walt Disney and others have done with the cartoon film. The subtle twisting of reality into a new world of the imagination is familiar to most of us in countless examples from Mickey Mouse to Tom and Jerry, and from the Beatles' *Yellow Submarine* to the moveable cut-outs of Monty Python.

It is also a technique we can apply in the classroom to help children generate and develop sound ideas and to 'work' these ideas beyond the level of mere effects. The raw materials of music are sounds, and all sound is potentially musical material. Musical sounds (in the most conventional sense) operate at a fairly sophisticated level, having been refined for their particular purposes. It could be easier to begin with 'raw' sounds whose 'meaning' is generally no more than simple *signals*. For example,

> roar of motorbike = 'a motorbike'!

Listening to recordings of familiar sounds and identifying them could be an important part of the process.

From there we could begin to set sounds in the framework of a time-scale. For example, we can 'lift out', say, thirty seconds of time and examine it in detail. We could do this by tape-recording for thirty seconds and then listening to the tape to see what happened during that period, or we could all sit still and listen attentively for thirty seconds noting down the sounds we hear and where in the time-scale they appear.

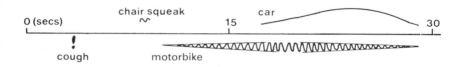

Before discussing what we heard as a whole-class group, it would be an interesting exercise to divide the class into small groups of about five or six and to ask each group to re-create the thirty seconds and what they heard in it, by imitating the sounds as exactly as possible with voices. At this stage, the sounds are not intended to be any more than 'effects' and the important thing is to imitate as closely as possible what we heard. This is a useful exercise in listening – an important preliminary to any study of music. Discussion could be based upon a comparison of what each group was able to re-create from the sounds they heard.

Having got the class making sounds with their voices in this way – sounds related to immediately identifiable familiar things – we can try to extend the work into the realms of feeling and imagination. Each group would choose one sound from those already imitated and improvise with it, allowing it to start off as the simple imitation it was before. Then, without substantially changing its characteristics, develop it into something different or into a greatly exaggerated version of the original sound. For example, the characteristic roar of a motorbike passing in the street outside, could be developed to become the roar of a totally different kind of engine or of an engine of a machine such as no-one had ever seen. What started as a straightforward imitative effect now becomes a world of sound in itself, a territory to be explored for its own sake, unrelated to the 'real' world of streets and motorbikes though still – at this stage – related to *something*. So that, for example, the 'motor-bike' could be transformed through development of the sound-image to the point where it takes off and becomes, say, a spaceship. In this way we can begin to disorientate the sound, removing it from its natural and most easily understood environment by allowing the imagination to work on the sounds themselves so that *they* generate the new images rather than having to rely on more literary or poetic ideas fed in as stimuli for further 'sound pictures'.

Although music may frequently be associated with other arts, it is crucial to musical understanding that we learn to work with sounds and to develop ideas within the medium itself. Even where visual images must form an integral part of the work, we should aim for a proper balance between the visual and the aural so that each complements the other, rather than one simply 'illustrating' the other. In this way something entirely new emerges.

A project in sound and vision

An example of just such a nice balance between music and visual art can be seen in the tape-slide programme *The Elf* (see p. 238). This is a complete audio-visual work created by a small group of 5th-form boys at Madeley Court School, Telford, Shropshire. The music came first, and its origins are discussed in the tape-slide programme *Music at Court*.

The Elf began as a classroom assignment in creative experiment. The boys in the group (playing trumpet, clarinet, guitar, percussion and saxophone) started with a rudimentary 'story line' about a group of elves living in an idyllic forest setting with little to do other than happily making music together. This tranquil life was to be disturbed by the coming of 'men'.

As a starting point for creative experiment the 'story line' is vague enough to be treated in very general terms and thus avoid the dangers of a too literal 'programme' interpretation. Apart from the ideas of a peaceful and happy life interrupted by the advent of a destructive and aggressive element, there is nothing so definite as an 'event'. The music can concentrate upon evoking the two broadly contrasting atmospheres. In the tape-slide programme *Music at Court* we see (and hear) the group begin work on the piece and take it to a reasonable stage of development in the course of one lesson period. This happened on the day in which the photography and recording for the *Music at Court* programme was being done, and there was some discussion among the group of boys about the possibilities of the tape-slide medium. The combination of music with visual images was attractive to them and they subsequently suggested completing their piece in such a way that the music could be integrated with photographs.

The music itself was composed by group improvisation, working over the ideas many times until they were finally confirmed. When the music was finished the group took photographs in the locality – pictures which not only 'illustrated' the ideas in the music but which also could be organised to complement the movement of the music and its overall design (see below and p. 111). For example, although the pictures change fairly rapidly (it would seem likely that the group was trying to get as close as possible to effects which are only really obtainable with ciné film), the pace of change in the first section is more relaxed than in the aggressive middle section. It is also worth noting the way in which, in the central section of the music, dramatic pauses are marked by comparable pauses in the slide changing. Then again, the pictures themselves are 'composed' in a way very similar to that which we adopt with musical sounds. The boys themselves appeared in the first section as the happy band living a life of 'art and music' in a woodland setting devoid of any reference to the progress of civilisation. By contrast the central section, suggesting the destruction of the idyllic life, has no human figures in any of its pictures. Instead we see only machines and buildings. The final section cleverly combines these two elements.

"THE ELF" was composed, performed,
photographed and produced by:

Stephen Brown:Guitar and Percussion
David Chatterton:Trumpet
Julian Dean:Clarinet and Saxophone
David Underwood:Clarinet
James Welch:Trumpet

MADELEY COURT SCHOOL
TELFORD SHROPSHIRE

All in all, *The Elf* turns out to be not simply a piece of music which by chance had some photographs attached to it but a vivid and compelling 'essay' on the development of new towns. Seen in the context of a classroom music course, it is clear that the strength of this work lies in the primacy of the music. Although in one sense the starting point was a visual/literary one, the music was not evolved as a straight 'translation' of visual or literary images. Rather the music was developed itself as a dramatic contrast of two sound ideas and, that much having been realised, the invention was extended into photography to make a truly integrated piece of work where music and visual elements are of equal importance.

Musically *The Elf* shows signs of having been influenced by some aspects of modern jazz. For example the modal and 'folksy' first section is reminiscent of John Coltrane or Graham Collier (cf. 'The Barley Mow' on *Down Another Road*, Fontana) and the wild gyrations of the aggressive middle section remind one of Ornette Coleman and the jazz *avant-garde*. This is not to say that the boys who made *The Elf* were deliberately copying the work of these jazz musicians but merely that we must assume that they had heard quite a lot of modern jazz and had already played in that style. Stylistic imitation is one of the ways in which we 'make music our own'. It is a way by which we engage with specific techniques in our attempt to make our own music sound like (but not identical with) music which we admire and to which we respond deeply. In this way we advance in improvisation and composition, ultimately dispensing with most of the props of other peoples' musical styles and developing along paths of our own.

How original is 'original'?

Teachers are sometimes disappointed when their pupils' improvisation and composition is obviously derivative. But genuine originality is very rare, and musical ideas which may be familiar to us as adults and musicians can still be, in a very real sense, 'new' for the pupils who discover them. That 'discovery' may take the form of exploring along clearly defined lines unashamedly derived from the work of a much admired composer or performing group. We can see this kind of creative imitation at work in the compositions of some of the upper school pupils illustrated in the tape-slide programme *Music at Notley High School Part 2*. The wide ranging use of electronic apparatus for music at Notley High School caught the imagination of some pupils who were well aware of the use of synthesizers by groups such as *Tangerine Dream*. Moreover, the multi-media presentation of such groups, making use of lighting effects, also had its influence on at least one young composer whose work is shown in the tape-slide programme.

Alberio, by 6th-form student Tim, was conceived with dance, lighting and background projections in mind. Musically, it relies heavily upon various aspects of electronic sound successfully combined with conventional melodic and chordal patterns. The piece is structured on the basis of contrasts; contrasting tone colours in music, contrasting colours and physical movements in the lighting and the dance. *Alberio* is an impressive composition but some teachers who have heard the piece, aware of the strong influences, have felt unable to accept this as evidence of 'creative' work. Its derivative nature is, for them, a stumbling block; it is not sufficiently original to be called 'creative'. But that is not how the composer himself thought of it:

> I never did get it exactly how I wanted it, because of my lack of technique . . . practice on the synthi . . . because I hadn't really been using it an awful lot before and I had to get used to it and obviously couldn't get exactly the right sound I wanted first of all. But I got it very, very near. It [music] is just a way of expressing myself; you know, like you can't express yourself in words. You take over from where the poets leave off. (*Music at Notley High School*, T/S frame 73)

Tim's own words make it clear that, although he must have been aware of the strong influences, he was genuinely exploring these sounds. The experience was *for him* new and 'creative'. If this form of creativity is perhaps closer to interpretation than invention, it is no less an exercise of the imagination than the work of artists within a 'school'. At any level composition is largely a process by which the composer sets himself problems and seeks solutions. This is not a mechanical procedure since, although compositional problems may often have elements in common, each situation is bound to have something new about it. There will be uncharted territory to explore, and this will probably mean trying a number of possibilities before the final solution is discovered. To ensure that he does not wander aimlessly, the composer must himself impose limitations. He may decide to work in certain timbral areas, or within limitations of specific scales or sets of notes. Students who take as starting points for their own exploration general stylistic features in the music of groups or composers they admire, are doing no more than make those features boundaries for creative experiment.

In the upper forms of the secondary school we should naturally expect to find musical pupils choosing their own starting points for work. Lower down in the school it is more likely to be the teacher who sets the boundaries through 'assignments' for creative exploration. These assignments can themselves be based upon specific and limiting features of style or technique. Invention needs something to work upon.

'Tangible' sound: materials and instruments

The teacher's first task is to help pupils to focus upon particular areas of sound exploration. There can be no hard and fast rules about how this should be done or about where we should start. We may decide that the old maxim of teaching 'from the known to the unknown' means starting where our pupils are – with their own musical tastes or at least with very familiar sounds. But it could equally be argued that 'starting where they are' has nothing to do with musical style or taste but merely with the common ground we all occupy in being able to hear sounds at all. Indeed, where very familiar musical styles produce barriers of prejudice, a new approach based upon unfamiliar sounds could be neutral territory from which substantial progress might be made unhindered by pre-conceived notions of what is or is not 'music'.* We have already mentioned the possibilities of 'found object sounds' and unconventional sound sources as starting points for creative experiment. The Project's tape-slide programme *Materials and Instruments* outlines the possibilities for a course in which students explore the sound properties of different materials and use their discoveries to invent and construct new instruments, and to make music with them. One of the biggest problems with music is its intangible nature. A course of the kind proposed in the tape-slide programme offers a line of sound-experiment which can lead to inventiveness on two fronts – the instruments and the music.

In schools up and down the country students are now creating music of their own. In much of the advanced work orchestral instruments are used, but probably most teachers rely on classroom instruments such as the 'Orff' xylophones, glockenspiels and metallophones. Useful as these instruments are, the range of sounds they offer – both in pitch and timbre – is severely limited. In the circumstances there is much to be said for going beyond that range of sounds but without having to encounter the considerable technical difficulties of orchestral instruments. Again, it is principally a question of focus. We could simply collect sounds and make music with them. But the additional feature of creating a musical instrument (possibly one that has not been thought of before) gives a measure of coherence that might otherwise be lacking in the exploration. This can be a useful way into creative experiment, improvisation and composition.

There is, of course, nothing very new about making musical instruments as part of the school music programme. In primary schools teachers and children have been making simple percussion instruments – such as jingles from metal bottle-tops, maracas from plastic bottles filled with dried peas,

---

* Music, like so many other things, is subject to fashion. In addition to having a general goal of musical understanding, the music teacher is working for an attitude to music which will transcend popular assumptions and prejudices.

claves from pieces of broom handle, and so on – for a very long time. One-stringed fiddles and xylophones are logical developments on the same lines and there are several books available offering helpful suggestions for this kind of work. That is a useful beginning. It calls for some degree of skill and care, not only in the making, but also in learning to listen carefully to the quality of the sounds the instruments produce. In particular, constructing pitched instruments such as xylophones and glockenspiels can be a useful training in pitch discrimination. The tape-slide programme *Materials and Instruments* gives examples of glockenspiels made by using nails 15 centimetres long or ceramic strips. But instruments of this kind, because they are so closely linked with traditional instruments of the same type, are unlikely to stimulate creative experiment much beyond conventional melodic patterns. And we are then still limited to more or less the same kind of instruments we have in the Orff Instrumentarium.

In the early 1960s Ronald Roberts, in his book *Musical Instruments Made to be Played*, promoted interest in a new direction. With chordal dulcimer, Nordic lyre and bowed psaltery we could provide pupils with a much needed alternative to the pervasive percussion sounds which have tended to characterise classroom music. Even though the Roberts' instruments are intended primarily for music in traditional forms, the string tone – plucked or bowed – does offer new scope for experiment.

In the main we shall probably use such instruments for the purpose for which they were intended. Thus, the chordal dulcimer is for accompanying songs. The strings are arranged in four groups of three – giving us the tonic, dominant, sub-dominant and supertonic triads. Without having to develop the more demanding techniques of the guitar, this instrument enables us to accompany simple tonal melodies. On the face of it there would seem to be little scope here for sound exploration. However, unlike the guitar, the chordal dulcimer does not have frets. It is therefore capable of producing some very interesting glissando effects – which have a strangely oriental flavour. A glass rod, fitting neatly between the string and the belly of the instrument, can be moved while the string is plucked. Alternatively, several small pieces of glass tubing can be placed between the strings and the sound board as moveable bridges, and by setting them at varying points along the strings we can create new scale patterns – even to the extent of using intervals smaller than the semitone. Arranged like this and plucked, the instrument sounds not unlike a Japanese koto. If we allow the imagination to develop along this line we might find ourselves inventing – and perhaps building – a new instrument based on this principle. In fact this is exactly what one student did and the result can be seen in the tape-slide programme. The instrument – called a 'Selecta' (because you select new scales for each new piece of music) – was in effect a very large chordal dulcimer with 24 strings instead of 12. Unlike the chordal dulcimer, the new instrument had strings all of equal thickness and all tuned to exactly the same note. Different pitches were obtained by sliding small metal bridges to different points on the strings. These points could be calculated mathematically to reproduce the intervals of ancient and oriental scales. (Details of these scale patterns can be found in Harry Partch, *The Genesis of a Music*, University of Wisconsin Press, obtainable from Da Capo Reprints, 3 Henrietta Street, London, WC2.)

In this instance the creative impetus was derived from the form of an existing instrument – the chordal dulcimer – which was adapted principally so that the student could experiment with unusual scale patterns. But no doubt it is such experiment that has, over the centuries, led to the development of musical instruments generally. A student who creates music for a new instrument developed from an older model, will perhaps be ready to find out a lot more about the development of musical instruments. He might be led to the study of dynamic problems such as those that faced the makers of keyboard instruments and brought about the invention of the piano. In the same way he might explore technical possibilities that are in common use on some instruments but not on others. For example, string harmonics are part of the standard repertoire of violin, viola and cello and also in music for harp and guitar. But until John Cage developed the 'prepared' piano in the early 1950s, the harmonics of piano strings had never been extensively used.

The tape-slide programme *Materials and Instruments* suggests possibilities for developing new instruments from old ideas: clay pots with whistle mouthpieces, and a glass 'glockenspiel' called the Fenetraphone. And from there the ideas can develop along entirely new lines. Examples are given of an instrument made from ping-pong balls whose tones are regulated by needles; a Musical Chair, the plucked and bowed string sounds of which are reminiscent of Indian classical music; and a 'composite instrument' made by a group of students using a variety of sound sources – metal, wood and glass. But *Materials and Instruments* is not a unit of work to be imitated. Its purpose is to suggest just one line of approach to creative experiment, and to emphasise the need for a focal point in such work, whatever the precise details of the course we devise.

Improvisation and composition in popular music idioms

Imitation is an aspect of creativity, and it can be of particular importance to teenagers. This is an age when there is often a strong desire for means of personal expression; a desire which can be satisfied by music if the young people are able to identify themselves with it. They will tend to have pronounced likes and dislikes and their first need will be to be able to play and sing what they like, in a style as near as possible to the model they admire. Something very similar seems to happen in visual arts work in schools. Teenagers are frequently anxious to be able to 'draw what we see' and to be able to make things appear on paper 'as we know they are'. In other words they experience 'a crisis of representation':

> . . . *often the child takes refuge behind* a mass of clichés and worn-out ideas. Within this age-group many children are sensitive and self-critical, and, easily discouraged into conventional materials they already know, need to explore new techniques and be subject to new stimuli. (Plaskow, 1964, p. 23).

Applied to music this statement might seem to suggest moving away from familiar pop, rock, reggae or whatever, and indeed a case can be made for starting afresh with new stimuli in a 'neutral' region of sound that does not automatically create associations with the 'classical'/'pop' dichotomy. Nevertheless it would be a mistake to overlook the value of imitation as a point from which creative ideas can flow. And imitation implies familiarity with what is imitated.

Piers Spencer (Woodberry Down School, London) has written extensively, from the background of his own teaching, about the use of pop music in class teaching (see Vulliamy and Lee 1980, and Piers Spencer, *The Influence of Pop on Creative Music in the Classroom*, Schools Council Secondary Music Project, York, *Working Paper 1*, 1975). He starts from his pupils' existing involvement with music:

> Pop music is central to the social life of perhaps the vast majority of adolescent children. They hear it on the radio, on records, they dance to it at discos and many of them perform it. With so much exposure to and evident enjoyment of pop music, one would expect it to influence the creative work they produce in the classroom.

Describing work with children at a Hull comprehensive school he says:

> I had a pleasant, mixed ability class, consisting of twenty-nine reasonably musical children. The class had not done a great deal of creative work before, so I spent the first three weeks giving formal lessons in which I got all of them to play as a group, exploring simple pieces which had the basic elements of the Afro-American style; that is, the style which still forms the backbone of nearly all present day pop. These elements are: riffs (ostinati), the pentatonic scale, syncopation and the blues chord sequence.

After three weeks the pupils were forming themselves into groups and composing short pieces. They were given a variety of possible arrangements. For example, to compose the words and music of a blues; to compose a short 'commercial' for radio; or to make up a song or instrumental number whose form or character they decided for themselves.

> I deliberately did not stress that I wanted them to compose in a pop style. On the other hand the music ethos of the school was such that they felt perfectly free to do so if they wished.

Piers Spencer wanted to find out whether the teacher-directed improvisations the class had made so far would affect their composing, and what correlation there might be between their enthusiasm for pop and the influence it might have on their creative work.

> One of the dangers inherent in any style is that, until it has been thoroughly assimilated, real expression is often replaced by insincere gestures – 'stock responses' . . . I heard two girls singing a recent hit song 'Sweet Talkin' Guy'. I recorded a short phrase from their singing of the song and then asked them to sing a phrase from 'Football Crazy', an English song which they knew well. It is interesting that the latter seems to come more spontaneously from their speech habits, whereas the former, in its Americanised vowels and in the different tone colour produced by head resonance, seems to have *assumed* a personality. In this, I feel, they are not being themselves, however skilful the imitation. This contrast is evident in many of the remaining recordings, which are all of unaided original work.

On a tape produced in association with his paper for the Project, Piers Spencer illustrates the progress of this work through a number of pieces by pupils. These pieces all come from the one school, but they are probably characteristic of what might be produced through a similar course elsewhere. Although the pupils, in their spoken and written declarations of musical taste, and in their social behaviour, appear to show a preference for certain kinds of pop music, 'when it comes to making up their own music they often show an assimilation of a variety of styles, both pop and non-pop'. The key is, of course, music *and* words with which they are familiar and which they feel they can imitate. As with their work in the visual arts, the music may initially be little more than 'a mass of clichés and worn-out ideas', but it is nevertheless the outcome of conscious choice and preference. It is a creative act, albeit at a humble level, and with encouragement it can certainly lead to more original work (see Malcolm Nicholls' account of the development of 'Dene' in Vulliamy & Lee, *Pop Music in School*, pp. 127–8, and Piers Spencer's analysis of music by the same boy in *An individual develops*, also in *Pop Music in School*, pp. 113–121).

The sound first, and then the sign

One cannot over-estimate the primacy of instinct and predilection in the development of creative ideas through improvisation and composition. Questions of musical style are, in a sense, irrelevant. The important thing is to start *where our pupils are*. Naturally, this could have stylistic implications: 'where they are' could mean 'the music they enjoy'. On the other hand as we have already emphasised above, it could mean quite simply 'the sounds they can perceive'. The fact that we have two ears and can hear and delight in or find an interest in sounds of all kinds is a valid starting point; it is something already experienced, something we 'know' and can build upon. Improvisation and composition are manifestly not rule-directed procedures, however large a part 'received techniques' may eventually play. Yet so powerful has the conventional approach been that we may find this a difficult proposition to accept. As Professor Alan Walker points out:

> The music Establishment has led us astray . . . One of its basic creeds is the cultivation of musical understanding via musical rationale . . . this is a fallacious principle despite the fact that most present-day musical education is based upon it. You cannot teach anybody anything that he does not already (intuitively) know. (Walker, 1962, p. 149)

And again:

> Music is non-conceptual. It neither requires nor demands an 'explanation'. It is purely musical truth which can be comprehended on a purely musical level . . . all our knowledge about it must flow out of our experience of it . . . there is no valid theoretical concept in the entire history of music which did not first emerge as an intuitive part of creative practice. Musical theory is always wise after the creative event . . . (Walker, 1966, p. 5)

If we set out to encourage young people to improvise and compose we must start with the youngsters themselves and the sounds. But this does not imply a totally 'free' process, uncontrolled and aimless. On the contrary, it should suggest clear lines of *work* with the sounds and the musical ideas, aimed either at careful imitation or at some form of motivic development. Whichever way it is approached, this is a *conscious* process, though not one that proceeds according to externally imposed 'rules'. There can surely be no better way of coming to understand music than to try to develop our own intuitive groping after a means of personal expression, however clumsy, derivative or humble that may be at first. The theory comes later to explain the experience.

Interpretation: the creativity of performance

We have dealt at some length with the *invention* of musical structures; the exercise of creativity in generating and developing musical ideas through improvisation and composition. As in any other art form, this is a process in which we strive to construct forms which will give a coherent 'external' identity to inwardly perceived (*felt*) ideas. From a multitude of possibilities we select some forms or strategies and reject others, continually weighing up the expressed detail in relation to a 'held' mental picture of the projected whole work. We do this until we arrive at a point where we are certain that what we have made is right for us, and that no other arrangement of the materials will provide (for us) a truly satisfactory expression. Only then do we declare the piece finished.

It is not difficult to envisage this process as it underlies the work of the painter or the writer; the one standing back from his easel and contemplating the work in progress, 'matching' it in his mind with the imagined ideas, the other pondering the words he has put on the paper, considering how far he needs to make alterations to bring utterance in line with the original concept. And all this is true, of course, of the composer in his own way.

But in music it also applies to the re-creator; the interpreter, the performer. He too must match outward expression with inward perception. Creativity is as important in the performance of music as it is in composition. At the highest levels this is obvious. In the writings of professional critics and in the self-criticism of performers we are frequently made aware of the shortfall between ideal and achievement, though we may feel that, when it comes to amateur or children's performance, such thinking cannot apply because in these instances the technical resources are so much more limited than in the case of the professional musician. Consequently, we may tend to believe that musical performance in schools must of necessity be primarily a *directed* activity, dependent upon the teacher's own interpretative ideas and thus offering no scope at all for pupil's inventiveness. The teacher is the one who 'knows how the music goes', so that rarely, if at all, shall we feel we can invite suggestions for interpretation from student players.

But is it any more unreasonable to expect pupils to have ideas about interpretation and performance than to expect them to generate and develop their own musical compositions? We have seen that, by offering pupils opportunity to use sound as a vehicle for invention and to experiment with musical structures, even at a very humble level results can be satisfying and productive and can lead to a deeper understanding of how music works. But it is also acknowledged that, while such experimentation may lead students to genuine 'discoveries' and produce what is *for them* 'new' music, they are nevertheless likely to be covering territory at least very similar to that already explored by professional composers. Indeed this is one way in which we can usefully draw attention to the work of other composers and relate it to the classroom activities. Strikingly original music is rare at any level of attainment and, even among professionals, conventions quickly establish themselves so that improvisation and composition inevitably become, to some extent, a kind of 'imitation with modifications'.

This is a perfectly natural and musical process. It is one of the ways in which styles develop. If we are to grow as composers we need to assimilate and 'to make our own', stylistic features which we glean from the work of others – especially where those features seem to have a particular meaning for us and are aligned with our own attempts at musical expression.* It is from there that we start to forge our own style. In a sense when we begin to explore possibilities for making up our own music, we may be doing very little more than re-interpreting 'generalities' of ideas and structural patterns that have sunk into preconsciousness,† either because we have at some time heard something similar and it is there deep in our memory, or because, if only in a general way, we are aware of certain trends in music.

The techniques which have been developed for encouraging 'creative' work in improvisation and composition in the classroom recognise and make use of these imitative and interpretive tendencies. The resulting work is no less 'personal' to the students, indeed the process can help to bring them closer to (and therefore make more 'personal' for them) the expressiveness of a wide range of musical styles. But for many of those teachers who have been keen to see classroom music-making develop along these lines, the concept of creativity has been limited to 'making up our own music'. Accepting, as we must, the importance of imitation in that process, it is difficult to see why teachers do not, in general, do more to encourage the most obvious aspects of creativity through *interpretation and performance of existing music* (see the Project's second film, *Arrangements* (1981)).

Here, just as in other musical 'creative' activities, work can be carried out by groups as well as by individuals. There is opportunity for experiment and for sharing different views of the same assignment. Variety of interpretation may spring from a broad and knowledgeable acquaintance with the repertoire, or it may be simply the result of varying technical accomplishments. For example, a whole class is taught a song. When everyone knows the tune well, the words are discussed and the different moods or events narrated are noted. The class is then divided into small

---

* 'It is also characteristic of the musical person to sink himself into the mood of the music and achieve a relation to it that has an effect on his whole spiritual being. He experiences the art-work so inwardly and so profoundly that he feels as though he were creating it.' (G. Révész *Introduction to the Psychology of Music*, 1953, p. 134.) See also the following (from James Britton, *Language and Learning* Penguin Books, 1970, p. 261) describing the work of a sixteen-year-old in an English class who had taken eagerly to the poetry of Dylan Thomas, and whose creative writing went through a phase of trying to emulate some of Thomas' idiosyncracies: 'Looking at her world through Dylan Thomas' spectacles was a way eventually of extending her view of it: as the balance righted itself, she found her own voice again, but richer for the experiment of using his. Trying other people's voices may for the adolescent be a natural and necessary part of the process of finding one's own.'

† i.e. ideas which can easily be recalled since they have not been unconsciously repressed.

working groups (e.g. groups of five or six) each of which produces its own version of the song. This could mean variety in accompaniments – anything from simple clapping patterns to more complicated percussion accompaniments or the addition of chords on guitar(s) or tuned percussion, or even the invention of some kind of counter-melody. A 'version' of the song could also imply an unaccompanied rendering which creates interest through varied vocal techniques and ornamentation, or through contrasts of solo and tutti sections, or contrasts of girls and boys voices. As with other forms of creative work, it is probably best to allow students the opportunity to experiment with their own ideas before looking at ways in which others have tackled a similar problem. Nevertheless, the different versions of the song having been made, performed and discussed, the teacher now has a good basis on which to demonstrate further possibilities (comparing different recordings of a folk song – including folk/pop presentations as well as 'authentic' or 'revival' versions – or discussing ways in which such a song has been made the basis of an orchestral work e.g. Delius's use of *Brigg Fair* or Bartók's use of Hungarian and Roumanian folksongs or his developments of 'folk-music style' as a basis for original composition). Then again, the work of one group might become the starting point for some class instruction, so that the skills that have been seen at work (say, guitar chords or whatever) can be learned and used by others. The manifest achievement of one group's version of a song can be a stronger motivation for others to learn these skills than would be a purely theoretical approach to chords, independent of any *necessary* musical use.

Instrumental skills are more likely to develop through performance of existing music than they are through improvisation. A large part of the satisfaction of playing a musical instrument is in the achievement of re-creating known music in accordance with performances we have heard and enjoyed. When *our* brass band begins to sound something like those that win the competitions, then we know we are getting somewhere and we are encouraged to improve our skills even more. Here a great deal depends upon the teacher's own skills as a conductor, and we should never underestimate the importance of direction and sound musical judgement in achieving worthwhile results. Naturally, in striving for high standards of ensemble playing, it is usually necessary for the school band or orchestra to become selective. Normally, it will follow that the group must be rehearsed outside the school timetable, and consequently, the tendency is for this kind of musical performance to be removed entirely from the classroom. The usual pattern of rehearsals – after school hours (or occasionally during lunch hours) – restricts the broader educational value of band or orchestra. It becomes (because it has to become) a training session, practising music for concerts, ironing out technical problems, getting music together for a deadline. Time is short. Pupils have other commitments and homework ahead of them. The best that can be done is for the teacher to take sole charge and become more of a trainer than an educator, putting forward his ideas rather than drawing out possibilities from the players.

No criticism is intended here of what has become the tradition in this kind of operation. By and large it is necessary and, in its own way, productive. There are many excellent school ensembles giving a great deal of pleasure to the players and often achieving quite extraordinarily high standards of performance. However, it is a pity if the pursuit of high standards within the selective orchestra and bands demands so much from teachers that they feel unable to encourage instrumental activity in the classroom. There, of course, standards would have to be relaxed to some extent if all the pupils were to be involved. In many ways this calls for greater skill on the teacher's part because he must provide music which will be attractive, stimulating *and practicable* for those with little or no conventional instrumental training, and at the same time will be worthwhile for those with more advanced skills. In addition, what is played must whet appetites so that both beginners and advanced players will want to go on improving their techniques. A more demanding situation for any conductor is hard to imagine! We have already (pp. 69–70 above) looked at some of the possibilities for *ad hoc* classroom bands. Further examples of such work are shown in the Project's film *A Place for Music*. There we see a balance between the teacher's direction (as conductor), his instruction in specific detail of technique (e.g. the notation of transposing instruments) and his wider educational role, drawing upon the players' own ideas and their suggestions for interpretation of the music.

From the start, the creativity of performance is linked to developing technical skill. Whether the techniques are simple or complex, only by mastering them are we able to use them expressively – creatively. It is a mistake to see the development of skills as a separate and preliminary stage in the process. Children need the creative stimulus of 'using' the skills they have acquired *as* they acquire them. We must try, therefore, to provide opportunities for interpretative decision-taking even at the most elementary levels. Pupils should get used to making up their own minds on 'how the music should go' (e.g. dynamics, speed, modes of attack, etc.: 'What is the mood of this music? What will be a suitable way of presenting it? What are the important features that need to become foreground? What is background? What do *you* think the composer wants us to feel through this piece, and what must we do to bring out that quality?'). No music, however simple, is outside the scope of such questions. Every performance must try to *present* the music; to re-*create* it sensitively and with the utmost skill the performer(s) can bring to the task.

And instrumental music can also have an important role in classroom music-making for the majority. Sadly, this is still overlooked in many schools where the opportunities for performance are restricted to the selective extra-curricular bands and orchestras, and the classroom music lessons are lecture-style presentations of 'theory' or 'appreciation' – with perhaps an occasional 'massed' singing session as a token of genuine music-*making*. It is possible for most pupils to acquire some degree of instrumental skill, sufficient to take part in simple ensemble performance in the class lessons. If, from the very beginning, this can be linked with opportunities for them to take their own interpretative decisions, both in larger ensembles (such as a band involving the whole class group) and in smaller groups (twos, threes, and fives, for example), the resulting confidence in dealing with musical ideas will not only produce added motivation for more ensemble participation but will feed back into other forms of musical creativity. Even quite elementary instrumental skill can be a useful spur to invention in improvisation and composition. More advanced instrumentalists will clearly have correspondingly increased scope for exploring their own melodic, harmonic and structural ideas, and for creating more complex pieces of music.

The Project observed very few instances where teachers seemed prepared to capitalise fully on the creative potential of musical performance. If we are to make the best educational use of musical experience it is essential that we do all we can to close the gap between composition and performance. It is in any case a false distinction and one which has appeared mainly as a result of misunderstanding; a mistaken view of music which sees amateur performance as possible only under the total direction of an instructor. This produces a distinction between 'experimental' or 'Creative Music' (sic) and the 'traditional', authoritative – and, by implication, musically more satisfactory – procedures of the school orchestra. But if we drive instrumental music out of the classroom, or use it in class lessons in a way that offers no opportunity for students to exercise their own interpretative judgements, not only do we confirm the majority in the view that musical accomplishment is really for the gifted minority, but also we diminish the opportunities for developing an all-embracing creative attitude to music in the curriculum. For nothing has been more damaging to progress in this area than the mistaken idea that 'Creative Music' is in some way an alternative to other forms of musical activity, or even that it is in opposition to 'traditional' musical performance.

If we have fostered this distinction we should not be surprised if those students who are instrumentalists find themselves helpless without the printed notes in front of them, never play from memory or 'by ear', never improvise, and never make any attempt at creative interpretative decisions for themselves. They will naturally come to rely entirely on their teachers as the only possible authorities, distrusting their own ears and aural sensitivity, perhaps completely unaware that the act of performance could ever demand anything from them other than simply doing what they are told to do. Understandably, for these students any kind of experimental activity with sounds will appear to be 'messing about'. Unused to taking decisions about sounds and sound structures they will almost certainly see what is presented to them as 'Creative Music' as something different from, and less valuable than 'proper music'. Regrettably there are more than a few teachers who also look at music in this way. As may be expected, their attempts to promote creativity in the classroom, sincere though they may be, have a tendency to failure because there is little incentive to extend techniques or to involve more advanced instrumentalists who have had substantial experience of improvisation and composition. Far from being at opposite poles, these are two aspects of the same thing and cannot flourish without one another.

A variety of musical material can be provided for small groups to rehearse and perform in timetabled music lessons. Groups should be encouraged to explore many different musical styles and to prepare pieces for presentation to the rest of the class, using, as far as possible, their own initiative in interpretation. As with group improvisation and composition, preparing a piece for performance needs time for ideas to generate and develop, and the teacher's role is perhaps best seen as an instructor, visiting each group in turn and asking appropriate questions to stimulate the students' exploration of the possibilities. Occasionally, of course, the teacher will find it necessary to take charge and help by directing a performance, either with a small group or with the whole class. We could try too to make better use of peripatetic instrumental teachers in class music lessons. And there is scope for experiment with different groupings of instruments (and voices); it may be helpful sometimes to have the more advanced instrumentalists work together, but there will be occasions when one or two advanced players could join with, and so encourage less experienced players, the latter providing – say – a simple percussion accompaniment or a harmonic accompaniment in the form of a short chordal ostinato.

Finally, we can stimulate interest in instrumental skills by occasionally inviting individuals (or small chamber-music groups/rock music groups/folk groups, etc.) to prepare items for performance to the rest of the class. These can be starting points for discussing interpretation, the players/singers offering their own views on their chosen styles of performance. Even players of elementary standard should be encouraged to present music in this way.

Growth-point: the creativity of listening

We are inclined to think of musical activity in terms of a hierarchy in which composer and performers figure above listeners. Doubtless this is because, for most people, listening to music in a concert hall, or from recordings or radio is a relatively passive business. Naturally, there will be times when we feel that what we want from music is an uncomplicated aid to relaxation; a pleasant but undemanding background to reverie. But such a view hardly does justice to the artistry of musical composition and performance. Music may not communicate like spoken language but it *does* have something to communicate in the beauty of its forms and structures. Unless we are prepared to give our full attention to music it becomes a pointless exercise; indeed we shall miss its meaning altogether. For music has not survived as an art merely by providing a pleasing background to other activities. It is clearly a worthwhile experience in itself, and it is essentially an aural experience. All the efforts of technique and skill on the part of performers and composers are aimed at one thing and one thing only – the coherent expression of sound ideas; and when all else has been said it is ultimately our ability to perceive, assimilate and *understand* the sound of music which matters. There is nothing else we can do with music but listen to it!

As we have already observed, the ear is really the only 'rule' that exists in music, and aural sensitivity is the key to all musical understanding. This is the point from which we grow musically, since listening is a creative act; a process by which we make the sounds part of ourselves and so assimilate their meaning *for us*. Active listening is fundamental at every stage of improvisation, composition, interpretation and presentation: we evaluate and take decisions on the basis of what we hear, and however much kinetic satisfaction we get from playing an instrument, the ultimate pleasure is *aural*. The argument, so often advanced as a justification for the traditional 'Music Appreciation' lessons in schools – that we should, in the main, enable pupils to become 'informed listeners' because only a small number of them will ever become practical musicians – may have distorted our view of the art of listening, and indeed of the importance of aural sensitivity throughout the entire range of musical practice. The implication that, if the majority cannot actually *make* music, then – as a second best – they can listen, is unfortunate. For listening is an aspect of music-*making*; it is the means by which music is re-made within anyone who properly and positively hears it. Far from being a third-order activity, it is basic to musical experience.

This does not, however, imply school music lessons focussed entirely on the record player. Indeed there is an illogicality in the 'disc-jockey' approach through which a teacher will attempt to introduce a whole class to certain musical works from the record player, talking about the compositions and the lives and times of the composers, and playing brief extracts as 'illustrations'. This method grew up with the gramophone itself and the consequent availability of many superb performances, more or less at the touch of a button. It was thus not difficult for us to convince ourselves that we could bring the concert hall experience into the classroom and fill the ears of whole classes of children with the sounds of great music; an experience they might otherwise miss.

Unfortunately we often seem to lack faith in the music itself, so that the musical experience which was our first aim may easily take second place to the explanation and the background information we feel obliged to impart – as though music would be meaningless without a spoken commentary. Moreover, however expert we are in our presentation, the obvious differences between pupils hearing music 'live' and from choice, and having it played at them from a loudspeaker in a classroom to which they have been directed by a school timetable must affect anyone's ability to inwardly 'receive' the music. In the 'academic' atmosphere of a classroom it is unlikely that those without previous practical experience of music will be able to respond very positively to the music; yet it is just those pupils for whom this method tries to cater.

Hand and ear

It is a truism to say that most of us, once we have mastered a skill, forget what life was like before we had that particular accomplishment. It seems possible – and indeed probable – that many school music teachers overlook the importance, in their own musical awareness, of an interaction between listening and the struggle for coherent expression through performance or composition/arrangement. Understanding music depends upon continuing *active* experience, not passive contemplation. Rarely is it easy. There are considerable physical barriers to overcome. In the performance of music there are the problems of getting our fingers to fit on to the keys or getting our hands to control simultaneously the stopping of strings and the movement of a bow, or – if we are singers – getting our vocal chords and breathing to act efficiently together to produce the right kind of sound at the right time. And there are also what might be called 'identity' problems for the ear since, as we strive for control of the medium with fingers or breath, we must at the same time learn to inhabit new worlds of sound and to make sense of the sounds we hear as we produce them. It is precisely in this, our striving to control the medium and to overcome the physical hurdles of hand and ear, that we reach deeply into the sounds of music, so that, with this sustained experience behind us, when we come to deal with the 'second-hand' presentation of music 'frozen' in a recorded

performance, even if the music is unfamiliar, we are automatically able to make the necessary mental adjustment and relate what we hear to the actuality we know. The majority of school pupils do not have that advantage. As teachers we may be inclined to assume that, because *we* find no obvious difficulty in assimilating music from recordings, it will be just as easy for our pupils. We forget that essential link: the first-hand work with sounds; the interaction between the physical and the aural.

Nowhere, perhaps, is this more obvious than when a teacher, dismayed by the lack of response to the recordings he has chosen, tries to capture pupils' interest by inviting them to bring their own pop music recordings and play them as part of the music lesson. Normally the response is not much better, for, in the case of most standard 'top twenty' material, this is unashamedly entertainment 'background', and with its familiar harmonic language and insistent beat it is not intended to engage us deeply beyond inspiring us to *move*. There's nothing wrong with that, of course; that *is* the appropriate 'physical' contact with the sound in this style of music – though doubtless few music teachers would think disco dancing particularly appropriate to the music lesson! What is interesting is to note that in those schools where considerable *musical* progress has been made through the medium of Afro-American styles it is always on the basis of practical music-making not simply listening to 'top twenty' records. Within the field of pop, rock, reggae, soul and so on there is manifestly as much variety as in any other area of music, and there is plenty of music which *is* intended to engage us thoughtfully. To respond to music, whatever the style – 'pop' or 'classical' – we have to learn to listen with care, and that is an active role not a passive one. It grows out of other musical activity; first-hand encounter with sounds and sound structures, and opportunities to take positive creative decisions about these things. Theoretical, historical and sociological explanations may be of interest to those who are already motivated to listen to music, but in the last analysis it is music itself which speaks to us, and unfamiliar music 'makes contact' through the agency of the sum of our previous musical experience, not through rational explanation:

> A listener who responds to music does so because he has unconsciously identified himself with it; it is not only true *for* him, it is true *of* him as well. No musician needs to be told that the intuitive musical experience is a vehicle of truth far superior to that of rational thought. (Walker, 1966, p. 9)

Constructive listening

Listening to music is a vital part of music education, but we must first see that our pupils know *how* to listen to sounds. This may well mean starting at a very simple level with whatever sounds can be heard around us, and working from there to 'musical' uses of sounds. Elsewhere we have given examples of the kind of work which can encourage careful and productive listening. When groups of students make up their own music, or devise arrangements, or organise performances of other people's music, it can be helpful to draw attention to recordings that in some way link with what the students themselves have done. Their own activity in putting sounds together, or in taking decisions about points of interpretation or style of presentation, technically simple though it may be, will provide the all important bridge between the reality of musical experience and the recorded sound.

Having approached recorded music by way of their own creative efforts, students will frequently take fresh impetus from recordings for the continuation and development of their own ideas. The Project's tape-slide programme *Music at Court* offer some examples of this process at work. The boys we see working on *The Elf* have clearly drawn inspiration from certain aspects of modern jazz. A rock music group is also strongly influenced by what they have heard – as we should expect. But perhaps the most striking example is a group of four girls shown working – as a classroom assignment – on a piece for clarinets and saxophone. In this group the player producing the main musical ideas talks about the ways in which her own thoughts for a piece of music have emerged from other music she has heard: she is not copying another style but is developing her own music from sounds which have excited her imagination. Two works in particular appeared to mean a lot to her, the Stravinsky *Octet* and Rimsky-Korsakoff's *Sheherazade*:

> . . . I was trying to compose for a string quartet, and I was trying to start off with an F-major arpeggio . . . So I said to Susan, 'Could you plan an arpeggio of F . . . Cecilia came in with A, and then C . . . so you get this arpeggio going up. And I came in with . . . kind of . . . Stravinsky 'Pagan' . . . F to E-flat, and it was all going down . . . arpeggio . . . and we worked it out from there. Usually, when we improvise, we have some form to work to, but we didn't in the case, except for the first movement . . . *We had to listen very carefully* to other people so that we knew where we were exactly. So it takes not only your own part but everybody else's part into consideration, and you work around that. We call it 'Conversations for Four' because we take it from one to another. Linda starts off with a very abstract theme, and then we sort of take over and 'chat' to each other and to one another . . . It sounds a bit like something from 'Sheherazade' – though it is not exactly.

Here we do indeed have a creative attitude towards listening to music, not simply because what is heard stimulates the production of music by the students themselves, but principally because the need to hear music and to 'make it one's own' arises from the classroom music *activities*. The student we have quoted above (then in the 5th year of the secondary school) is the product of class teaching which gives priority to music-making (in every sense of the word). As the teacher, Grenville Hancox, has said himself:

> . . . I was determined that . . . I should try to do everything in my power to involve everybody in making music – not just to look after the small band who would be able to look after themselves anyway, but to make everybody aware and conscious of music-making, socially, artistically – creatively, recreatively . . . To me it is important that they are able *to listen to each other's music* and develop a critical awareness for each other's classroom compositions . . . One of the most pleasing things is that they are able *to listen to each other's music in a responsible way*, and . . . if they can take that attitude . . . and listen to other composers' music – classical composers or Stockhausen or Baroque composers – and apply the same sort of . . . critical approach, then I think we may be on the way to achieving some progress . . .

The music curriculum at Madeley Court School recognises the need for significant interaction between all modes of music activity – improvising and composing, skill-learning, performing and listening. It is largely the provision of opportunity for this interaction that produces the essential feedback between what the pupils do themselves and what they hear done by others (e.g. on recordings), and it is this which makes the musical activity in the school grow and spread so that it becomes realistically available for the majority of pupils.

A 'syllabus' of listening

Like Grenville Hancox's course at Madeley, the music curriculum devised by Tom Gamble at Manland School, Harpenden also places emphasis upon making and listening. We have described this course in detail elsewhere (see pp. 39–43 and Appendix I). It may nevertheless be helpful to reiterate here Tom Gamble's principle that 'Musical activities in the classroom should include all three basic modes of musical experience – the creative, the re-creative and the perceptual' and that 'Working with sounds; ordering developing and shaping them to form a coherent sound object which is musically expressive and interesting . . . helps to develop an understanding of the basic concepts of music and encourages a deeper response to all kinds of music'. With this as his starting point, Tom Gamble has structured a course which quite deliberately links pupils' work with recorded examples – particularly from the music of our own time:

> In Michael's composition, the wind motif at the beginning and the short bursts of sound energy from the xylophone led me to draw the class's attention to the opening of Sir Michael Tippett's Third Symphony, which generates a similar kind of musical energy. (Tape-slide programme *Music at Manland*, part 2. frames 26/27)

The Manland School music curriculum ranges widely, though it does give some prominence to the mainstreams of European music, including the traditional organisational patterns, such as rondo, sonata, ternary and binary forms. Tom Gamble believes that his pupils should be aware of the important structural devices of all periods; they are therefore given some opportunity to work with simple serial techniques:

> . . . young people can be introduced to this idiom *through practical work before listening to the music of Schoenberg* . . .

The important 'method' point here is that the recordings of serial music are not used as models but as follow-up to the pupils' own exploration of twelve-note music. They begin with, say, a whole-class improvisation on a note-row, probably resulting in a set of variations. From there pupils go on to compose short pieces of serial music, working in small groups. Only when they have completed their own pieces and discussed them will the recorded examples be played. But to approach the recorded music by way of their own work helps pupils to make more sense of the work of the professional composer when they do hear it.

Obviously, it has been necessary for Tom Gamble to build up a large collection of gramophone records, a collection that goes far beyond the standard orchestral repertoire. Although the course is structured around a 'syllabus' of music for listening, the teacher must be ready for the unexpected to arise in class or small-group compositions. For example, the tape-slide programme gives an account of a student piece entitled 'Heaven and Hell' which 'evokes a primitive sound-world reminiscent of Harry Partch or a Balinese gamelan orchestra'. It would be quite important, in a music course of this kind, to have speedy access to recordings of Partch or of an Indonesian gamelan. In this way, recorded music contributes usefully to development of musical understanding.

Attentive listening

It is clear that bridges need to be built in many directions simultaneously:

> The way in which new music can cross from one mind to another is by unconsciously 'linking up' with music which both minds know. Musical foregrounds are comprehended in terms of the common musical backgrounds across which they unfold; that is to say, where there is no common background, incomprehension ensues. (Walker, 1966, p. 98)

It is tempting to think that we can cause school students to listen to and develop an understanding of a multiplicity of 'musical foregrounds' (i.e. different styles and varied treatments of musical material) by providing 'common musical backgrounds' which consist of peripheral information (e.g. the lives and times of composers, abstract descriptions of 'musical form', and so on). Unfortunately, it is all too often evident that this approach has not produced the hoped-for public of 'informed listeners'. Indeed, for many who have no doubt been through that kind of school music education, there seems still to be a basic lack of understanding about music's function, even if they are the kind of people who attend musical performances, as the following heartfelt letter to the *Guardian* (February 1980) tells us so clearly:

> Sir.—Having sat through most of Act I of a ballet at the Royal Opera House while two ladies next to me talked incessantly, I risked a polite remonstrance. One of them replied : " But it's only music."
>
> Is there any reply to this ?—Yours faithfully,
> **Derek Parker**
> 37 Camden Hill Towers,
> London W11.

This curious lack of *respect* for music can be found even among musicians. It is not at all uncommon to find that, at conferences and courses for music teachers, audiences will listen attentively while a lecturer is speaking, but as soon as he puts on a gramophone record to illustrate a point someone will talk! Does this perhaps suggest that for many people there is a feeling of 'remoteness' about recorded music? We do not feel the same compulsion to give it our full attention as we would were the player and singer there in front of us. Or is it that we have become too used to the idea of the record player merely as an instrument for illustration? In the classroom we may find ourselves putting on a record and *talking over it*, drawing the attention of the class to the composer's development of ideas *while the music is heard*. If we want our pupils to listen carefully, perhaps we should remind ourselves of the importance of attentive listening, even when it's to the 'unreal' music of the gramophone.

In Sean O'Casey's *Juno and the Paycock* (1928), 'Captain' Jack Boyle, having had it suggested to him that gramophones are 'destructive of real music', replies:

All a gramophone wants is to be properly played; its thrue wondher is only felt when everythins quiet – what a gramophone wants is dead silence! (Act II, p. 51)

There is probably no similarly succinct reply that would immediately help the ladies who talked during the ballet to realise what they were missing, but in the long term music education in schools should try to provide the experience of positive and creative listening which will make all music meaningful in its own terms. Simply putting on records and 'introducing' the music to classes of children is not enough. We should regard listening as an aspect of creativity, and, in consequence, try to organise our programme of music activities so that children learn to keep their ears open, to use their own judgement and discrimination about sounds and, through first-hand practical work in improvisation, composition and performance, come to understand how composers create worlds of sound which any of us can inhabit just by using our ears, and by giving the sounds our undivided attention.

Transformation and integration: the power of creative imagination

Ideally education is a unified and a unifying process. It should be an experience which helps us to make sense of life's contradictions and, while developing minds of our own, to recognise the possibility of differing points of view. It should also help us to face problems for which no-one as yet has answers.

Experience of art making and appreciation is central to this view of education, not merely because the arts are an important part of our general cultural understanding and awareness, nor yet because they offer opportunities for individual 'expression', but primarily because the processes of creativity, brought to the fore through artistic activity, involve not only origination and invention but also *the reconstruction and re-integration of existing products or ideas.*' (Hildreth, 1966, p. 440).

We have already commented upon the danger of emphasising 'self-expression' as a justification for the arts in the curriculum. As Susanne Langer says,

> Sheer self-expression requires no artistic form. A lynching-party howling round the gallows-tree . . . is giving vent to intense feelings; but such scenes are not occasions for music, least of all for composing. (Langer, 1942, p. 216)

Equally hazardous is the line of argument that assumes an almost 'therapeutic' role for the arts in school; helping children to become balanced and emotionally healthy individuals. Whilst it is true that the arts are 'about' feeling and sensory/emotional response, we have to be careful to avoid making this an end in itself – as though our main function was to 'treat' neurotic invalids.

The fact is that, with any artistic activity *used* educationally, we walk a tight-rope. Outside the context of education the arts need no justification. Experience of music, painting, dance, poetry or whatever speaks for itself and 'justifies' the art without further qualification. But it is also clear that the process of inward symbolisation is educative in a special way; whoever strives for the 'wholeness' of coherent expression in sounds or words, paint or clay or bodily movement, seeks to 'make sense' not only of the materials but also of his own experience. From this point of view, the arts occupy a unique position in the school curriculum, and we should certainly be prepared to take them much more seriously than we do.

Music has particular strengths of its own. Symbolisation in musical sound is entirely abstract, or if identifiable 'real' sounds are used they must be transformed or combined surrealistically to make them distinct from mere sound-effects.

In many ways, therefore, it is easier in music than in other arts to draw attention to the inherent expressive qualities of the medium. Obviously words with music (e.g. in a song) have direct links with the world of events, but musical symbolisation itself is not 'representational'. Thus we are concerned in the main with problems of selecting and defining the appropriate areas of sound, and with organising initially unconnected ideas. Whether we start from our own 'sound ideas' or from previously composed pieces of music in which the 'connections' have been made but now require interpreting, in both cases we use imagination to create new order.

It is only human to want to bring chaos into order; in this respect the processes of art reflect a fundamental need. For we could surely not conceive of a work of art without system or arrangement. Art has always been closely associated with the 'forming' process of ritual, and with attempts to understand existence through inward symbolisation:

> Although music and the dance will not in fact assist the crops to ripen, nor any religious rite control the motions of the earth or sun, it would be a mistake to dismiss all ritual action as serving no practical purpose. In these attempts to make order out of chaos, man was able to enlarge and deepen his perception of the external world, and thus become better able to understand, appreciate, and eventually control at least some of its aspects. At the same time, the rituals which he practised led him to the discovery of what we should now call art. (Storr, 1972, p. 177)

Thus the true 'value' of art or music lies not in its capacity to entertain us, or to add that 'little something' a cultural gloss to our lives, but rather in the way in which, through active involvement with it, we gain insight into what Langer has called 'the central facts of our sentient existence'.

An effective policy for music in the school curriculum will probably elude us until such time as we can evolve programmes of work which are firmly rooted in music's deepest functions. The teacher's approach to creativity 'must be more than a "bag of tricks" brought out at infrequent interval for a change of instruction pace' (A. H. Passow, *Gifted children: looking to their future*, Latimer/NAGC). We must be clear about what we are doing, and we must tackle our task systematically.

Thus, Brian Loane, Head of Music at Boldon Comprehensive School, South Tyneside, begins the outline statement of his music curriculum with the aim for his department: 'To make music' (see Appendix I). Open-ended this may be; vague it is not. Indeed it goes to the heart of the matter. For as the work in this school has so successfully shown, a properly workable syllabus ought to be able to gather together all aspects of music, including skill learning and the study of music theory, simply by giving priority to 'making' (which is 'creativity' in the broadest sense of the word), and ensuring appropriate musical *action* which transforms instinctual energy, integrating emotion and intellect. A syllabus like this takes its momentum from the pupils' own imaginative work, but that is not to say that the teacher merely 'waits to see what will happen'. On the contrary, very careful planning and considerable forethought is required to define a progression of techniques which may sometimes be used to stimulate pupils' inventiveness (i.e. skills 'fed in' by the teacher) and at other times will supply the means of fulfilling ideas (i.e. skills taught to meet specific needs made apparent in the pupils' work). In this way not only is the work itself 'creative' but the teaching method also exemplifies the creative process, drawing both inspiration and help from established skills but keeping the *imaginative application* of skills always to the fore. This is surely what must be implied by Carl Seashore's dictum that 'Music is an art, and he who plies it successfully has the *power* of creative imagination'. (Seashore, 1938)

Conclusion

In the mid-1950s and the early 1960s a number of teachers, many of whom were also composers, began to develop new approaches to music in the classroom by stressing the importance of creativity. In the main the 'method' was to encourage pupils to explore sounds and to develop short pieces of music of their own by a process of 'empirical' composition – improvisation reinforced and gradually 'refined' by frequent repetition until ideas took shape and 'gelled'. There was often an emphasis upon the 'experimental' music of the contemporary (1960s) *avant-garde* – since this tended to take a usefully 'open' view of musical sound and so broadened the scope of music for those pupils who had no previous conventional training. At the time it seemed right to lay stress upon 'experiment' and inventiveness, if only because traditional methods had offered so little opportunity for pupils to participate in class music lessons in self-directed ways.

Arising from this work in schools a literature grew up which by its nature may seem to some to be offering not so much a complement to the older style of class music work but rather a stark and uncompromising *alternative*. Some, at least, of the early publications were careful to say that what was being proposed was only a part of the overall picture of music in education, albeit a part we should try to develop. But in spite of those cautious 'disclaimers', the contrast between 'traditional methods' and 'new developments' was at first so striking that many teachers were baffled and could see what was happening only in terms of 'either/or'. In this way

'Creative Music' came to be regarded by some as an 'absolute'; an alternative *method* rather than a fresh and possibly wider view of music in education that could be both forward-looking *and* embrace the best of traditional attitudes.

It is regrettable that the term 'creative music' has taken on this exclusive meaning, suggesting a dichotomy between these activities and other aspects of school music-making. This may have been due partly to the need, in the first instance, to draw attention to procedures stressing inventiveness and imagination, but it has also arisen because some teachers have distrusted these developments and so tended to use the idea of 'Creative Music' to express their unease. In much the same way that we find those who, without giving the matter much thought, lump together all Afro-American music styles and call them 'pop', so there has been a tendency in some quarters for 'Creative Music' to be used to sum up classroom methods which are thought to be 'experimental' or 'untried', and which are held to be in opposition to the 'proven', 'tried and tested', 'traditional' methods. This is unfortunate because it is simplistic and distorts the aims of those who have tried to widen the impact of music in the curriculum. It also ignores the progress that has been made.

Teaching techniques have developed, and it is probably time we stopped talking about 'creative music'! All musical knowledge and skill can be put to creative use, and if it isn't it has very little value musically. It might have something interesting to tell us about sociology or history or physics, and for that we should be grateful. But in the end *our* business is the art of music.

5 Timetable, staffing and accommodation

It is impossible for curriculum re-appraisal or development to avoid questions of timetabling. We can try to ignore the implications and 'make do' as best we can, but in the end either new approaches must be tailored to work within the existing timetable and staff allocation, or the provision must be modified to allow innovations to work properly – in some cases to work at all. Music is an area which could benefit from a great deal more timetable experiment than it has been given so far. There should be closer examination of the way in which we use existing provision. We should also be prepared to define our priorities in music education and in the timetable and staff organisation needed to reach these goals. Even so, it is important to bear in mind that no single mode of organisation will cope with every eventuality. Guidelines can indicate possibilities; thereafter it is a matter for individual schools to decide what suits their needs. Clearly there is room for modifications which do not require more time and staff. Equally, there are some things which are not going to be possible within the current working arrangements of most music teachers. We must recognise these distinctions and if necessary be prepared to act accordingly. But any change involves a complicated balancing act between assumptions and attitudes, circumstances and history. It is easy enough to believe that we could do a better job if we had more time and more assistance but, economic considerations apart, the present climate of uncertainty about the role of the arts in education does not make it any easier to justify increases. Until we can reach some measure of agreement among ourselves and can convincingly demonstrate the importance of music and the other arts in *general* education, the position is unlikely to change. For to allocate substantially more time for music implies a radical re-appraisal of the whole school curriculum.

Working within existing limits

It is not unusual to find schools with more than 1,000 pupils on roll having only one full-time music teacher working in a single music room to all intents and purposes exactly like any other classroom. Sometimes there will be a second member of staff (though perhaps not giving more than half time to music) and this could mean a second room for music with, possibly, two or three very small practice rooms nearby. This kind of provision is almost certainly based on the old assumption that music is 'extra' to the curriculum; that the teacher's main work is organising orchestra and choir activities (which would normally take place in the school hall), that this work *is* well-served by additional peripatetic teachers, and that therefore the general curriculum work in music cannot warrant more time, staff or accommodation. Music lessons are still seen mainly in terms of singing, 'music appreciation', or 'theory' with classes of 25 or more working as single units. It is extremely difficult to effect any kind of change in this pattern, since to do so would require an act of faith not only on the part of those who organise the timetable and allocate space but also on the part of music teachers themselves, and without opportunity to experiment there is little we can do other than guess at the possible outcome of large-scale changes. For the most part, then, we are faced with a concept of curriculum development that, if it is to work at all, must work within whatever constraints currently apply.

This is not as serious a problem as might at first appear. Some possibilities have already been touched upon (pp. 78 *et seq.*). If we can make up our minds about the kind of course we want to offer for the majority of pupils, then it should be possible to devise a way of making it work within the scope of a particular school. For example, if we cannot have classes divided into several small groups operating simultaneously, then the work can be adapted so that one group each week prepares and performs its finished piece of music (composition or arrangement) for the following lesson. Activities for the whole class can also be devised to encompass many of the points we would normally wish to make by a small-group 'discovery' method. Obviously working with the class as a single unit will mean that for much of the time the teacher has to direct operations, but we can try to involve individual pupils in the directing role as well (see p. 41).

Alternatively, it may be decided that, in spite of the limitations, we should try to operate a small-group workshop in the one classroom. A careful strategy must then be planned to make this work. For example, organising the group activity in a series of relatively short periods of time (e.g. 3–5 minutes each) interspersed with similarly short periods of class discussion and demonstration. The extent to which small groups can work on their own for any length of time is directly related to the availability of work spaces. If the groups can be given places outside the music room they will work better, with occasional visits from the teacher to encourage and help as necessary. But even with the most highly-motivated pupils this is a noisy activity and some co-operation from other members of staff will no doubt be necessary.

Again, it is an arrangement that could be approached by easy stages. Rather than sending five or six groups out from the very beginning, the majority could work in the main music room whilst two groups (or three at most) are given separate work spaces (an entrance vestibule, an instrument store, and so on). These groups would have to show that they could be trusted to work in this way and the privilege could be given on a rotating basis as appropriate. When weather permits, some groups might be allowed to work in the open air.

A sufficient number of teachers have already show that, given determination, this kind of activity can be made to work, even in very restricted conditions. As time goes by and there is evidence of successful curriculum work in music, it is usually possible to arrange for additional space.* Additional staff is another matter altogether, but there again the 'workshop' method of organisation can have advantages. Discipline problems generally arise from boredom and lack of involvement. This is more likely to occur when a subject such as music is taught on a 'whole-class' basis. Then it is essential that the teacher does have *complete* control over every part of the work, demanding a similar response from everyone in the class. It is unrealistic to expect development of individual ideas – except in the most straightforward kind of 'information'-based written work – and the content of the lesson has to be geared throughout to what is controllable by the teacher. The risk of some pupils lagging behind and becoming bored is high, and the teacher will often find himself expending more energy on class discipline than on music-making. The commonest cause of boredom among pupils in music lessons is the 'unreality' of the lesson content. Taught as a purely 'information' subject (with lecture presentation and dictated notes) it bears little relation to the reality of music outside the classroom. Yet this methodology may be the only possible approach if the teacher has to work with the conventional class organisation, maintaining proper discipline. This can be true even with some forms of music *activity*, if the participation must be organised so that the class always operates as a single unit, everyone doing the same thing; for example class singing. During the Project we observed some massed singing lessons in which it was extremely difficult for the teacher in charge to involve all the pupils and where a second member of staff was required to 'police' the back rows. Remove that concept of discipline and we might begin to think of an alternative methodology.

---

* As, for example, in the case of one teacher associated with the Project who, in the course of several years in a school, was able bit by bit to acquire the use of additional space for group work in music to the point where the 'odd' corners, etc., totalled just twice the square footage officially allocated for music (i.e. the two music rooms).

If the class is working in several self-selecting groups the distribution of ability should make it possible for everyone to find his/her right level. The chances of involvement are thereby increased. Abler pupils will be able to get on without too much attention from the teacher (though attention when it is given must be appropriate to the group's level of work and the assignments given to such groups must be substantial enough to engage their interest). Other groups – perhaps containing some of the less able – can be given more attention (see pp. 73–4). In some ways this requires more careful pre-planning than the 'whole-class' organisation but at least we can feel that our energy is being given in the main to musical matters rather than merely to maintaining order. The noise levels need controlling if several groups work in the same room, but if spaces can be found where groups can be sent to work it will normally be found that, simply because it can generate a much higher level of involvement in the majority of pupils, group-work eases problems of control rather than increasing them. From time to time we are bound to find pupils who cannot work unsupervised however much we show that they are trusted to get on with the job. But again, it is generally easier to keep a helpful eye on these less co-operative pupils if the majority of the class are working at group assignments which they can identify with and become involved with.

Obviously the element of trust is very important in the development of group-work. As a method of organisation it will be most successful if it can be seen to be the norm rather than the exception. A workshop 'event' inserted as light relief into a traditional academic programme may easily be mistaken for a kind of game; it will be difficult to get pupils to take it seriously, and as a result it will probably not be very useful or productive. Treated as the normal method of organisation, the workshop principle can become a much more effective way of using a teacher's time. It can free him to give help where help is needed. If necessary, different levels of work can be run simultaneously. The Project recorded examples of work organised in this way over a period of years developing into a 5th- and 6th-form composition course without extra timetable allocation. The 5th- and 6th-formers having moved up through the school within a system where increasingly the teacher was able to trust them to work on their own in small groups, were able to pursue individual composition projects, often involving elaborate electronic equipment, in a small room associated with the main music room simultaneously with lower forms working in the main room and at various points around the school. The teacher made his 'rounds' of the lower form groups, taking in the 6th-form pupils on his way. Their work needed more detailed help but on the whole less frequently than, say, the 2nd- or 3rd-form groups. It would be as natural to have groups from different years working in the music area on a variety of projects as it would be to have groups from a single year or class working on different things at the same time. If the work spaces are available there is no reason why they should not be used. The main organisational problem for the teacher is then to decide how much time to give to advanced or elementary groups or individuals, though to a large extent that will be dictated by the nature of the work, and will vary to meet specific needs as projects proceed. In a school with only one music teacher, the 'small-group workshop' arrangement can be a distinct advantage, enabling the teacher to cope with a wider range of work than the conventional class lesson organisation (see pp. 84–5).

There is much to be said for doing what we can with what we have got but even so there should be a recognised minimum of time and accommodation below which no music teacher should be expected to operate. One 40-minute period each week is really minimal. There is very little of educational or musical significance that we can do with that kind of time (though *something* is possible). No teacher should be forced to teach music in such a way that it is impossible for pupils to be musically active. This means there will be sound – sometimes a lot of sound – and there must be reasonable space. Again, *something* is possible in a single music room, but if that room has to accommodate rows of desks that cannot be moved then that will severely restrict active music-making. It isn't even any good for class singing because it is virtually impossible to ensure that children behind desks can sit properly to sing.

We have already observed that music is not just another classroom subject that can be taught in more or less any room that will hold thirty pupils. Like crafts and sciences, music has special requirements which must be met if it is to operate properly. Music needs its own workshop or laboratory. And it needs time for ideas to develop – just as cookery needs time for bread to rise or a cake to bake! And like work in craft rooms or science laboratories – indeed anything that is active and involves pupils with the use of equipment – there are many aspects of music-making which are unthinkable with groups of more than fifteen or twenty. Any conditions other than these inevitably impose serious constraints upon the teacher and the subject; constraints which can be a real barrier to effective education. As one teacher has written:

> A pupil-teacher ratio of 20 : 1 would be acceptable. Larger numbers than this seriously limit the possible success of the work. Teachers working with larger numbers *often fail for for this reason alone.*

Others describe the problems of trying to develop interesting music work with limited facilities:

> Accommodation restrictions in this school are still acute: two huts with storage area for instruments; floors unstable for stereo or for creative dance; no practice

rooms and nowhere to send groups for composition. Woodwind, string and guitar teachers work under great difficulty.

We had very limited scope for group work; usually two guitar groups could work at each end of the main music room, another in a practice-cum-storage room, and a fourth on a landing or outside a cloakroom.

In spite of the difficulties, these teachers have made an effort to develop active courses. Certainly it is worth trying to do something, however limited; were we to wait for better facilities we might wait for ever. Yet it is also arguable that so long as we are prepared to make do in this way, our willingness and compliance will be accepted, possibly without any feeling of obligation on anyone's part to improve facilities for music. We should be prepared to take a stand for minimum facilities which include perhaps sufficient work spaces for five or six small groups plus a large clear area (i.e. without desks) for 'plenary' activities, all, if possible, set apart from other subject accommodation so that the musicians can produce the sounds they need without disturbing other work. At the same time, we must recognise the need for secure educational principles on which to argue for better accommodation, especially if what we want is very different from what has previously been considered adequate for music.

This applies with equal force to timetable provision if it is to involve any kind of re-arrangement. The question of the *amount* of time allocated to music is, again, a separate issue. So much must depend upon what we see as the principal aims of music in education. If our objective is large 'O' and 'A' level sets, then it could be said that extending time for music in the first four years might give us the opportunity to identify more potential 'examination' candidates and give them the necessary training. But that does not in itself provide justification for music as a part of everyone's general education. In principle we should expect to offer a course in years 1–3 (or 1–4) which caters for *all* pupils and which gives adequate support to potential 'examination' candidates and others alike (see pp. 71–2). A comprehensive course such as that would certainly seem to warrant more than a single weekly period.

Minor modifications

Two factors are of crucial importance; time and numbers. A teacher writes:

I am amazed at some secondary school time-tables where children change classes every thirty-five minutes. Creative work is impossible in this situation. Double lessons (at least an hour) are essential for real work to take place . . . if necessary, half a day once a fortnight . . .

If music is taught creatively (in the widest application of the word, i.e. making-interpreting-listening: see Chapter 4) time must be allowed for generating and developing ideas. This is a totally different process from the one in which information is given out by the teacher, taken in by the pupils and 'digested' later through exercises – possibly as homework. The 'information' lesson does not necessarily call for extended contact time between teacher and class. But where learning takes place through ideas generated by pupils from a brief stimulus provided by the teacher, continuing contact on an informal basis (the occasional word of encouragement or a helpful question from time to time as the work proceeds) is vitally important. This way of working should not be rushed, so there is clearly a case for a minimum of 'double periods'. We can, of course, achieve this by a relatively simple re-arrangement. If a class has two 35-minute lessons each week these could reasonably be combined to make a single unit of one hour or thereabouts.

Some comprehensive schools work on a system of block timetabling, by which all or half the classes in a year group have the same subject at the same time. This allows departments to organise the teaching units in whatever way they choose, grouping by ability or in sets for particular kinds of work, or in broad mixed-ability classes. The numbers in any given group can be varied so that, in music for example, a relatively large performance ensemble (choir or band) might draw students from across the whole year, leaving smaller sets for more specialised instrumental work, examination work, composition or improvisation. Staff can also be deployed in a number of different ways; some taking single sets, others working as a team – perhaps with larger groups.

It has sometimes been suggested that block timetabling can lead to a restrictive kind of subject-department autonomy; a form of 'empire building' which tends to look inwards and so ignore opportunities and responsibilities in the curriculum as a whole. The development of 'faculties' combining related subjects might be seen as an attempt to overcome the potential disadvantages of block timetabling. But, as we might imagine, 'faculties' have their own problems – as indeed will any system we adopt – and these are frequently problems of co-operation. A faculty of creative arts will only operate successfully if all the subjects included agree on a creative policy. Sadly, it would seem that music is often the 'odd man out', the music teacher finding it difficult to see how he can organise his subject so that it 'works' like the visual arts, drama and dance. This is not so much a matter of combination or integration (though some collaboration can certainly help pupils' general understanding of what the arts do). Primarily the 'faculty' promotes a common philosophy, and if that is understood and agreed arts teachers can feel they are making their mark on the curriculum even if subjects within the faculty have to be timetabled and accommodated individually.

More extensive developments

As with so many other things in education, it is neither possible nor
sensible to try to determine the 'best' system. Streaming, setting, total non-
selection, block timetables or faculties will all find their advocates. It is
more profitable to start with the needs of the subject or subject area and
with the underlying philosophy which determines the particular form of
music's contribution to the curriculum. What works satisfactorily for a
basically 'information' subject will not necessarily be the best system for a
subject like music or drama, but it should not be beyond the bounds of
possibility for different systems to be operated simultaneously in the same
school. A combination of the block timetabling and 'faculty' organisation
mentioned above would make possible combined arts projects or integrated
programmes without upsetting the wider timetable considerations in the
school. At the same time, sustained periods of work within the single
subject 'blocks' would be perfectly natural and could lead in and out of
combined or integrated courses.

A more unusual arrangement for combined arts projects would be half-
day or whole-day workshops. It could be argued that the real potential of
the arts in education is unrealised; that it is dissipated by the once-a-week
or twice-a-week lesson, however flexible the system within normal
timetable constraints. By contrast, Theatre-in-Education groups up and
down the country have shown that a worthwhile impact can be made with a
one-day workshop involving large numbers of children. The theatre group
'takes over' from the normal timetable and for one day only involves pupils
in a totally absorbing experience – all the more powerful artistically
because it is an uncommon event. A theme is explored, developed and
brought to fruition in a 'performance' at the end of the day. The Theatre
group leaves but the feeling of having taken part in a *real* theatre experience
remains. Perhaps we have something to learn from this example. Whilst a
one-off event of that kind cannot deal with the sort of skills that require
constant practice and frequent re-inforcement, it can nevertheless reach the
delight – the magic – which is at the heart of artistic experience. With the
best will in the world, it is difficult for us to sustain that level of
involvement in short bursts of activity week by week. Indeed, in some
ways class-work in music not only fails to sustain itself, but actually loses
impact, just because the weekly 'lessons' are so regular and predictable.
Art, after all, strives against such regularity. One of the most remarkable
features of the Sonata Principle is not the way in which works conform to a
pattern but the truly amazing diversity of expression that has been possible
within the scheme. Art is concerned with revealing and asserting new ways
of looking at things. It is not about making unchangeable forms which will

at all costs stand for ever. Rather its principles allow for and encourage a continuous regeneration of ideas, thoughts and feelings. Like the Hindu deity Siva, whose powers embrace equally the forces of reproduction and dissolution, artistic creativity involves both making and destroying. If we are seeking a realistic timetabling for music and the other arts in schools (realistic in artistic terms, that is), we should perhaps be considering an *irregular* arrangement which could generate and sustain a feeling of excitement with the work in hand akin to the working life of the artist. There is a great deal of very ordinary drudgery in the practice of an art; it isn't all living on a high plateau. Nevertheless, it is not mechanical and it does have a strong element of variety coupled with a sense of purpose and direction within each creative project. Something of this is evident in the preparation for any school concert, play, opera or 'musical'.

If music could be timetabled within the framework of an 'arts workshop' which operated in a variety of ways according to the demands of each project, a great deal more enthusiasm and insight might result all round. Instead of the weekly music, art or drama 'lesson', the workshop would organise a programme of 'events', some drama, some dance, some music; or combinations of the arts giving prominence to one or other aspect. For example, music might take the lead on one occasion, while dance took the lead at another time. For a different event the visual arts could provide a starting point, not necessarily for a combined production but perhaps for an integrated exploration of a theme. The central idea would be explored through improvisation and composition in dance and drama and music separately, the results being shared at the end of the session. Events of this kind need time to expand ideas, and a half-day 'block' would really be the minimum suitable. Whole-day courses could achieve a great deal more. There is value in working through ideas as thoroughly as possible and tying up the ends, as it were, in some form of presentation. Without additional time or staff, this might be achieved by putting together, say, six twice-weekly one-hour periods to make a single one-day workshop allocated as a timetable block to the arts faculty. Thus, in the first three years, each year group might have four such days in a term. This would make it possible for the arts faculty to plan large-scale projects each of which could be completed in a single day or extended across the four 'workshops' of the term. Other timetabled time would then be available for specialist courses in years 4–6. The importance of the years 1–3 'arts workshop' courses would be that they could implant a good working understanding of what the arts *generally* have to offer, with appropriate skills of a limited nature encountered as work proceeded. This could be a satisfactory basis from which to proceed to more advanced and detailed work in *one* art form. A variation on this plan might be to put each year group's four workshop days together to make one four-day event per term during which time

everyone would be involved with a 'production' of some kind – say, a
music-theatre piece or a dance-drama.

There are obvious objections to this way of working, principally in
relation to skills. For certain kinds of skill 'little and often' is the only
effective method. On the other hand, delight in taking part in artistic work
– whatever the medium – is a pre-requisite for understanding, and
sensitivity to the medium *is* a basic 'skill' which needs to be learned like
any other skill. Too often we take such things for granted and launch into
the theoretical details without proper foundation. But the purpose of
theory is to explain experience, and to spend the first three years in
'workshop' projects as has been suggested *could* be a much better basis for
future work than week-by-week one-hour (or even two-hour) 'theory and
appreciation' lessons in abstract and without reference to first-hand
experience. It is in those first years that we should hope to generate
enthusiasm for the arts, and we need a timetable structure that will assist
us in this, not one which works against it.

A number of examples come to mind in exciting 'workshop' projects
mounted outside the school system and funded entirely or partially by
Education Authorities. Courses such as those provided (under the auspices
of the ILEA) by the Cockpit Theatre and the Central London Youth
Project Music Workshop have made a powerful contribution to education.
Elsewhere, local arts centres with an 'educational' bias – such as the
Dovecot Arts Centre in Stockton, Teesside – have organised dance and
drama events involving music. Perhaps such things are effective *because*
they are independent of schooling and all that 'school' suggests. But if we
believe that music does have a contribution to make in education we could
do worse than trying to find a way of organising music within the school
timetable so that it could operate with the assurance and effectiveness of
these out-of-school projects.

Similar in spirit to such proposals is the radical change of approach
suggested on p. 54 above. 'Vertically streamed' music classes on the
timetable would open up a range of performance possibilities that have so
far been completely untapped. These too could be linked with work in
allied arts to place the emphasis upon practical participation; for surely the
arts are nothing unless they 'happen'?

One way of making music 'happen' with something of the reality it has
outside schooling, is to operate what has come to be known as an 'open'
music department. Malcolm Nicholls described such a department – at
Countesthorpe Community College, Leicester – in *Pop Music in School*
(Vulliamy and Lee, 1976, revised edition 1980):

> Countesthorpe College, a secondary comprehensive school for fourteen- to
> eighteen-year-olds, was opened in 1970, and is a part of the Leicestershire Plan
> of upper schools and age eleven to fourteen high schools. Its catchment area

includes pupils from the immediate country area and from a nearby council estate in Leicester. The buildings were designed for the innovatory teaching methods which Tim McMullen had planned and discussed with his new staff before opening. As the first principal of the college, he established procedures of participatory government by the staff and pupils, who in turn established organisational and curriculum policies which five years later remain largely unchanged. The principal characteristics are:

1 Participatory government: major decisions are made as necessary by the 'Moot', a meeting of staff and pupils. The 'Moot's' rotating standing committee meets weekly to make everyday decisions. Urgent or minor decisions may be made unilaterally.

2 The 'teams': areas of the college are allotted to 'mini-schools' as homes where the pupils spend half of their timetable with their tutor (or 'form-teacher') or one of his team.

3 The remaining half of the pupils' time is spent in 'activities', all of which are optional. All college work is based upon the principle of an individualised, 'pupil-centred' curriculum . . . I feel it is valuable for a music department to be run on these lines, since each individual, even at the age of fourteen, will have different technical needs and aspirations and unique aesthetic values.

Organisation of the music timetable. In the Countesthorpe 'team/option' curriculum the music teacher has the essential right to arrange the basic constitution of his groups to make each of them include a number of pupils who are self-directing, some who require more attention, as well as some who are compatible in that they can, for example, share guitar techniques or can play a useful combination of instruments. Thus the teacher can at least expect not to be landed with fifteen prospective pianists at one session. However, the flexibility of the team system not only allows these arrangements to be made but also allows the occasional arrangement of 'one-off' and very specialised groups. With advanced notice tutors can make arrangements for pupils to change their music time temporarily so that, for example, the music wing and I are left free for a musical afternoon on the theme of 'The First World War' with a group of thirty or so pupils and their tutor. The regular groups, therefore, usually of about ten to fifteen pupils, are the basis of the music provision. On top of this come the 'casual' visitors – pupils who are known to be able to use their time profitably or with particular directions from their tutors as to the requirements. These on average make five to ten extra and include pupils who in fact visit us fairly regularly. Occasionally there may be thirty or thirty-five pupils engaged in various activities in the music wing, without any other member of staff present.

It is clear that in arts education (and particularly in music) there is a lot of scope for timetable experiment. One thing is fairly certain, and that is that if we are to make any significant impact educationally with music a single 35-minute period once a week is not much use. But how do we begin to explore the possibilities for change? It isn't necessarily the timetable makers who are standing in the way. Music teachers are often themselves the very last people to want change. Should we infer from this that the majority feel they can do a perfectly good job with what they have at present? Perhaps that is so, but there might also be an indication that long-established attitudes towards music, placing it low in the educational hierarchy, have produced a defeatist outlook amongst music teachers. By and large teachers in the other arts do not seem quite so inward looking and dispirited as some of their music colleagues. There must be an explanation. Then again, when we look at exciting projects mounted by out-of-school organisations, such as those mentioned above, we may wonder where in the schools we should look for a similar expression of educational vision in music. Whilst there are certainly some very encouraging signs of innovation in school music, on the whole suggestions for 'workshop' projects over extended periods of time do not meet with much show of approval from music teachers. And even proposals for half-day timetable blocks have been known to produce hostility from those who feel it would call for unusual feats of planning to fill that kind of time: 'What about the weak teacher who is praying for the bell to go?' is a not uncommon question.

Yet how often are we guilty of creating 'weak' teachers by asking them to do the impossible; to generate enthusiasm for music and a genuine involvement with music in mixed ability classes on 40 minutes once a week? If there was ever an undertaking that required unusual skill in the handling it is surely the single-period once-a-week music lesson. There is so little time to develop even the simplest of ideas. The bell goes and the impetus is lost. Next week the whole process must begin again – and because we made such little headway in the previous week we may well have actually lost ground. Progress is slow, pupils become bored, and the teachers feels he/she is fighting a losing battle. It is this kind of thing, as much as anything, that can make a teacher appear 'weak'. Given a little more time to work through a theme with a class, getting a worthwhile response from pupils because there is not the immediate pressure of the bell which may go before anything can be achieved: *that* can do a lot to encourage a teacher and strengthen his technique.

Do we need more music teachers?

Music in school probably suffers as much from under-staffing as it does from inadequate accommodation and unrealistic timetabling. Once again, this is largely the result of popular misconceptions about the music teacher's role. In the minds of most people (including quite a few Heads and education administrators), the image of the school music teacher is that of the 'Director of Music' conducting choirs, orchestras or bands, and organising concerts. Class teaching he is expected to take in his stride, and it is generally assumed that this will not be particularly demanding; a little 'Music Appreciation', perhaps, or some class singing and 'theory'. No doubt many Heads are simply unaware of music's *curriculum* potential, but at present it often appears that, given the choice, they would prefer to see the specialist extra-curricular groups flourish even if this had to be at the expense of lively and interesting work in the classroom.

The reason is not hard to find. A school band that goes to the festivals and wins all the prizes or appears on television, can bring the same kind of credit to a school as would a highly successful football team. That may indeed be a crucial ingredient of school life, and certainly we should not despise it. But, at the same time, we should be wary of this becoming the main justification for music in the school; for where it happens its effects are often not without significance. On the one hand it may encourage the music teacher to put all his efforts into the choirs and orchestras, for which he knows he is most appreciated, even to the extent of abandoning any real concern for his class teaching. On the other hand, a teacher who tries to maintain a high level of general music activity in class lessons but is well aware that, from the point of view of the administration, it is the band (or whatever) that really matters, can easily find himself seriously overworked. Such a teacher will not necessarily find it easy to convince those responsible that he needs assistance, if only because there *is* a popular assumption that class teaching plus extra-curricular music activities should be well within the capabilities of a single music teacher. Moreover, in many schools that single teacher would be expected to offer a subsidiary subject in addition to music. This is by no means a thing of the past, as the following extract (from a recent letter requesting a testimonial for a teacher) so clearly shows:

> . . . Our requirement is for a proficient musician on her specialist instrument . . . prepared to contribute to the life of the school in other ways . . . perhaps by coaching games . . . If an academic subject can also be taught, that would be an advantage. I am especially wanting help with Religious Education.

It is interesting to note how, although music is valued in the curriculum of this school, the Head does not regard it as an 'academic' subject on a par with, for example, Religious Education. Reading between the lines, there does seem to be an assumption that the teacher, having acquired her musical skills will simply pour them out, for the benefit of the pupils, without much intellectual effort or detailed preparation. It is enough that she is 'a proficient musician'. The rest, presumably, happens by magic, leaving her plenty of time to coach for games and teach Religious Education. Suppositions such as this have had their effect upon the general status of music in education and almost certainly upon the level of staffing for music too.

In the first place, we shall need to demonstrate music's importance and value within the general educational scheme. Music has much more to offer for the majority of pupils, through class music activities, than is normally acknowledged. Very few Heads are aware of the possibilities for music in general education; they cannot, therefore, be blamed for thinking that music is a minority subject and that the teacher's main responsibilities are outside the timetabled curriculum.

In the second place music teachers themselves will need to develop much more clearly defined ideas about music's 'academic' nature, and be ready to stand by their belief in the value of music for the majority. Because only a small number of pupils may wish to take music in public examinations this does not mean that music is limited 'academically' to the contents of the 'O' or 'A' level syllabus. As we have tried to show elsewhere, there are plenty of activities suitable for general class music lessons that manifestly have substantial educational value. This work requires a high level of skill and preparation from the teacher; as much indeed as any other conventionally 'academic' subject. It is not something to be thrown off almost without thought, and since it makes a significant contribution to the education of all pupils, rather than a gifted minority, it is surely just as important as the extra-curricular choirs or bands which generally cater for smaller and selective groups.

It has been suggested that we might do well to adopt the North American system of having separate teachers for the class work and for the instrumental ensembles. No doubt this would be helpful in some cases, for some teachers do show particular skill in one area or the other. However, if the arrangement were to be effective we should still need to see radical changes in attitudes elsewhere. If not, it is probable that a 'hierarchy' would speedily develop in which the conductors of selective bands, choirs and orchestras received greater recognition than the teachers responsible for the general music classes.

It would seem to be preferable to retain and expand our present system to give equal importance to all aspects of music in school, but to try to ensure that activities stem in the first place from a wide-ranging and lively approach to music in the classroom. Such a programme calls for flexibility in staffing, and whilst it is obviously sensible to make the fullest use of a particular teacher's talents, the music curriculum would undoubtedly gain in educational standing if the extra-curricular work were seen to have its roots in the class-teaching and if, at the same time, there could be positive feedback from a teacher's work with, say, the orchestra into the work he organised for the general class lessons. At the moment it is precisely this kind of productive interaction between the timetabled classes and the 'out of timetable' work that is lacking in so many schools.

If we are ever to be in a position to capitalise upon this inter-action and so to develop fully music's potential in the curriculum, it is clear that we shall need more timetabled allocation and increased staffing. Ultimately this rests upon how others see us and see our job. As things are we have a long way to go. By and large the present image of the music teacher is not a particularly helpful one, and where music education does receive praise it is quite often for the wrong thing. Two examples from a recent DES publication will suffice. In one we are given a glimpse of work done under the heading of 'Music' by 'an able boy in the second term of his fourth year'. It consisted of 'A book of *10,000 words* of copied notes, some (with the teacher's approval) copied from the book of another pupil who had taken the course the year before'. And we are told that this is 'an example which could too easily be replicated'. Another paragraph gives details of a school which had 'a strong tradition of liveliness, *creativeness* and *independence of thought*', and where 'the girls were encouraged to *explore ideas* and to *exercise critical judgements*'. Yet the only mention of music in this school is in a reference to the 'out of class provision' of 'opportunities for choral and instrumental music'; not areas of music-making in which we commonly find pupils exercising critical judgements, exploring ideas and/or displaying creativeness and independence of thought. (DES, 1979)

Neither of these examples is likely to produce support for extending music time or staffing in the schools. The first paints a sad picture of a teacher who seems to be doing his best to avoid the reality of music (or even the necessity of being present at all, since notes can apparently be copied from past pupils!). And although the second school is quite rightly praised for offering 'a good range' of musical opportunities, these are of a limited nature and are 'out of class'. We must conclude that this was the priority for the school and for the music teacher, since the class music teaching does not appear to warrant a mention.

As we can see, a depressed state of *class* music teaching can easily become a major factor in maintaining a low level of staffing for the subject. Because there is no strong agreement among music teachers and Heads about the role of music in the classroom, and because this work is so often subordinate to the selective out-of-timetable ensembles, opinion is confident that we are unlikely to need more than one music teacher for an average sized school. The consequent isolation of the musician in education is decidedly relevant. It completes yet another 'circle of constraints'. Uncertainty among music teachers about their educational role tends to produce half-hearted class-teaching; as a result Heads are disinclined to put much faith in music as a curriculum subject or even to try to understand its potential. This prevents the appointment of additional staff, and so a single music teacher remains the norm. Cut off from the kind of productive interchange of ideas that is typical within a reasonably sized department, and overworked by the pressures of coping with music in and out of the timetable, the isolated music teacher may quickly lose whatever confidence he/she had in the educative values of the subject. The consequent uncertainty . . . tends to produce half-hearted class-teaching . . . and so the circle continues without a break.

To some extent the situation has been improved by the institution of 'faculties of creative arts'. Even though there may be no increase in the music teaching staff as such, a hitherto isolated music teacher can be brought into contact with positive and developmental ideas within the 'arts' group, and that may well strengthen the music teaching. Similarly, it is to be hoped that the establishment of music curriculum development groups in many parts of the country (some under the auspices of the Schools Council Secondary Music Project working through its regional centres (see p. 235) will help to break down the isolation many music teachers feel, and so increase their confidence and their resolve to work for wider educational recognition for class music activities.

Making room for music

Frequently it has been said that 'buildings don't make schools'. Nevertheless, good space encourages and bad space inhibits; teachers can be helped by their environment – and may just as easily be frustrated by unhelpful accommodation, even if it is newly built. This is particularly true in the arts, which need not only the right number and size of spaces but also a sympathetic milieu in which to generate and develop ideas. Regrettably, new school building during the past twenty years or so has not often recognised advances and changes in the arts areas of the curriculum.

As in so many other respects, Music has suffered more than most subjects from inadequate or unhelpful accommodation. In older schools music teachers commonly find themselves allocated rooms no-one else wants. In new schools, where a purpose-built music room (or even a music 'suite') may be provided, it is often a token conception of what is needed, based on those same assumptions that inform staffing and timetable; notions of a teaching style which is static and unlikely to change. Splendid though these buildings usually *look*, they may nevertheless inhibit curriculum development. Thus in new schools and old, for many music teachers it is 'a story of improvisation':

> Resources, not only of staff and equipment, but also of building must be considered. My pupils cannot work at the optimum rate with six groups in one room. The work lacks sensitivity – rather like asking an artist to create some sensitive work while others are scribbling on his paper! My pupils demand a clean atmosphere in which to try out sounds – no blots from others. Until buildings are right this must be a matter for classroom organisation.

County architects are busy people, coping with an enormous variety of building problems; a primary school one day, a secondary school another, an extension to the Town Hall this week and a new Fire Station after that. No doubt they would say – perhaps with some justification – that if music teachers do not get what they want this is yet another example of what can happen when teachers are irresolute or divided about the role of their

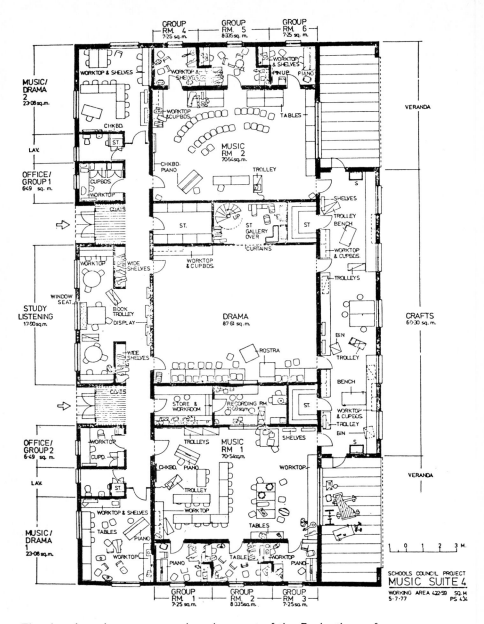

The drawing above was produced as part of the Project's conference on music accommodation in school. A complex very similar to this is in the process of being built at the Margaret Dane School, Hertfordshire.

subject. Even so, teachers have been trying for a good many years now to broaden the impact of music in the school curriculum, and it is sad that so little notice seems to have been taken of their needs. It may be that they are too good at improvising! Many, like the teacher quoted above, take a philosophical view and deal with the problems organisationally; for to wait 'until the buildings are right' could mean waiting for ever! Some of the organisational possibilities have been outlined above (on pp. 78–86). Obviously it makes good sense to get on with the job and to do the best we can with what is provided. But should we not also be seen to be making a case for *proper* accommodation for our subject; accommodation that will be suitable for all the traditional forms of school music-making and which will also offer the flexibility we need to develop in particular the curriculum aspects of the subject as they affect the majority of pupils?

The Project's initiative

Right from the start of its investigation, the Schools Council Secondary Music Project took the view that any attempt to improve the status of music in schools would be bound to have implications for the accommodation of the subject, either through the design of new school buildings or in the up-grading and adaptation of existing buildings. Whichever way we looked at it, it was obvious that music required specialist accommodation to cater for a number of very different activities.

The Project set up a working party of teachers, HMI, Music Advisers and representatives of the Department of Education and Science Architects and Building Branch – the latter including David and Mary Medd, internationally recognised for their imaginative and forward-looking work in the design of music and drama accommodation in schools and for their work on *Building Bulletin 30: Drama and Music* (HMSO, 1966), still an inspiring work of reference in the field of school design. With Derek Poole (also of the DES Architects and Building Branch), David and Mary Medd visited a number of schools associated with the Project, examining at first hand the teacher's requirements for class music activities, and producing detailed drawings showing how existing accommodation was being used and how it might be modified or developed where necessary. In addition, a number of drawings were produced in which prognostications were made for types of accommodation which would allow for greater flexibility than the traditional forms of music teaching rooms.

Teachers' views on accommodation

The Project also sought advice from a large number of Heads and music teachers, many of whom generously gave their time to provide substantial

written accounts of what they felt was needed. It is evident from the high
level of response to this enquiry that there is deep and widespread concern
among teachers about their facilities. In the light of the detailed comments
received it is interesting to speculate on why so little seems to have been
done to meet the needs of music teachers. An analysis of these reports,
undertaken by John Bryan, the Project's research officer, tended to
confirm the principal conclusions reached at the working party conferences;
that is to say:

Siting

Music accommodation must be specifically designated: we can no longer
expect music teaching to happen in an assembly hall.

Type of accommodation

Music must be recognised as a *practical* subject and therefore needs
'workshop' or 'laboratory' style accommodation rather than conventional
classrooms. We should be thinking now in terms of 'music activity areas'.

Flexibility

(a) Designs should be adaptable; it would be impossible to design a block
    of rooms that would fulfil the needs of every teacher.
(b) Designs should be able to cover the wide variety of activities which
    may occur under the heading of 'music': instrumental teaching
    individually and in groups, extra-curricular ensemble rehearsals (choirs,
    bands, orchestras, etc.), class-singing, class-orchestra, large-group (e.g.
    whole-class) improvisation/composition, recorder groups and other
    small/medium-sized ensembles, small-group (e.g. five or six pupils)
    improvisation/composition/arrangement, individual composition/
    arrangement, electro-acoustic music and work with tape-recorders/
    synthesizers/electric instruments (e.g. rock groups), dance-drama,
    movement with music, links with visual art work and with craft,
    listening to music (in groups and individually), *and* music examination
    classes (e.g. 'O' and 'A' level – or similar – preparation).

Space

Evidence does not necessarily always indicate a need for an increase in
area, but it does suggest that in many cases a redistribution of space for
music might help to increase flexibility.

Adaptation

Whilst we must think carefully about new building, and be prepared to say
clearly what we feel is essential for future development, we should not
overlook the quite considerable scope for modification and adaptation
where older buildings can be up-graded.

There was a reasonable measure of agreement on the main issues as stated above. On detailed points opinion tended to vary, as the remainder of the analysis shows:

The siting of music accommodation

To what extent should music rooms be integrated with the rest of the school?

(a) The music block should be a separate, self-contained set of rooms, or should be situated at the end of a building well away from the traditional 'academic' teaching areas. Music teachers feel inhibited by the thought that their work may disturb other classes, but music classes also require freedom from unwanted sounds and should not, therefore, have to compete with the noise of service departments (e.g. the school kitchens).

(b) The music facilities must be sited so that the specialist needs of the subject can be developed; at the same time the positioning of music should not prevent or discourage active association with other subjects (e.g. the other arts, but see also Tom Gamble's paper, Appx V, part 2).

(c) Further suggestions include:

Integrating music with PE and/or drama space

Placing music close to drama and art for easy liaison

Grouping music, dance and drama together in a single building

Siting music near to and on the same level as the assembly hall for easy transport of instruments for rehearsal and performance

Ensuring that music is sited away from the main thoroughfares so that instrumental lessons can take place at break and lunchtime unhindered by other pupils moving about the school

(d) Careful thought should be given to the relationship between class music areas and instrumental tuition/performance and practice areas. Some felt that these two functions should be separated in the design of the building to minimise sound transference. This might be achieved with a corridor between the two sections. Alternatively rooms for instrumental tuition could be sited in a completely separate block.

The music department as a whole

It is generally recognised that there is need for a variety of rooms, large and small. Perhaps because they have suffered for so long from poor facilities in which any attempt to change a room's function is a major undertaking, some music teachers favour rooms with specific designations, permanently set up and with specialist storage (e.g. a 'band' room with chairs and music stands and instrument storage, the room ready at all times for instrumental ensembles – including classroom orchestras – but not used for other forms of music class teaching).

Heads, on the other hand, tend to think of any large space, even if it is designed as a music 'studio', in terms of multi-purpose use ('. . . large enough to be used for assemblies, lectures, examinations, parents' meetings, further education and community use'). Between these extremes are those who believe that music should have its nominated areas, free of obligation to share with any other department or function which needs a large space, but designed to provide a variety of *musical* activities in any one room. For example, a large 'studio' that would accommodate a choir and orchestra with a grand piano but which could *easily* be made available for music class teaching (implying facilities for *quickly* moving and storing chairs/tables/music stands/instruments).

(a) For class-teaching it is desirable to have, as a basic unit, a large room with small spaces/rooms on the perimeter for group work. The main area should be able to take classes of maximum 30 with instruments and other equipment as necessary. The 'group' spaces should be able to accommodate five or six pupils with instruments, chairs and a table or worktop, plus if possible, a piano. These small-group rooms should *not* have to be used for instrumental tuition.

(b) Children working in small groups tend to produce better results if they are not distracted by extraneous sound. Some preference is therefore shown for making the 'group spaces' small sound-insulated rooms. A few teachers suggested 'cabins' or 'cubicles' that need not be completely sound-proof ('semi-sound-proof booths as in record shops'). It would, in any event, be important for the teacher to be able to see what was going on in each group space and to be easily accessible when help or encouragement was needed for work in progress. Certainly if group rooms have doors then it is essential to have a window in each door. Two teachers submitted diagrams showing group spaces related to main teaching area:

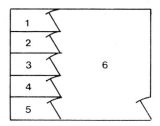 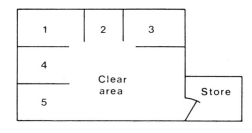

(c) If the group rooms are not to be used by peripatetic instrumental teachers, then separate accommodation for their teaching and for pupils' practice must be provided. Practice rooms should not be too reverberant; loud instruments in small rooms can be overpowering.

(d) Storage is of the utmost importance in any music department. Teachers mentioned the need to provide storage (preferably lockable) for the following: classroom instruments; orchestral and band instruments were available. Shelves should be 50–65 cm apart, with roll-down shutters fitted if security is a problem. An alternative might be lockable cupboards under work surfaces all round the room.

Classroom instruments: The main consideration here is ease of access so that instruments can be collected or distributed quickly and easily (e.g. not a corner cupboard that creates bottlenecks). One teacher suggested that one large store room could be made to serve two main teaching areas and so help with sound insulation. However, the general consensus seems to be that instruments should not be kept in a store room but should be accessible within each teaching area. Open shelves all round the classroom is one solution. This would reduce unnecessary movement of instruments, and make it easy to check to see which instruments were available. Shelves should be 50–65 cm apart, with roll-down shutters fitted if security is a problem. An alternative might be lockable cupboards under work surfaces all round the room.

Wall cupboards will normally be satisfactory for the larger percussion instruments such as glockenspiels, xylophones and drums, but not especially suitable for smaller items. A combination of wall-mounted cupboards (for drums, etc.) above the work-surfaces and shallow drawers (for various kinds of beaters, triangles, finger cymbals, etc.) below the work-surfaces might be the answer. Another possibility for the smaller items is a trolley or a box on wheels – but then storage would also have to be provided for the trolley itself. Some teachers express a preference for keeping *all* their classroom instruments on trolleys, having six for each class so that each group of pupils simply takes a trolley containing a selection of the instruments available.

There is particular need for a convenient method of storing percussion beaters so that it is easy to check if any are missing or damaged: 'something like a pipe-rack' and 'a shelf with holes in' were recommended by teachers.

Orchestral and band instruments: There was some disagreement about the relationship of storage for orchestral instruments and classroom instruments – which perhaps reflects the relationship of class-teaching to instrumental instruction. Some teachers felt it was important to have orchestral instruments stored apart from the class-teaching areas and accessible only from an instrumental teaching area to avoid disruption of lessons. Others felt that they would wish to keep an eye on the orchestral store and suggested that it should be accessible only from the main teaching room. Yet another point of view suggests that some orchestral instruments (e.g. large percussion) may frequently be needed for general class work, and that if the instrumental teaching areas are separated from the main classrooms storage for orchestral instruments should be easily accessible from both sides.

For instrument storage, teachers comments on the type of shelving required generally align with the suggestions made in *Building Bulletin 30*, although since that publication some new requirements have arisen. For example, more room may now be needed for storing guitars. Facility for storing music stands *without having to fold them* would also be an advantage: perhaps some kind of rack?

If a music block has separate practice rooms for instrumental tuition, there seems to be no reason why some small amount of additional storage (again preferably lockable) should not be provided in each of these rooms.

Audio equipment: The type of storage facilities needed will obviously depend on the amount and distribution of the equipment (e.g. whether it is permanently installed or on moveable trolleys). However, there will need to be plentiful storage for records, open reel tapes and cassettes – and with reasonable 'spare' space for the collection to be expanded. The storage should be purpose-built, possibly incorporating commercially available holders with slots for records and tapes, and it should be in a dry and well-aired part of the room.

Books and sheet music: Text books and exercise books seem not to present any serious problems, but purpose-built storage is needed for orchestral parts, choral and sheet music, which is difficult to keep tidy: cupboards with vertical slots are suggested.

Storage is also required for worksheets and other printed material for *class* use. One suggestion was that an ordinary office filing cabinet might be kept in a storeroom or in the main teaching room so that pupils could help themselves to what they needed.

Under this heading we should perhaps also note the need for a separate 'office' where the music staff can keep their own books and materials, private information on tutor groups, and correspondence.

Other materials: In addition to the specific storage mentioned above, some teachers require space to store miscellaneous 'inspirational' materials for use in projects that link music with drama and with dance. For example:

costumes (preferably a wardrobe or small room which can contain hampers)

art materials (ranging in size from large sheets of card and paper to scissors and pots of glue)

scrap materials (scrap metal, wood, glass, instrument strings, etc.)

(e) Some teachers would like a separate listening room. Preferably this should not be part of the main teaching unit (which would need its own sound system for records and tapes), but should be set apart so that pupils who wished to would 'be able to listen to music quietly at any time, in the same way that library facilities are available'. If a designated room were not available, these listening facilities might be sited in carrels to one side of a wide corridor (it is assumed that in either case listening via headphones would be available).

(f) If a music department includes classrooms of different sizes (i.e. instead of or in addition to small-group rooms and practice rooms), it could be useful to set aside one moderately-sized classroom for 5th and 6th form and/or examination work. This could include suitable storage for collections of study scores and, if possible, its own listening facilities.

(g) Very surprisingly, the question of acoustics was referred to by not more than three teachers, who asked for consideration to be given to reducing reverberation, perhaps by using carpets ('hardwearing carpets') and curtains rather than wood floors and reflective wall surfaces. Certainly there is a tendency in some school building to provide the 'music room' with a 'lively' acoustic that would be encouraging to class-singing but which would be likely to make for difficulties in small-group work. Doubtless this arises from a view of 'school music' based on class-singing and unlikely to change. Obviously we do need suitable acoustics for singing, but ideally the building should also provide spaces with acoustic design suitable for other music activities.

Supplementing Building Bulletin 30

Building Bulletin 30 (DES, 1966) continues to provide a good basis for the design of music accommodation. However, developments which have taken place since it first appeared in 1966 suggest that, while most of the information given is still relevant, some small extensions to the Bulletin could be helpful. For example, the music section of the Bulletin tends to be weighted in favour of facilities for extra-curricular performance. This perhaps needs to be balanced now with more focus upon classroom activity.

Whilst flexibility in the use of accommodation is important, giving teachers opportunity to develop new techniques and organisation in their work, the economics of building will almost always mean that we cannot have everything we want just as we want it. Decisions to include some facilities and leave out others will have to be made, but hopefully these would be made by teachers and architects in consultation with one another. From this point of view the Project would most certainly wish to endorse the general premises of Building Bulletin 30:

> This bulletin and others in the series give indications of the choices available to the designer in relation to a particular subject or aspect of the curriculum; *they do not tell him what choice he should make.*

It is also significant that much of what was written in 1966 about providing spaces for drama and movement as 'curriculum' activities now has close parallels in music. For example:

> The place of drama [music] is often too narrowly conceived – the presentation of an annual play [concert] within the limitations imposed by a school hall of rigid and conventional design. In fact, where accommodation permits, skilled and imaginative teachers have shown that a wide variety of dramatic [musical] activities has its place in school.
>
> *The first need is to clarify the meaning and purpose of* drama [*music*] in education in so far as it affects accommodation, *and then to consider what kind of facilities it is really likely to need in years to come.*

Moreover, the general features outlined in the Bulletin's description (in BB30, para. 19) of a 'good drama studio' might also now be applied to a 'good music activity area'.

The kinds of spaces that may be needed

(See BB30, para. 82 *et seq.*) Some activities which hitherto were thought to be more appropriate to 'clubs and societies' may now find a place in the classroom curriculum. The categories 'class-teaching', 'instrumental tuition and practice', 'orchestras and other ensembles' still apply, of course, but are likely to have wider implications when we examine the details. For instance, we may now wish to add 'electronic music-making' (considered broadly enough to include pop/rock groups, tape composition, recording techniques).

The provision for extra-curricular music-making should be considered in relation to developments in class music teaching. Changes of emphasis here will affect specifications in building. For example, where a large music 'studio' may have to accommodate a variety of class work as well as orchestra/choir rehearsals, raised 'staging' (see BB30, diagram 55: '5 ft wide hollow steps') may now be less useful than it was formerly. Similarly, diagrams in the Bulletin which show the space required for players of orchestral instruments (e.g. BB30, diagram 56) may need supplementing with details of the space required by rock bands with amplification equipment, drumkit, etc., steel band instruments, guitar groups, and electro-acoustic music equipment (synthesizers, mixers, tape-recorders, etc.).

Any discussion of spaces for large-scale performances would need to take into account requirements for productions which might be rather more flexible than those envisaged by the Bulletin (see BB30, paras 102–4). It could be useful now to be able to plan for music-dance-drama-visual arts mixed-media events which may be initiated by a music department).

Storage

(See BB30, para. 105 *et seq*.) Again it is principally a matter of adding information. Electronic equipment and hi-fi equipment need to be considered, and a distinction should be drawn between orchestral/band instruments and classroom instruments (e.g. 'Orff Instrumentarium'); each category requires separate storage. It is perhaps also worth noting that orchestral instrument storage may be affected by changes that have taken place in the size of cases (for example, some woodwind instrument cases tend to be larger nowadays than those illustrated in diagram 61 of the Bulletin). The Bulletin's information about record storage (para. 113) also needs modification in the light of developments; very few 10-inch records are produced now, and there should, of course, be provision now for reels of tape and cassettes.

Better spaces for music

The Project frequently met teachers who were dissatisfied with the accommodation and facilities for music in their schools. Generally the complaints were more than justified, as investigation revealed; for example:

> Areas temporarily allocated to music, originally planned as sixth-form accommodation (lockers, etc.).

> Music taught in a room adjacent to an indoor swimming pool (and with an 'observation window' on to the pool!). Considerable disturbance from the noise of those using the pool.

> Music 'workshop' originally designed for sixth form dining and adjacent to the kitchen, with servery. (Complaints of noise from the kitchen staff, but it is often the other way about.)

> The school was designed with no accommodation for music, but later a primitive temporary prefab structure was used. There have been many discussions for development, some of which have included Music, but the only proposal to reach a planning stage included a sixth form centre and provision for drama – but this has not been executed.

> A school for 1000 pupils has two music staff and one room for music plus a small maths classroom. Neither room offers any scope for group work, one being furnished with tables and desks.

Most of the rooms used for instrumental teaching or for 'small-group' work were without ventilation or daylight, and were contrived from partially used stores – some containing abandoned furniture.

Seven of the nine spaces used for music teaching fall very short of the minimum mandatory requirements for teaching accommodation.

The small music room is furnished with large tables because of its use for R.E.

The store has to be used as a staff office.

One music room, three practice rooms, no separate store; this is the total provision in a school for 900 pupils. The three practice rooms have virtually no sound insulation, either between them and the music room or the hall. Nor has the music room itself. The room, with three outside walls – one with an outside door – and a single storey structure, can be very cold. There is one convector heater.

Noise penetrates to other areas . . . the school doctor asked if the music class could be quieter as he could not hear through his stethoscope . . . work therefore somewhat inhibited!

All the accommodation used for music has 'bathroom' acoustics and suffers from lack of insulation.

Many music teachers believe they are powerless to affect decisions which might improve their facilities, and although they continue (understandably) to complain, most do their best to get on with the job, and in consequence develop an indifference to the quality of the space provided. As David Medd has said, 'For generations there have been teachers who have had no control over the nature of space in which they work. They have to accept the buildings rather like the weather.' However, when, on a small number of occasions, the Project did meet with teachers and Heads who were being invited to offer their comments on proposals to extend or modify the music accommodation, or even to build new accommodation, surprisingly few had much idea of the choices available to them or indeed of the nature of the questions they should be asking. Most were ignorant of the existence of *Building Bulletin 30*.

It is useful for teachers to know what the possibilities are, and what factors the architects will need to keep in mind, but in the end it is of course the architect's job to work out the spacial implications from the evidence of educational activity. If we are to see improvements in facilities for music it is vitally important for the teachers to convey to the architects the clearest possible picture of the *music activities* themselves, and of relationships and points of emphasis between different activities.

Equipment and finance

. . . music is frequently the worst equipped and accommodated subject in the curriculum . . . Whereas with the other 'practical' subjects the equipment is installed before any teaching can begin, with music the reverse practice is commonly followed: the teacher has to begin with virtually nothing and build up very slowly through the years, with his equipment supplied by small grudging instalments, often of poor quality. (*Half Our Future* (the 'Newsom Report'), DES, 1963, paras 418/419)

Seventeen years after those words appeared in print the situation for music teachers has changed very little. Here and there, of course, we find schools with outstanding resources for music, but the circumstances are almost always exceptional: an LEA with money available at exactly the moment when it was needed, a far-sighted Head, a music teacher appointed specifically to 'rescue' the subject after a 'difficult' period in the school's history. Most music teachers speak despairingly of their task, for example: 'How *do* we do everything *and* examinations . . . with so little money?'. And understandably many find it laughable even to contemplate the possibility of developing the music curriculum. Another teacher writes, 'How do you do it without equipment?' As with the provision of space for music, it would seem that – in some quarters at least – there is still a strongly held view that the subject *should not need* much more than a piano, a blackboard and some chairs. The Project found instances of work being done which would have been impossible had not the teacher himself supplied the equipment. For example, teachers may find it necessary to bring into school their own tape-recorders or records, or their own percussion instruments.

Knowing what we want

The 'deprivation' of music in schools should not necessarily be blamed on hard-up or tight-fisted LEAs! Where we find good resources for music it is usually because the teacher knows exactly what he wants to do and what equipment he needs to do it, *and* is ready to present a convincing educational case for the work. Many are undecided about the direction in which they should move, and uncertain of the equipment they may need, or even about what is available. Again we should ensure that teachers know what choices they have, but we cannot tell them what choice they should make. Everyone's circumstances are different and to some extent equipment needed will depend upon specific local conditions (e.g. a school with a high proportion of West Indian pupils who could make very good use of steel band instruments).

Teachers' enthusiasms are important; at the same time we should remember that advice and the *offer* of certain types of equipment may help to develop new enthusiasms in previously unexplored areas of music. Costs of instruments in particular can vary (e.g. with locally available discounts). Prices are rising all the time and it would therefore be pointless to estimate here a 'reasonable' budget for a music department. But it could be helpful if LEA music advisers would research the position in their own areas and provide all their teachers with lists and suggestions, updated from time to time. No doubt it would be essential to make it clear that these lists did not imply the immediate availability of unlimited finance! Nevertheless, it could be encouraging and stimulating for teachers to know what the possibilities were. Some authorities are already offering this kind of help, but comments received by the Project suggest that more guidance is needed and would be appreciated. For example:

> What classroom instruments other than Orff-type are available cheaply? Will they be acceptable to the secondary age-range pupils?
>
> We need advice on acquiring classroom instruments on a limited budget; e.g. how to spend £30, £50, £100 or more . . . Instruments that could be made in school . . . sounds from other sources.
>
> Suggest some order in which instruments, other sound sources, and electronic equipment might be acquired.
>
> Instruments for *class use* – guidance in building up a stock; which instruments should be bought first?

Obviously answers to questions about order of priority in buying equipment would have to be related to curriculum content; there is a 'chicken and egg' element which we can't ignore. If we know with certainty what we want to do, we can try to define the resources we need to do it. On the other hand, knowing what equipment is available can stimulate ideas for classroom activities.

In the first instance we might decide to embark on a programme of sound exploration and improvisation leading eventually to group and individual compositions/arrangements. We should want the course to have substance and progression, perhaps leading to an investigation of certain styles of music and a knowledge of various kinds of notation (including staff notation). We could begin such a course with the minimum of equipment; for example, we could start with various kinds of vocal sounds and with group improvisations and compositions based on these sounds, 'made up and remembered' without the need for notation. We could continue with a similar exploration of 'found object' sounds, again making minimal demands financially. Thereafter, however, it would be essential to know that specific items of equipment were going to be available. We should need a good record-player, records, and possibly facilities for recording and playing tapes; we should certainly need pitched instruments in sufficient numbers for the class and of types that would be acceptable and stimulating for secondary age-range pupils. Anticipating the kinds of music which would be developed by the pupils, we should have to make sure that suitable instruments were available to match various levels of skill. This might include some 'Orff' instruments (which are useful because the notes are easily identified; they can therefore be helpful in linking sound with notation), but it might be essential to provide other resources that offered a wider range of timbres and which were not too strongly associated with the junior school (as the 'Orff' instruments undoubtedly are for many secondary pupils). It might be possible to achieve what was needed with an even wider variety of 'found' sounds, but even so it could still be necessary to acquire *some* fairly expensive equipment for this stage (e.g. large orchestral percussion; gongs, vibraphone, drums of various sizes, electric guitars and amplifiers).

The Project's tape-slide programme *Music in Inner Urban Schools* demonstrates Alan Renshaw's approach at Islington Green School. He is shown combining a range of instruments with tape and electronic effects to involve the pupils in a sophisticated thematic composition about *Faces*. The results are impressive, but as Alan Renshaw says,

> We're very, very fortunate to have some of the most amazing professional instruments. And to actually have a real vibrating vibraphone in a music room not only helps my task in selling the subject and getting it going, but it's an amazing sound machine. So I think it's worthwhile for music departments to invest in the real stuff, in the real McCoy!

Another teacher makes a similar point:

> Orff-type classroom instruments have only limited usefulness, and non-traditional use of them should be encouraged. Expensive percussion instruments are preferred – gongs, metallophones, and so on . . . cymbals and triangles of all sizes [should be] available. Cello bows, metal sheets, and old pianos are also very useful.
> Children should be encouraged to brings sounds into school.

Without a doubt one of the most trying things for a teacher, working in an intangible 'material' like sound, is to have to attempt to stimulate imagination, inventiveness and enthusiasm for music either with no hope of moving beyond the most elementary level or – possibly worse – with the prospect of alienating pupils through the use of apparatus which appears 'childish'. But knowing the kind of course on which we want to embark at least provides a starting point. From there we should set out to acquire the equipment, and where it cannot be acquired we should either have to tailor our course accordingly – or abandon it altogether and think again! If only the most elementary equipment was available, we should have to decide how best to make a progressing and stimulating course with what we'd got; although knowing clearly what our goal was, we should at least be able to continue to press for improvements while doing our best with limited resources.

If, on the other hand, we are at all uncertain about the kind of course we should be offering, some indication of equipment that might be available for work at different levels can stimulate ideas and help us to design a scheme of work appropriate to our pupils. The teacher who asks for a graded and budget-linked list of classroom instruments may well know what he wants to do but is at the same time conscious that his ideas will have to be tempered by what he can buy with his limited financing.

Given a particular sum he could have this or that and so follow a particular programme of class work. Given more money (now or later) he could try to extend the work already begun or develop some entirely new plans. Conversely, this teacher may feel that a defined list of equipment within a specified budget limit will in itself help to stimulate ideas and enable him to plan a course. Either way, a list, linked where possible to local costs, can be useful. It may be accompanied by curriculum suggestions from the Music Adviser based upon his special knowledge of schools in the area, information which can help teachers to work together on projects involving particular resources (e.g. aspects of ethnic musics).

Between the conventional classroom instruments and the very expensive professional equipment, there are a number of possibilities that might help to get over the difficulties of 'acceptability' for secondary age pupils. Tin whistles may be more acceptable than recorders because, although they are only diatonic, they do not present the problems of intonation that can be a major difficulty for elementary recorder players. The true recorder repertoire is remote from the average teenager but whistles have continuing connections with 'popular' music of many different kinds in some areas of Britain and have featured in folk/pop groups in recent years. And of course they are cheaper than recorders! Chord instruments are useful for accompanying melodies and for filling out the harmonic background in small-group arrangements. Guitars are obviously popular and players may be led on to more adventurous playing than simply chord strumming), but chordal dulcimers and the cheaper models of chord organ can be useful and stimulating instruments, even for very elementary players.

Many teenagers have quite a range of electric instruments themselves at home and could be encouraged to bring them into school for class music-making. The 'stylophone', for example, may be rather limited in timbre but it has its uses. Boys are often very skilful in building electronic gadgets for music (see Vulliamy and Lee, *Pop Music in School* pp. 135, 193), and there is a lot that can be done in electro-acoustic music with quite simple equipment. Although one teacher, who obviously had strong feelings on the subject, wrote (to the Project) 'a synthesizer is an essential piece of school equipment', others have shown that some very convincing music can be made with a single tape-recorder and some simple home-made equipment (see Orton, *Electronic Music for Schools*, Cambridge University Press, 1981).

Another possibility worth exploring is to make our own instruments. The Project's tape-slide programme *Materials and Instruments* demonstrates one approach (see p. 114 above), and other uncommon instruments – which might be built by setting up joint courses with a craft department – can be found in David Sawyer's book *Vibrations: making unorthodox musical instruments* (Cambridge University Press, 1977).

The basic list

It is difficult to say what would be an appropriate minimum collection of instruments for classroom work. If we want to concentrate on staff notation we shall need simple pitched instruments for a whole-class group, but variety may not be important. It could be sufficient to have, say, 12 or 15 alto glockenspiels (or soprano glockenspiels) plus the same number of descant recorders (or tin whistles). On the other hand, a teacher who wished to follow a course based on principles such as those evolved by Carl Orff would need a variety of 'bar' instruments plus some tuned drums and some un-pitched percussion. The following is one teacher's suggestion for a basic collection of 'Orff' instruments (with certain additions):

1 chromatic bass xylophone	2 alto glockenspiels
2–3 alto xylophones	1 soprano glockenspiel
1 soprano xylophone	various sizes of drums, cymbals
1 diatonic chime bar set	and triangles
1 chromatic chime bar set	

Another teacher lists a mixture of 'Orff' instruments and other pitched instruments:

2 soprano chromatic metallophones	12 Spanish guitars
1 soprano recorder	6 acoustic guitars
2 descant recorders	1 12-string guitar
2 treble recorders	1 banjo
2 tenor recorders	4 Aulos 'fifes
1 bass recorder	4 harmonicas

And to this basic list he adds a collection of orchestral instruments which includes not only the full range of woodwind, brass and strings but also a set of saxophones and a good range of the large orchestral percussion.

Obviously to set up a school with resources as extensive as that would cost many thousands of pounds, even if the orchestral instruments were second-hand. Traditionally it has been the custom for schools to build up collections of orchestral and band instruments, and to make them available on loan to pupils. This is a great encouragement to beginners, especially on the larger and more expensive instruments, and schools with these resources usually find there is no shortage of 'takers' for instruments whenever they become available. But it has become more and more difficult for individual schools (particularly new schools) to establish such collections, so that any worthwhile orchestral activity (or brass band or jazz orchestra) tends now to depend quite a lot on pupils buying their own instruments. Is there, then, any point in a school trying to provide anything other than the large items (timpani, double bass, bassoon, bass trombone)?

Some would argue even that the days of the separate school orchestra/ band are over and that it would be wiser to concentrate now upon pooling resources for *area* orchestras incorporating players from several different schools. In the end this may be the only feasible thing to do, but it would be a pity if individual schools could no longer contemplate any form of extra-curricular music-making at reasonably high levels of attainment. Although it is to be hoped that class music activities for the majority of pupils would be regarded as the priority, a successful extra-curricular programme can feed back into the class work and add considerable strength to the 'general' music-making.

Perhaps the most difficult choice for the music teacher working on a limited budget, and trying to build up his instrumental resources little by little over a period of years, is between the selective music-making of the orchestra/band and the 'majority' music-making of the classroom. If he spends several hundred pounds on a bassoon, that may increase the scope of music the orchestra can tackle but that one instrument will probably be on loan to a single student for some time, perhaps several years. If, on the other hand, the teacher spends a large part of his allocation on classroom glockenspiels and xylophones he may be able to extend his class work but he inhibits the scope of the orchestra and the potential for encouraging more advanced musicians. The glockenspiels and xylophones, useful as they are, will have limited application. One solution would be abandon the traditional 'out-of-class' ensembles (such as the conventional instrumentation of orchestra or brass band), and develop new groups (folk music groups, rock bands, 'New Music' ensembles) using instruments which would not necessarily have to be loaned to individual students or taken off the premises for practice, and which could therefore be available for wider use in classroom work as well as for the 'specialist' players.

Teachers' views on other equipment

Our use of space is affected by the equipment and furniture that has to go into it. The Project's survey of teachers' views on accommodation produced a number of interesting comments on these related matters.

Pianos

These were thought to be 'very useful whatever the context/content of musical activity.' It is the only harmonic instrument with an extensive pitch range generally available to us, and therefore remains an important 'tool' in music education. Good quality instruments are needed that will withstand hard and prolonged use.

However, the majority of teachers seem to feel that a grand piano is an unnecessary luxury in the main teaching room, though many thought it important (or 'essential') to have access to one somewhere in the school (e.g. the assembly hall) for assemblies and concerts. A piano (preferably a good upright – to save space) should be provided for the main teaching room, and if possible pianos should be available in small-group rooms as well. And '*adjustable* stools should be provided for *every* piano'.

Some teachers suggested that other forms of keyboard instrument might be considered. For example, small electronic or reed organs are popular with children and are useful in tape and pop music.

Audio equipment

Most teachers feel there is a need for a 'Listening Centre' which should be equipped with good quality record deck, cassette or open-reel tape deck linked to more than one set of headphones. Some, however, strongly prefer to use loudspeakers for group listening and believe there are always likely to be occasions when it will be necessary to play records to a whole class or a large group. This is probably best done with a fixed hi-fi 'centre' housed in one security unit.

Opinion is divided on the merits of permanent hi-fi installations or trolleys. Having all the equipment, including loudspeakers, mounted on a trolley offers flexibility of use in different locations, but the advantages may to some extent be offset by the greater hazard and liability to damage or technical breakdown. In general, it seems, portable recording facilities are more important than portable playback facilities. Fixed installations will require long leads for microphones to achieve the same recording flexibility.

Although some teachers feel it is essential to have both open-reel and cassette tape-recorders, most seem to prefer open-reel machines since these are still likely to give the best quality reproduction, and the tape can be edited. However, they are not so easily transported and are generally more difficult than cassette-recorders for pupils to operate. Portable cassette machines are useful for collecting sounds outside (i.e. for copying and using in tape transformations – e.g. for 'musique concrète'), and one teacher suggests a 'stereo cassette deck . . . in addition to the open-reel deck so that copies of children's compositions may be made . . . to take home – just as they are able to do with paintings and poems'.

Equipment for electro-acoustic music

Although, as we have seen already, some very useful work can be done without expensive or elaborate equipment, if there is to be substantial commitment to this field of music-making a teacher will no doubt want to set up some kind of small studio containing tape recorders, mixers, and synthesizer. The studio would be used for the composition of electro-acoustic music, both by means of synthesized sounds and tape-transformation of other sounds, but it could also double as a recording studio (perhaps with microphone links to the main teaching rooms). If a large enough room can be set aside for this work it could also serve as a base for the 'electronics' of rock groups. Good sound-proofing would be essential for all these functions.

Furniture

Music teachers generally dislike heavy desks, but work surfaces of one kind or another are likely to be needed from time to time in all music rooms. Small tables are particularly useful for work with tuned percussion instruments.

Light, stackable tables are recommended by some teachers. These tables are 'easily groupable' or can be used individually. Six would normally be enough for an average sized class. Too many tables can be a nuisance.

Another suggestion is for laboratory-type worktops around the perimeter of the room, with shelves above and cupboards beneath, leaving the centre of the room free for music performances or for dance/drama activities with music. The worktops should be approximately 76 cm from the ground and 92 cm deep.

Light and stackable chairs seem to be generally preferred, possibly with arm tablets as another way of providing work surfaces. However, one teacher made the comment that 'rooms need character and consistency, and so some sense of permanent set-up is important'. Rather than have stackable furniture, he preferred to divide the room into two, one half being permanently set up as a 'workshop' with equipment set out on fixed work surfaces, the other half being empty except for a few items of furniture that could quickly be moved or re-arranged.

Other considerations

A number of teachers point out that chalk-dust and hi-fi equipment don't mix! They advocate white plastic boards and felt-tip pens.

Music teachers are as likely as any other to require plenty of pin-board space for art-work and 'inspirational' material. Some would also like music rooms to have black-out and slide/film/film-strip projection facilities.

Heating may be a problem; it can damage instruments and equipment, therefore care should be exercised in siting radiators and ducts. The pipes of hot water radiators also transmit sounds from one room to another and may thus totally defeat the best efforts at sound insulation.

Value for money

In the end, like everything else in education, it comes down to a matter of finance. No LEA has a bottomless well of cash from which to draw for every need a school can think of. Inevitably there will be arguments and negotiations, claims and counter-claims about different aspects of the curriculum. As music teachers we have no more right than any other group to expect that our claims for increased time, space, staff or equipment should be given preference. But we should not expect to have to operate in seriously disadvantageous circumstances. If we believe in ourselves as educators and in what our subject has to contribute to general education, we must press for the kind of funding that will make possible at least a moderately realistic approach to music in school. At the present time too many music teachers are expected to produce worthwhile results under conditions that would not be tolerated in other subjects, and this is largely because of deep-seated misunderstandings about music's curriculum potential.

Obviously this is not universally the case, and we should be very grateful for those Authorities who have responded to developments in music education and have done their best to give it support. But elsewhere the message is plain: music doesn't matter as a curriculum subject, therefore it cannot expect funding comparable with other subjects.

Music in education *can* give value for money, but there are still too many people who have little or no idea of what that 'value' is likely to be. It is now clearly up to music teachers to demonstrate the case for music education, and to say what is possible with the funding that is available. Only music teachers themselves can show that there have to be understood minimum standards of accommodation, staffing and equipment below which music ceases to be viable as a subject for the majority of pupils.

6 Examinations and assessment

Opening the door – or closing it?

One of the effects of extending the scope of music in the curriculum has been the highlighting of some long-standing worries about music examinations. There was already some concern about the way in which the conventional patterns of public examinations were inclined to restrict teaching, for example:

> An examination syllabus tends to determine what is taught in the two years leading up to it . . . it also determines how many students will opt for that subject.
>
> The work of most school music departments is influenced by the *constraints* of GCE/CSE.

But further to that, the evidence now of pupils producing their own music in many different styles, often without much in the way of conventional training and sometimes without the ability to read and write traditional music notation, has led some to question the value of examinations in any form:

> Assessment – is it relevant? Or is it indulged in to conform with the rest of the school procedure?
>
> Does the exam have any useful part to play?

Others apparently see the new developments as something of a threat, and so hasten to defend the *status quo*; reluctant, it would seem, to admit even to themselves that there could be much of value in that significant proportion of the world's music which, while it is not notated is nevertheless invented, performed, enjoyed and understood (and 'evaluated'?) entirely on the basis of the sound it makes. The chairman of one examination board's music panel told the Project that he would '*never* be prepared to make a final judgement on a piece of music – even a piece of electronic music – without seeing the score'. Such a statement, which appears to imply that no music is worthy of a musician's attention unless it is notated, would automatically exclude from examinations a great deal of aurally successful music which is being produced by young people in schools today, especially in the fields of rock and ethnic musics.

'Academic standing'

Nevertheless, there are people who would like to see a *development* of assessment techniques, broadening the range of opportunity for students to submit work in both conventional and unconventional forms, by placing less emphasis upon mere 'information about music' and giving more attention to the *sound* of music itself – with or without notations. There are, however, doubts about how this should be done. Teachers write of the 'need to design a totally new examination to take account of the changes taking place', but at the same time are conscious of accountability: 'We are answerable to so many agencies: surely we ought be be able to show standards of attainment?' Some feel that we have allowed ourselves to be overtaken by events, and that we have not given enough thought to matching new classroom activities with suitable assessment procedures *as these things grew up*. If we are not careful, they argue, we may now miss vital opportunities for our pupils and for the future development of the subject because our 'academic' rating is low and therefore we are not to be taken seriously:

> Is the subject [music] capable of assessment? The implication seems to be that if it is not it could be at risk.

Is this in fact the case? Are we really threatened by ogres of the examination system? Have we been presented with an ultimatum: 'assess or disappear'? Possibly the threat, if it does exist, is from within. In our uncertainty about some of the new directions that music has taken in schools are we inclined to take refuge in the conventional forms of syllabus and examination, afraid perhaps that, without the 'proof' these seem to offer we may be accused of turning our backs on 'academic rigour' and becoming 'undemanding' or 'non-intellectual' in our approach to music?

It would be very sad if this were so since 'academic' standing is not something which can be imposed from outside the content of a subject; and it is presumably not worth a great deal if it is totally incapable of embracing new developments. Obviously all skills (including the 'skills' of imagination and inventiveness) have their 'rigour', and within their own terms can be handled with varying degrees of success, which it should not be beyond us to evaluate. The important thing would be to make sure that we do not try to evaluate against each other, things which have little in common. The terms of reference must be found within the skills, musical styles or whatever, related specifically to what is being presented for assessment. Thus there would be little to be gained in assessing a violinist whose techniques were specifically developed for 'folk fiddling' by asking him to play a Mozart sonata (or vice versa; it does not follow that the competent performer of Mozart will necessarily be able to give a convincing performance of folk music). By the same token, it is difficult to see why we should regard as 'unassessable' a piece of music made by empirical means, formed and held in the memory but not notated (because the composer/ performer did not need that aid), and dismiss it *because* it is not notated! Surely it should be assessed on the same terms as those on which it was made?

The broad and the narrow ways

Are there not simply two possibilities? Either we accept the many-sidedness of music and, starting from the music itself, determine criteria for evaluation which will embrace all styles and techniques, or we define *our* terms of acceptability for music, deliberately ignoring and excluding anything that does not fit that model (e.g. the rock guitarist, the 'folk' fiddler, the 'empirical'/intuitive composer).

There are advantages and disadvantages in both approaches. The first may commend itself to those who would like to see music in education broaden its scope still more to encourage and include the widest possible range of music-making. But the problems of reaching agreement on comparability of achievement cannot be overlooked. It might therefore be difficult to convince others that a certificate of attainment awarded on this basis was worth anything. The other method, which selects and defines what is to be examined, and excludes everything else, may be somewhat unrealistic musically but, because the area covered is limited, clear and easy to grasp, there can be little doubt about comparisons. The examiners can quite properly argue that if we want their certificate it must be on their (the examiners') terms; no-one is compelling us to enter the examination, but if we do, and if we pass, the 'meaning' of the award will be clear. Regrettably, though, this may be the only form of accepted music examination. And there is the rub; it's all very well to argue that such an examination does not in fact prevent young people from developing other kinds of musicianship; it doesn't actually stop them playing their guitars or whatever. But if their musicianship does develop significantly within its own sphere (and the evidence is overwhelming that this is possible), then why should their skills not have the recognition accorded to others?

Whichever course we take the lesson to be learned is clear: we must be quite sure that everyone understands what we are examining and what our 'certification' actually means. It's no use pretending that we can demonstrate exactly comparable standards in extremely diverse forms of music-making. But neither should we pretend that we are conducting the only meaningful kind of music examination if we have started by deliberately excluding a great deal of widely recognised music.

Why examine music?

There is one further point which should perhaps concern us, and that is *who* is the examination for? One correspondent suggests that 'Assessment procedures are worth close scrutiny because so many teachers have to complete reports.' Is there a link here with the fears of another teacher (quoted above) that if we do not find the answers to our assessment problems 'the subject . . . could be at risk'? Are some of us more worried about ourselves than about our pupils? It is strange how many music teachers seem to be obsessed with examinations. Is it important to be able to measure the achievement of our students in terms readily acceptable to others (standardised and well-established techniques, straightforward repetition of information, and so on) because this gives *us* reassurance about the value and the success of what *we* do? No-one would deny that teachers need confidence in themselves if their work is to grow usefully, but this is a side of the job that should be kept in perspective and about which we have to be completely realistic. It would be a poor sort of confidence that was dependent mainly upon 'pointers' from outside: the need to supply marks for reports, the ready-made curriculum of the external examination syllabus relieving us of the responsibility of selecting material, comfortingly showing us 'where it all leads', providing the clearly signposted journey in a progression of techniques and information to be assimilated by students and tested by the teacher, and – the 'trump card' in many cases – the belief that 'the examinations represent what the Universities demand'. Obviously there is some truth in this; universities *have* had their influence on the school curriculum and they do expect their entrants to be competent, although most will be looking for more than the mere mechanical application of formulae or the ability to regurgitate second-hand information. They will also be hoping for some indication of musical insights being developed. And it could be salutary to remind ourselves that the universities themselves cannot look to externally imposed syllabuses to provide guidance; they must rely primarily upon their own judgement.

It is not being suggested that marks for reports or examination syllabuses are 'wrong' in themselves, but simply that we should be careful to use them as means, not ends. It is preferable that our confidence should come from sincere convictions about the educational value of *all* the music-making we organise, across the whole ability spectrum. For perhaps the greatest danger of concentrating too much upon marks and examinations is the underlying assumption that our work in schools is finally geared to those few who will be going on to music courses in higher education. What about the rest? To them it matters little what universities or colleges want or don't want from their students. Music in school must have something to offer to the vast majority, those who are not heading in the higher academic direction. Unfortunately, as we have seen, public examinations very rarely recognise the existence of such pupils and in consequence their needs may easily be overlooked.

An experiment in assessment

If the idea of 'music as a creative art' is central to music in education, any consequent attempt to develop the curriculum, although it will presumably include a wide variety of musical activities and skill learning, must surely give some prominence to composition, both as small-group work and as an individual activity. Indeed, it would be reasonable to want to see work of this kind organised so that pupils' skill could grow from simple beginnings in group improvisation, through a substantial composition course leading to advanced individual work: in parallel with similar development through instrumental tuition.

Already a number of schools are attempting to design and operate composition courses leading to the submission of work in public examinations. At present this is normally possible through a CSE Mode 3 syllabus and may include the work of young people who would not normally be encouraged to compose music. The teachers who organise these courses generally have an open mind about the role of music notation; scores may or may not be necessary, depending upon the composers' experience and the nature of the music itself. Obviously pupils will make maximum use of their skills, and course work will aim to extend their technique. But in general the emphasis is towards the sound of the music itself, and teachers tend to favour the submission of tape recordings for assessment of pupils' compositions.

In 1977 the Project invited Robert Bunting, a teacher who had already undertaken research in this field, to organise a conference on the subject of examinations and assessment with particular reference to the composition elements in some CSE Mode 3 examinations. The problems of assessing creative work at this level had not been widely discussed, and it was therefore agreed that the conference should devote a major part of its time to an 'assessment exercise' in which delegates would listen to tape recordings of pupils' compositions and attempt, by means of a series of assessments and reassessments, to reach consensus views on the grading of the pieces heard. Although in some cases scores were available, it was agreed that judgements would be made as far as possible on what the 'examiners' could derive from the recordings alone.

To begin with, each member of the conference listened privately to the tape which included eleven pieces, selected by Robert Bunting from tapes

submitted by three schools. These pieces demonstrated a range of techniques
– some elementary, others quite advanced – in music for instrumental
ensemble, electric organ, solo bamboo flute, piano duet, xylophone and
drum, together with a variety of 'tape' music including 'concrete' sounds
and synthesized sounds, and recording of live electronic performance with
piano and synthesizer. When all the conference members had individually
made a preliminary assessment of what they heard on the tape, they came
together, first in small groups and then, merging these groups, working
gradually towards a gathering of everyone in a single large group. The aim
at each stage was to pool ideas and, through discussion, to resolve
differences as far as possible until the whole conference could reach
agreement on criteria for judging the pieces of music, and if possible award
a series of marks – or at least define a rank order.

It was generally felt that this was a useful experiment (and indeed it has
been repeated since by other groups using the same tape), though naturally
everyone had certain reservations after the event. Detailed descriptions of
the proceedings, together with comments on the 'marking', plus other
observations on assessment of work in this area, were assembled by Robert
Bunting and published by the Project as one of its working papers. This is
reproduced here as Appendix II.

The examiners' views

Examination boards throughout the country were invited to comment on
the Project's attempts to initiate discussion on content and method for music
examinations. In particular they were asked for their views on the tape of
pupils' compositions and the assessment exercise which the Project had
promoted. Moderators and Chief Examiners were sent copies of the tape
and the conference paper. The latter was, of course, intended as a starting
point for discussion and was not presented as an authoritarian statement on
what should or should not be done in examinations. However, some of the
replies received suggest that if worthwhile discussion is to develop it may
first be necessary for some examiners to experience at first hand the kind
of work that leads up to the production of compositions such as those
reproduced on the tape.

(a) 'Depressed and sickened'

I found reading it a depressing and sickening experience, not only because of the
self-righteous, one-sided and iconoclastic views expressed, but also because of the
familiar clichés (so excitingly breathcatching in the Sixties, and so jaded in the
late Seventies) by which the views were presented. It was dangerously depressing
because I began not merely to question but to mistrust my judgement and the
experience behind it, e.g. 'Surely nothing could really be that bad – this work
must have intrinsic values to which your biased outlook has blinded you'. I found
myself re-examining other turbulent situations in Musical History, the rivalry

between the prima and seconda prattica in 1600, the Baroque and Style Galant, Romanticism and Impressionism, Folk music and the Tone Row as rival claimants to replace outmoded Romanticism, and the post war *informed* experiments in Aleatory Music.

Whereas in all the earlier situations the amateur copyists of the new experimenters had a rigorous training and technical skill, the post war fashionable aleatory style has provided a happy hunting ground for quick and easy 'creative' composition requiring no intellectual study or acquisition of technical skill equivalent to either 'orthodox' musical education, modern language fluency, scientific numeracy, or the precise practical skills of Design and Technology. Whereas a music student used to expect to have to work at music in order to play it, it seems now that he/she is often led to play at it in order to be ephemerally entertained by it. When in contrast one considers the progress made since the war in instrumental playing as illustrated by Youth Orchestras, Bands and Choirs, the dichotomy between the maturity of performing and the 'creative' composing in schools is – to say the least – remarkable.

Having made the general observations quoted above, the writer continues in a similar vein with criticism of particular points in the conference paper, though expending most effort on attacking phraseology rather than commenting on the substance. For example:

> . . . 'quality or orthodox exam courses' – their weaknesses mentioned but not specified – '*working* teachers – radical new approaches – changes of this dimension can only be carried out by individual schools working in isolation with CSE Mode III'. Such claptrap is designed to revile the 'reactionary' and to revitalise the poor hardworking faithful with tear jerking references to radical and lonely heroism.

Here, it would seem, we have an illustration of the extremes of misunderstanding that apparently can arise between teachers, endeavouring with sincerity to broaden the scope of music in schools, and those who exercise some control in public examinations. The Board concerned was at pains to point out that the feelings expressed did not necessarily represent the considered view of the Music Committee as a whole but were the personal opinions of the writer. Obviously we should have regard for any expression of views that helps us to see the problems more clearly, and although writing from an alien standpoint about the work which was offered for review, this examiner has values and standards that deserve respect. As Robert Bunting comments:

> I agree that, compared with the skills of instrumental teaching, composition teaching in schools is in its infancy. If X is saying that radical rhetoric is not enough, I agree wholeheartedly. Until we can teach skills, concepts and attitudes to creative work in a really thoroughgoing way, responding in detail to each individual's problems, we have to accept that we are only beginners.

Nevertheless, the criticism does reveal a lack of experience as well as a lack of sympathy. There seems to be no awareness or appreciation of the techniques of creative work in other areas of education (art, drama, dance, English), and no recognition of the way in which teachers are using examinations other than 'O' and 'A' level to develop the potential in pupils who would otherwise be ignored by the system. Most of the pupils whose work was heard on the tape were entered for the CSE. The references to 'new movements' in musical history do not seem particularly relevant; again Robert Bunting replies:

> . . . it would have been more to the point if he had considered revolutions in educational philosophy, particularly with the aim of adapting traditional techniques to the average child in a mass education system – a long way from the Florentine Academy of 1600 or the drawing rooms of 18th century Paris!

And the strongly worded attack on 'fashionable aleatory style' as a 'happy hunting ground for quick and easy composition' has no real bearing in this case since there was not a single passage of aleatory music presented on the tape. Moreover, all the pupils concerned were attempting to compose using what skills they had, and the tape set out quite deliberately to demonstrate a range of work from the highly skilled to the rudimentary, with no special claims made for the musical quality of the less advanced pieces.

(b) 'Fair comparison impossible'
I have read the document a couple of times and listened to the tape several times and found both extremely interesting . . . However in my personal view, pupils who are interested in this kind of approach to music would be better advised to follow a non-examination course, partly because I find it extremely difficult if not impossible to fairly award marks and partly because I feel the *musical* skill and understanding involved is far removed from that required from a pupil likely to gain a grade I after following a Mode I course. I consider fair comparison impossible and in many ways undesirable. However, having said all this I have still found the exercise useful and interesting.

This writer's own teaching was described as being 'in the more traditional style', though there is clear evidence of experience in handling a wide ability-range in a large school. Ideas about what can and cannot be usefully examined are strongly expressed, and are on the whole restricting. They revolve around a concept of '*musical* skill' which is not fully explained. The significance of the emphasised '*musical*' is not clear, but seems to suggest that the work presented on the tape was neither very musical nor skilful. What should we assume from the observation that the musicianship displayed was 'far removed from that required from a pupil likely to gain a grade I'? That these pupils are 'far *below*' the required standard, or simply 'different from' those who would gain a grade I? The accent here appears to be upon finding the easiest material to assess rather than finding ways of assessing unorthodox submissions that might encourage more pupils to show an interest in music.

(c) 'Purpose and sincerity in a student's work'

The project deals with creative art – in this case music of non-traditional kind, but rather original – even abstract – in form, and if provision for this is to be made in school curricula, then what form of assessment should be devised. A cassette tape with five such pieces is available and documents giving assessments made by one person and comments by others.

My reaction on first hearing the tape was one of wonderment. Was the whole thing a hoax just to see what high powered assessors might make of these presentations by 16-year-old students who are probably musically immature? Would the composer of 'Wind on the Waves' for example be laughing up his sleeve at finding that the Assessor had discovered that the piece contained a mixture of phrygian and dorian modes, of which modes the composer himself might not have had any such knowledge. Indeed it all seemed a waste of time and money. Most of the pieces were, to my mind, not suitable for concert performance, but might be useful for 'effect' music. Indeed, the BBC Radiophonic Workshop, had it been approached, could no doubt easily have competed.

However, I have re-read the Report of the Conference and listened again to the tape. I appreciate that with any form of creative art a problem does arise when attempting to lay down criteria for assessing such work. I thought that the Chart given in the paper was a good attempt to meet the problem. Nevertheless, it seems to me that to attempt to prescribe rules of assessment must inevitably tend to inhibit the innovator.

Surely the final assessment is really determined by the merit each piece attains when presented publicly. If a composition is intended to serve a purpose – perhaps for enjoyment in performing, for pleasurable listening, or for providing 'effect' for a film or play – then it will stand or fall on its own merit.

Naturally no-one wants to stifle innovation. Indeed without innovation in the past the world would hardly have progressed. I liked Richard Orton's LDI method – like, dislike or indifference – as a first approach, and I agree with the need to ensure that criticisms of students' work, whether by an individual or by a panel, should be constructive. Since, however, most of us probably had traditional musical training, clearly in the field of innovation this will not be an easy task. Close contact with the student would appear to be essential to establish the purpose and sincerity of his work.

To conclude. The Institute sets examinations based upon accepted syllabuses and its certificates record levels achieved in particular skills. A totally different situation exists when students are invited, in the field of music, to have 'freedom of expression'. If such expression produces something with a purpose acceptable to the majority – perhaps that will be merit enough.

This report is made not by a music examiner but by a teacher on the staff of an Institute which organises public examinations in many subjects, though not in music. The writer is described as 'a very active amateur musician' and the comments are of particular interest because, although it would seem likely that the writer has little contact with music in schools, and probably no experience of creative work in that connection, some trouble has been taken to understand the proposals being made and to evaluate the evidence of the tape-recordings. The report is critical of some things, sympathetic to others, and while the criteria suggested for assessment may sometimes beg more questions than they answer (e.g. 'Surely the final assessment is really determined by the merit each piece attains *when presented publicly.*'), the open-minded approach has a lot to teach us. Of particular interest is the view that, in assessing work of this kind, we need to know something of the person who has made it – and presumably of the preliminary work that has led up to the final submission. This idea is further developed by the assessor quoted in report (e) below.

(d) 'A problem of values'
It is appreciated that the scrutiny of existing methods and procedures has led some school musicians to question the validity of the courses they teach to the modern child in the classroom. New ideas are obviously welcome and stimulate an evaluation of what is generally accepted as appropriate.

It is appreciated that the notion of employing music in a much freer and uninhibited 'creative' manner has been one of the main avenues of development for the Project, that these approaches owe much to the activities of contemporary composers, and that the authors have endeavoured to adapt many of the 'avant-garde' practices to an educational context.

[The examiner] comments that it might be held that the new Music itself, divorced largely from the traditional approach, has yet to establish its values. He suggests that there has been a vigorous foray into new realms of composition, employing new sounds, vocal, instrumental and electronic, a wide variety of performance practice and a diversity of notations, but also that this music has yet to be widely accepted by musicians and the public, and that the criteria for its communication and judgement have yet to be established. This fundamental, yet unresolved, problem of values, impinges directly upon examination procedures. In its novelty it may be that the new Creative Music needs to be thought of as a new aspect of music which, given time, will evolve and codify its aesthetic canons. The dilemma for an examination board at present would be to decide in what way it should react to an obvious educational development in music education and yet uphold established ideas of competence in the subject. It seems that time needs to elapse so that the music itself can stabilise and that more knowledge can be gained of the extent to which Creative Music is a major and lasting element in the music curriculum.

The Board will certainly continue to be alert to developments in this field but the question of evaluation would as yet seem to involve issues which are not resolved in a wider context.

Here, clearly, there is a degree of goodwill and some desire to come to terms with 'an obvious *educational* development in music education'. But it seems likely that, even if the examiner has seen examples of this way of working in schools, it has not been a part of personal teaching methods. The report makes certain unsupported assertions about the work of the Project and about 'Creative Music'* and these assumptions create a barrier between the writer and the pupils' music on the tape. For example, the comment on 'the new Music itself' which is claimed to be 'divorced largely from the traditional approach'. This seems to have prevented the examiner

---

* See above, pages 136/137.

from hearing the unequivocally 'traditional' harmonic and melodic writing of the third piece on the tape, *Zeitgeist*, which is clearly in the key of D major. The report goes on to perpetuate the mistaken belief that attempts to encourage pupils' composition must inevitably draw upon non-traditional 'avant-garde practices'. A more worrying feature is the suggestion that examinations in music can never relate to anything other than that which has been 'given time' to 'evolve and codify its aesthetic canons'. This would appear to separate school music-making for ever from its contemporary musical environment. There is an implication that no worthwhile judgements can be made about new music. Yet reputable critics manage to deal quite well with first performances week by week in the national newspapers,* and as far as most of the 'experimental' music we may find in schools is concerned, the techniques are by and large the now well-established procedures of the 1950s and 1960s.

In the main this report is encouraging. There is appreciation of the aims of teachers who are trying to 'teach the modern child', and a welcome for the stimulation of new ideas. And there is a clear indication of willingness to 'be alert to developments'. Ultimately, though, we are left with a picture of an examiner who is extremely cautious and whose philosophy is really 'let's wait and see; when time has elapsed and the stimulating new ideas have become old ideas, then – and only then – shall we be able to decide what to do about them'.

(e) 'Progress as well as product'

. . . if pupils are to be judged as fairly as possible a 'profile' of them as creative musicians must be provided for the assessor. This must be supplied by the teachers concerned. A written report should accompany the pupil's course work, along with tapes, scores, etc.; and it should be possible for the assessor to spend some time with the pupil in a viva voce of practical performance. This is done already under my own Examining Board, where at present we have only a handful of Mode 3 syllabuses, but obviously considerations of time and expense become vital where there are very large numbers of candidates, and here the Moderator has to rely more heavily on the reports from the schools.

If we are concerned with the overall musical growth of our pupils, it would seem that an assessment should include *both* the inherent nature of the piece *and* the pupil's technical achievement.

The 'guidelines for getting to know a piece'/'parameters'/measures are essentially those which are already in operation, and although it is helpful to have them stated in print . . .I for one would welcome a further statement in the 'overall trends' area . . . The most important addition to the parameters listed here is an open mind on the part of the examiner. It is important to assess each piece of work individually, but if education is growth, then surely there must be

---

* e.g. William Mann, *The Times* music critic, who in reviewing a first performance wrote of himself as 'one whose greatest stimulus in all music is the first impact of a new piece' (*The Times*, 17 May 1980).

an assessment of the pupil's progress throughout the course; otherwise we may have been occupying him but not necessarily educating him.

Teacher guidance is very important, and too often there is little enough sign of it throughout the Mode 3 courses. This does not mean comments in red biro all over the folio, but an occasional short, well calculated statement to focus the verbal comment. It should be designed to be supportive as possible and to help the pupils towards musical insights.

This is a refreshing view of the examination as a positive and productive part of the whole educational process. The views expressed show none of the anxiety and cautiousness of the previous report, since the Board represented here has already taken the plunge and is trying to do something to meet the new developments. The techniques being used have much in common with those proposed by the Project conference, but there is a firm commitment to an overview of a student's work: '. . . we are concerned with overall musical growth . . . there must be an assessment of the pupil's progress throughout the course . . .' This is important. In our endeavour to give priority to the *sound* of music we may incline to the view that the realistic way to approach pupils' compositions is to treat them as we would any new work which we might hear in a concert hall. Without a score, and possibly with nothing more than a brief programme note, we should have only our ears to help us. On that basis we might prefer not to have to make a judgement of any kind, but if we were pressed to do so we should no doubt make some response even if it were a qualified one. A chance of a second hearing (or a third) would increase our confidence in our evaluation, even though we might still have had no sight of the score. Is this not the way we should deal with student compositions, especially when we can replay the tape as many times as we wish?

Obviously there is much to be said for approaching an aural art aurally! A proportion of our judgement of work of this kind, submitted for assessment, must certainly be made upon the effectiveness of what we hear. But in the case of these young composers we need to know more about their work leading up to the pieces submitted. For we are not critics making a judgement about a single work but educators with an overall responsibility for the development of musical understanding in those we teach. This examiner sees the assessment as a very useful tool for the teacher, and the Moderator's task is to work *with* the teacher in the education of the student.

(f) 'Showing the world what the pupils have done'
When I think of examinations in Creative Music there is always one very large query in my mind: what does society, particularly the employer, make of it? Society is mentioned as being the recipient of assessments, and examinations are to show the world what the pupils have done. We as music teachers know the value of Creative Music (though not necessarily examinations in it) but does it

mean anything to the average employer? Unfortunately I am rather inclined to think not . . .

These comments are pertinent at a time of economic restraint. Now more than ever, if music in education is to get support for expansion, we need to demonstrate its 'usefulness' as a part of majority education. As we have seen, the traditional view of music examinations is geared almost exclusively to conventional skill and techniques, placing the main emphasis upon the 'received wisdom' that will 'uphold established ideas of competence in the subject'. In general this tends to exclude not only that which is 'new' or 'untried', but also the inventiveness and imaginative skill of the students themselves. In consequence, the conventional music examination has little to offer to the average secondary school pupil, and it is unlikely to be very convincing as a demonstration of music's general educative values. In the eyes of most people, traditional syllabuses, limiting the 'acceptable' forms of musicianship and expression, emphasise musical training for a minority of relatively gifted pupils.

Yet there are aspects of music-making which, even at a very humble level of achievement, can make a worthwhile contribution to general education by developing pupils' powers of decision-making, and self-discipline, and their ability to co-operate with others; qualities much needed in our modern industrial society. Early in 1980, Grenville Hancox, in association with the CBI and its offshoot the Project *Understanding British Industry*, organised a conference of music teachers to examine music's potential in general education and the consequent implications for fulfilling the expectations of industry today. The results of the conference were very encouraging and a full report by Grenville Hancox is given in Appendix V, part 1. As will be seen, it concludes with the assertion: 'Music *is useful*. Music matters.' Appropriate examination and assessment procedures could do much to reinforce this view and to convince those in the world beyond school that there are indeed values in musical experience which are not reserved exclusively for the traditionally 'musical' minority.

Appendix I
Four programmes of work

The following outline plans for courses of music in school are reproduced here by kind permission of the teachers who have devised them. We offer each as an example of planning rather than as a syllabus to be adopted and copied by another teacher. The four teachers concerned would doubtless wish to emphasise that a syllabus must change as pupils, school and society changes. Thus a syllabus is always a guide and never a formula.

Programme 1 : Outline of creative work for first three years   1981 – 2

Tom Gamble, Manland School, Harpenden

Year 1

Sound, noise and silence

Listening and discussion

Related listening

Prepared tape of vocal, instrumental, natural and electronic sounds, all juxtaposed to provoke thought and discussion about the nature of sound and music.

Tone colour
1. Experimentation and exploration of sounds produced by:
   (a) Hands
   (b) Voice

CAGE: A Flower
CASTIGLIONI: Gyro (beginning)
BERIO: Sequenza III
BERBERIAN: Stripsody
KARE KOLBERG: Plym-Plym

   (c) Chime bars – using a variety of beaters

HARRY PARTCH: Cloud – Chamber Music etc.

   (d) Materials – such as wood, metal

Cambodian stone gongs
ANNA LOCKWOOD: The Glass World of Anna Lockwood

   (e) Triangles, cymbals, gongs etc.

Music of Bhutan, China, Japan
GILBERT AMY: Cycles

(f) Melodic percussion

Balinese Gamelan Music
STOCKHAUSEN: Refrain

(g) Melodic percussion

GILBERT AMY: Cycles
Simantra of Greece
XENAKIS: Persephassa
MAXWELL DAVIES: Ave Maris Stella,
marimba cadenza

(h) Drums

Music of Africa, India, Persia
XENAKIS: Persephassa [beginning]
CHAVEZ: Toccata for Percussion

(i) Strings – bowed and plucked

Music of the Middle East and Far East
MONTEVERDI: 'Cambattimento di
Tancredi e Clorinda' – use of col
legno, pizzicato, tremolo
String Quartets of BARTOK, BERG,
SCHOENBERG, WEBERN,
SHOSTAKOVICH, ELLIOTT CARTER
PENDERECKI: String Quartet No. 1
XENAKIS: Nomos Alpha, for cello
BRITTEN: Variations on a theme of
Frank Bridge

(j) Wind – including melodica,
recorders

BERIO: 'Gesti' for recorder, Sequenza V
for trombone
XENAKIS: Akrata, for 16 wind
instruments
BOULEZ: 'Domaines' (Bartolozzi
effects)
MAXWELL DAVIES: Hymnos
LIGETI: Ten pieces for wind quintet
MOZART: Wind Divertimenti and
Serenades
VAN EYCK: Pieces for descant and
sopranino recorders
BRIAN FERNEYHOUGH: Time and
Motion Study I, for bass clarinet
ELLIOTT CARTER: Canon for three
muted trumpets, Clarinet quartet
Music of the East: ceremonial trumpets,
Shakuhachi, etc.

Each small group of children rotates
from (e) to (j) so that all children gain
experience with each type of instrument.

2. Class, group and individual
compositions with sounds of the same
type, e.g. vocal, metal melodic, and
possibly construct scores.

Recordings of children's compositions
Excerpts from music listed above,
related to the 'family' of instruments
used by a particular group

3. Class and group compositions with
'mixed' sounds – either (a) or (b) to be
followed:

(a) Descriptive pieces composed to a title, e.g. 'Moonlight', 'Desert', 'Raindrops', 'Nightmusic', 'Jungle'.

SCHAFER: Epitaph for Moonlight
SCHOENBERG: 'Nacht' (Pierrot Lunaire)
LIGETI: 'Night', 'Atmospheres'
HENZE: El Cimmaron
BRITTEN: Nocturne
DALLAPICCOLA: Piccola Musica Notturna
GEORGE CRUMB: Nightmusic I

(b) Abstract pieces – groups of 4 or 5 children select instruments, and through experiment and improvisation, organise sounds to form a short piece lasting about two minutes.

NORDHEIM: 'Signals' for accordian, electric guitar and percussion
BOULEZ: Le Marteau sans Maître (Sections 1, 2, 4 & 8)
VARESE: Ionisation
XENAKIS: Persephassa, Nomos Gamma
STOCKHAUSEN: Refrain
GERHARD: Libra, Gemini
CARTER: Duo for violin and piano
MOZART: Trio for clarinet, violin and piano
HOLMBOE: Concerto for recorder, vibraphone, celeste, and strings

4. Discussion:
   (a) Repetition and contrast

BEETHOVEN: Pastoral Symphony (opening)
BARBER: Adagio for strings
ELGAR: Enigma Variations: Nimrod
STEVE REICH: Music for Eighteen Players
VARESE: Intégrales

   (b) Climax, shape, tension
   (c) Ordering and development of ideas
   (d) Foreground and background

Class work on the elements of music

1. Timbre and texture (also sonority, 'sound-mass'):
   Using as great a variety of instruments as are available, class forms a semi-circle – one instrument to each child.
   By conducting from centre of semi-circle, the teacher directs children to play in clockwise or anti-clockwise order, producing a variety of timbres and textures.

Recordings of class 'experiments'
BOULEZ: Marteau [sections 1 and 8]
PENDERECKI: Symphony [opening]
MESSIAEN: Turangalila Symphony
LIGETI: Lontano, San Francisco Polyphony
SEROCKI: Episodes
JEAN-CLAUDE ELOY: Equivalences
XENAKIS: Nomos Gamma
VARESE: Amériques

2. Duration, dynamics, tempo:
   Concentrating on one of these three elements at a time, teacher and pupils construct short pieces, conducting the class by the use of hand signals.

STOCKHAUSEN: Refrain
BOULEZ: Marteau [section 4]
WEBERN: Symphony op. 21
MESSIAEN: Quatuor pour la Fin du Temps
ELOY: Equivalences

LIGETI: Chamber Concerto
ELLIOTT CARTER: Symphony of Three
   Orchestras

3. Rhythm:
   (a) Regular rhythm and pulse   Marches and Dances:
                                   LIGETI: Continuum
   (b) Using rhythm to achieve unity BEETHOVEN: 7th symphony [slow
                                     movement]
                                   5th symphony
                                 HAYDN: Symphony No. 73; No. 10
      Ostinato   VARESE: Intégrales
                                   HOLST: 'Mars' and 'Saturn'
                                   RAVEL: Bolero
                                   STRAVINSKY: Symphony of Psalms
                                     'Les Noces'
   (c) Irregular rhythms   BOULEZ: Le Marteau
                                   BARTOK: Piano concertos
                                   STRAVINSKY: Le Sacre du Printemps
                                   HARRY PARTCH: Daphne of the Dunes
   (d) Proportional structures   Music of India, Indonesia
                                   MESSIAEN: Chronochromie
   (e) Random rhythms   XENAKIS: Nomos Gamma, Persephassa
                                   RANDS: Wildtrack I
   (f) Statistical rhythms   PENDERECKI: De Natura Sonoris
4. Pitch:
   Construction of short pieces which Recordings of class experiments
   exploit a wide range of pitch – non- ELOY: 'Equivalences' [range
   melodic instruments supply   alternatively restricted and 'free']
   accompaniment.
   (a) Unison, octaves, contrast   XENAKIS: Terretektohr; Empreinte
                                   PENDERECKI: Sonata for cello and
                                   orchestra
                                   LIGETI: Chamber Concerto
   (b) Sound-mass: chords, clusters PENDERECKI: Anaklasis [opening]
   (c) Pitch related to timbre   WEBERN: String quartet op. 28
                                     [opening]
                                   XENAKIS: Terretektohr, Akrata
                                   GERHARD: Libra [especially the
                                   opening]
   (d) Pitch related to texture   LIGETI: Atmosphères, cello concerto
   (e) Melodic patterns: sequence, canon VIVALDI; BARBER: Adagio for strings
                                   ELLIOTT CARTER: Canon for 3 muted
                                   trumpets
                                   BACH; WEBERN; ZELENKA
      Melodic patterns: use of birdsong MESSIAEN: Oiseaux Exotiques
                                   VIVALDI

5. Form and structure:
   Construction of short pieces by teacher
   and pupils by:
   (a) Combining features in 1–4 above
   (b) Juxtaposing 'sound events' – use of
       silence
   Discussion about unity, continuity, etc.

Children's compositions
LIGETI: Chamber Concerto
XENAKIS: Antikthon
SEROCKI: Segments
BOULEZ: Pli Selon Pli
GERHARD: Epithalameum
HENZE: 6th Symphony

Exploring the piano and 'piano-harp'

Group compositions:
(a) Clusters, chords
(b) Pitch – contrast of high and low
(c) Duration and dynamics – use of pedal
(d) Melodic pattern

SATIE: Gymnopédies
DUTILLEUX: Piano Duet: 'Figures
    Resonances'
MESSIAEN: Etudes: Ile de Feu I and II
HENRY COWELL: 'Banshee' etc.
BARTOK: Mikrokosmos: Allegro
    Barbaro
BOULEZ: Piano Sonatas
XENAKIS: Evryalyi
RACHMANINOV: Suite No. 1 for two
    pianos: 'Les Larmes' [based on
    4-note motif]
LISZT: Czardas obstine; Transcendental
    studies
CHOPIN: Mazurkas, Nocturnes,
    Ballades
ART TATUM: Jazz Improvisations
BEETHOVEN: Sonata op. 111
    ['Improvisatory' passages]

Prepared piano

JOHN CAGE: Sonatas and Interludes
GEORGE CRUMB: Makrokosmos II
STOCKHAUSEN: Mantra

Group compositions for piano and percussion

Construct scores for piano and percussion

Children's compositions.
BARTOK: Sonata for 2 pianos and
    percussion
GEORGE CRUMB: Music for a Summer
    Evening
STOCKHAUSEN: Refrain
BERIO: Linea
CAGE: Amores
GUNNAR SØNSTEVOLD: Quadri, for
    piano, harp and percussion

Variation form

Class and group compositions:

(a) Elaboration of a simple musical idea

(b) Use of ostinato

(c) Gradual transformation of original
idea until it changes completely.
Perform John Paynter's
Metamorphosis

Mediaeval elaboration, e.g. The Song
of the Ass

SCHUBERT: Trout Quintet; HAYDN:
Symphony No. 94

BEETHOVEN: Septet
LUTOSLAWSKI: Concerto for orchestra,
Passacaglia

FRANCK: Symphonic variations
MAXWELL DAVIES: Fantasia No. 2 for
orchestra – continuous variation
MAXWELL DAVIES: Taverner – Points
and Dances [distortion and blurring
of theme]
ELLIOTT CARTER: Variations for
orchestra
GORDON CROSSE: Epiphany Variations
THOMMESSEN: Barbaresk
THELONIUS MONK: Jazz improvisations
BEETHOVEN: 'Eroica' symphony, last
movement

Year 2

Spatial music

Related listening

1. Class organised in semi-circle, circle
   and other spatial configurations. Music
   conducted by teacher or pupils.

STOCKHAUSEN: Gruppen, Mixtur
XENAKIS: Eonta, Nomos Gamma
GABRIELI: Canzone, Motets
IVES: Putnam's Camp
HENZE: 6th Symphony, SEROCKI
BOULEZ: Domaines
PANUFNIK: Symphony of the Spheres

2. Group compositions based upon either:
   (a) 'Space' as a stimulus e.g.
       'Moonscape', 'Desert', or
   (b) Spatial location of instruments or
   (c) Combined use of (a) and (b).

Children's compositions.
LIGETI: Atmosphères
MESSIAEN: Et Expecto Resurrectionem
Mortuorum, section 3
GERHARD: Symphony No. 3, opening
HINDEMITH: Die Harmonie der Welt
VAUGHAN WILLIAMS: Sinfonia
Antarctica

**Class organised 'orchestrally' into
groups**

The groups may be:
(a) of various sizes
(b) instrumentally homogeneous

(c) instrumentally heterogeneous

The Symphony Orchestra – sections
Big Band Jazz – Duke Ellington etc.
Renaissance consorts

1. Comparison and contrasts of *timbres and textures* by using various combinations of groups, and by directing groups to play in different order

   Experimentation and discussion about: duration, dynamics, sonority, juxtaposition of sound events, etc.

   CARTER: Double Concerto for piano, harpsichord and two string orchestras
   SKALKOTTAS: Octet, 1st and 3rd movements
   JANACEK: Sinfonietta
   TIPPETT: 3rd Symphony, 1st movement, scherzo
   SIBELIUS: Finlandia
   PER NORGAARD: 3rd Symphony
   EDWIN ROXBURGH: Montage

2. Individual pupils conduct class ensemble and 'compose' piece by directing particular groups or combinations of groups to play in a specific manner as indicated by hand signals – followed by a discussion about the need for a balance between *repetition* and *contrast*.

   Children's compositions.
   SEROCKI: Segments, Symphonic Frescoes
   AMY: Cycles
   GERHARD: Epithalameum, 4th Symphony
   R. R. BENNETT: 1st Symphony, beginning
   BOULEZ: Domaines
   BERIO: Tempi Concertati, or
   FERNEYHOUGH: 'Transit', and
   BOULEZ: Eclat/Multiples for 'mixed groups'

3. Introducing standardised notation: After discussion about the need for a standardised notation derived from conductors' hand signals, children compose scores for class ensemble.

   Children's compositions (following score)
   PENDERECKI: Symphony – follow simplified score, 2nd movement
   PENDERECKI: De Natura Sonoris – following excerpts from score

4. Class performance of printed scores: George Self's New Sounds in Class, especially Nos. 5, 6, 11–14 – children also conduct.

   Bernard Rands: Sound patterns 2
   Children's scores from previous years.

   Compare different versions of some pieces
   LIGETI: Chamber Concerto [especially last half]
   RANDS: Wildtrack 1

Words and music 1

1. Group compositions to accompany the reading of a poem:
   For example, James Joyce's 'Chamber Music'; Arthur Waley's 'Translations from the Chinese'; Shakespeare (especially The Tempest); Tennyson.

   William Carlos Williams: Dylan Thomas,

   BERIO: Chamber Music, Folk Songs
   BRITTEN: Nocturne, Serenade
   Songs from the Chinese
   SAMUEL BARBER: Hermit Songs
   COPLAND: Songs; IVES: Songs
   STRAVINSKY: Babel, A Sermon, a Narrative and a Prayer, Cantata on Old English Texts
   WERLE: Nautical Preludes

A Lyke Wake Dirge – compare
Britten's and Stravinsky's settings.

NICOLA LEFANU: The Same Day
  Dawns, for sorprano and
  instrumental ensemble
CLEO LAINE and
J. DANKWORTH: Wordsongs
LUTOSLAWSKI: Les Espaces du sommeil

2. Chants and incantations
  (a) Class and group work [see
      J. Paynter and P. Aston: *Sound and
      Silence*]

Bhutanese chants; Polynesian chants,
  e.g. Ramayan chant of Bali
Early Christian Chant
STRAVINSKY: Les Noces; Symphony of
  psalms

  (b) Group compositions based on:
      ritual, magic, witchcraft

BERIO: A-Ronne
BOULEZ: Rituel

  (c) Ancient myths – sections of the
      myth given to different groups,
      forming a composite class
      composition, e.g. *The Odyssey*
      [see M. Schafer's *When Words
      Sing*]

WEBER: Der Freischutz
XENAKIS: Oresteia Suite [includes
  chanting]
DALLAPICCOLA: Ulysses
SKALKOTTAS: Ulysses

Aleatoric music

1. Class performance of 'chance' score.

Compare recordings of two
  performances:
EARLE BROWN: Available Forms I

2. Class performance of scores by teacher
   and pupils, based on 'Available
   Forms I'.

LUTOSLAWSKI: Jeux Vénetiens –
  contrasts 'ordinary' with 'aleatory'
  sections

3. Group compositions.

BERNARD RANDS: Wildtrack I
BOULEZ: Domaines, Rituel

Form

1. Cyclical repetition

Ritualistic forms of non-Western music

2. (a) Symmetry, palindrome

JEAN-PAPINEAU COUTURE: Pièce
  Concertante No. 1
MACHAUT: Ma fin est mon
  commencement

  (b) Class instrumental work

HAYDN: Symphony No. 47, Minuet and
  Trio

  (c) Overall symmetry

BARTOK: String Quartet No. 4

3. Binary form – group compositions

Dances of the Renaissance
COUPERIN; D. SCARLATTI: Keyboard
  music

4. Rondo
  (a) Class improvisation – contrasted
      groups

Recordings of class improvisation

  (b) Class rondo with soloist playing
      section A

Recordings of class performances
MESSIAEN: Chronochromie

(c) Rondos with soloist attached to each group in class

GOEHR: Lyric Pieces, No. 6
MESSIAEN: Et Expecto Resurrectionem Mortuorum
BOULEZ: Domaines
STRAVINSKY: Symphonies for Wind Instruments

(d) Concertante group play 'A'

STRAVINSKY: Requiem Canticles (Dies Irae)

(e) Group compositions

HAYDN; MOZART

Group compositions based on the idea of 'growth' and 'decay'

Compositions based on titles such as: 'Creation', 'Dawn', 'The City', 'Sunrise', 'The Black Hole', 'The Beginning of Time', 'Clouds', 'Anti-Earth', 'The Oscillating Universe'.

STOCKHAUSEN: Genesis; Ylem
HAYDN: 'The Creation'
BRITTEN: Sea Interludes: 'Dawn'
VARESE: Intégrales, Ionisation
GERHARD: Symphony No. 3 [opening]
LIGETI: Atmosphères
XENAKIS: Nomos Gamma; Terretektohr; Antikthon; Jonchaies
DONATONI: Lumen
NORDHEIM: Epitaffio
SALLINEN: 3rd Symphony
NIELSEN: 3rd Symphony, 'Espansiva'

Year 3

Words and music 2

Group compositions

1. Discussion about the relationship between words and music: union or dualism (meaning versus sound)

2. Examination of Luciano Berio's use of the sounds of words as a structural element in his music, of the way he disintegrates the text and thus the linguistic meaning – producing a new synthesis of words and music.
   E.g. in 'Circles' instrumental sounds are derived from the consonantal sounds of the text, and in 'Sinfonia', vowel sounds of the text are used for a similar purpose.

Related listening

In this section a few examples should be chosen from the list of related listening to illustrate the variety of ways in which words can be used with music
Speech and Music:
SCHÖENBERG: A Survivor from Warsaw
STRAVINSKY: 'Babel'
M. SCHAFER: Threnody
H. SEARLE: Riverrun (based on James Joyce's 'Finnegans Wake')
HARRY PARTCH: Barstow

The voice as instrument:
Swingle Singers; Jazz 'scat' singing; Coloratura soprano (Mozart's Magic Flute)
VILLA-LOBOS: Aria, for soprano and 8 celli
TOR BREVIK: Elegy for soprano and chamber ensemble

3. Onomatopoeic use of words– see
   M. Schafer's 'When Words Sing'
4. Pictorial treatment of words – see
   J. Paynter and P. Aston: Sound and
   Silence Ch. 4
5. Selection of material for compositions –
   on the basis of its musical potential i.e.
   for the sound quality and rhythmic
   possibilities alone, for example:
   G. M. Hopkins; e. e. cummings;
   William Carlos Williams; Tennyson;
   Shakespeare; Wilfred Owen; James
   Joyce – selected passages from
   'Ulysses'; 'Portrait of the Artist', and
   'Finnegan's Wake'; Nonsense verse;
   comics; French Symbolists; children's
   own poems.

Syllabic setting of words

BERIO: Folk Songs especially 'I wonder
   as I wander'
Songs of Carole King, James Taylor,
   Carly Simon, Lennon and McCartney,
   Simon and Garfunkel, Bob Dylan,
   Joan Armitrading
BRITTEN: War Requiem
Melismatic treatment:
BOULEZ: Marteau sans Maître, Pli
   Selon Pli
Vocal music of the Middle East
Tournai Mass (14th century)
   especially Sanctus
MACHAUT: Ma Fin est mon
   commencement
Gregorian chant
DUFAY: Kyrie
MONTEVERDI: Duo Seraphim –
   'Vespers' [vocal tremolo]
XENAKIS: N'shima
Parlando and Recitative:
chants; opera and oratio
Sprechstimme
SCHOENBERG: 'Pierrot Lunaire', Moses
   and Aaron
HENZE: El Cimmaron
Pictorial Treatment of words:
JANNEQUIN: Les chansons des Oiseaux
JOSQUIN DES PRES: El Grillo
BACH: Magnificat
HANDEL: Messiah
MONTEVERDI: Madrigals
BOULEZ: Improvisation sur Mallarmé II
   [Pli Selon Pli]
Vocalise:
HENZE: Arioso, for mezzo-soprano and
   orchestra
VILLA-LOBOS: Aria, for soprano and 8
   celli
BOULEZ: Le Marteau sans Maître,
   Section IX
KLAUS HUBER: Soliloquia
HOLST: Neptune
VAUGHAN WILLIAMS: Flos Campi
LIGETI: Requiem

NICOLA LEFANU: The Same Day Dawns
Vocal 'noise' – laughter, shouting, etc.
MAXWELL DAVIES: Eight Songs for a
    Mad King
PENDERECKI: St Luke Passion
BERIO: Laborintus II; A-Ronne
LUTOSLAWSKI: Trois Poèmes d'Henri
    Michaux – 2nd movement

Form

1. Melodic and rhythmic devices:
    (a) Ostinato – class improvisation;   Recording of class pieces.
        performance of G. Self: STAN KENTON: 23°N 82°W, Jazz Riffs
        Relentless   STRAVINSKY: Rite of Spring
                                             HINDEMITH: Clarinet Concerto
                                             MESSIAEN: Quatuor pour La Fin du
                                                 Temps
                                             PURCELL; ZELENKA; BACH; etc.

    (b) Canon – performance of Brian   BACH, SCHOENBERG, WEBERN
        Dennis: Echoes

2. Ternary form   Recordings of class performances
                                             PENDERECKI: Anaklasis – following
                                                 simplified graphic score of this work
    (a) Individual compositions for class   PENDERECKI: Threnody – follow score
        ensemble – scores duplicated   LUTOSLAWSKI: Concerto for Orchestra
                                                 – 2nd movement
                                             HINDEMITH: Concert Music for Strings
                                                 and Brass

    (b) Group compositions   Slow movements from symphonies by
                                                 BRAHMS, BEETHOVEN,
                                                 SHOSTAKOVITCH
                                             DVORAK: 'New World' Symphony –
                                                 following score
                                             Classical Minuets and Trios

Group compositions

Compositions in groups based upon   GORDON CROSSE: Dreamsongs
dreams, fantasy, the supernatural, science MESSIAEN: Turangalila Symphony,
fiction, visions of heaven and hell.   Quatuor, Les Corps Glorieux, Le
                                                Banquet Céleste, Et Expecto etc.
                                             MAHLER: 8th Symphony, 10th
                                                 (Purgatorio)
                                             MONTEVERDI: L'Orfeo
                                             LUIGI NONO: Ricorda . . . in Auschwitz
                                             PENDERECKI: Threnody, St Luke
                                                 Passion, Polymorphia, The Devils of
                                                 Loudun
                                             GEORGE CRUMB: Dream Sequence
Read parts of Dante's Inferno   BERIO: Laborintus II
                                             LIGETI: Requiem; Atmosphères

VERDI: Dies Irae
BRITTEN: Dies Irae – War Requiem
BERLIOZ: Symphonie Fantastique
   The Witches' Sabbath
BRIAN FERNEYHOUGH: Transit
CARRISSIMI: Lucifer, for Bass voice and
   continuo
LUTOSLAWSKI: Les espaces du Sommeil

Class vocal work

1. Electronic distortion of vocal sounds.
   Members of class read from different
   texts, boys reading slowly with low pitch
   – girls reading quickly with high pitch,
   recorded at different speeds. Other
   vocal sounds can be added as directed.
   Add echo

   Class performance played back at one
   speed on tape recorder.
   BERIO: Visages; Omaggio à Joyce
   NONO: La Fabbrica Illuminata
   STOCKHAUSEN: Microphonie II

2. Vocal textures
   (a) Class in unison, changing vowels as
       directed.

       STOCKHAUSEN: Stimmung

   (b) Two or three groups sustaining
       pitches at wide intervals.

       BERIO: Sinfonia – Martin Luther King
       section

   (c) Two or three groups sustain pitches
       at wide intervals while individuals
       'sing' a wide variety of vocal sounds
       when given cue e.g. speech,
       whispering, etc.

       PENDERECKI: St Luke Passion
       BERIO: Sinfonia, section 1
       WERLE: Nautical Preludes
       PETRASSI: Nonsense Rhymes

   (d) Class in unison – some singers hold
       the given pitch while others widen
       out in glissandos to extremes of
       pitch.

   (e) Overlapping held pitches (close
       intervals), glissandi and clusters

       LIGETI: Requiem

3. Performance of B. Rands 'Sound
   Patterns 3'

   BERIO: A-Ronne, Laborintus II
   LIGETI: Aventures

Serial music

1. Class ensemble
   (a) Variations on a 12-note row – each
       soloist improvises on a different
       version of the note row.

       Recordings of class performances
       SEROCKI: Musica concertante
       SCHOENBERG: Variations for Orchestra,
       Violin Concerto
       BRITTEN: Cantata Academica
       EGIL HOVLAND: Lamenti per orchestra

   (b) Webernian style – pointillistic
       fragmentation of all four versions of
       the note row – soloists play only a
       few notes of the row each.

       BERIO: Nones, Concertino
       WEBERN: Symphony op 21 – following
       score; children's piece, for piano
       KRENEK: Twelve Pieces for piano
       STRAVINSKY: Variations for Orchestra
       [Aldous Huxley in Memoriam]

DALLAPICCOLA: Piccola Musica
 Notturnaa
HENZE: Symphonies
WEBERN: Variations for orchestra

2. Group compositions
 Compositions based on 12-note or
 shorter series

Recordings of group compositions:
SCHOENBERG: Serenade
BOULEZ: La Marteau – following score
SKALKOTTAS: String Quartet No. 3
WEBERN: Quartet op. 22 for violin,
 clarinet, saxophone, and piano

Aleatoric music in class

Perform G. Self's New Sounds in Class
Nos. 19–22 and B. Rands: Sound
Patterns 4

Class performances of these scores:
STOCKHAUSEN: Mixtur
LUTOSLAWSKI: Symphony No. 2

Form

1. Compositions in more than 3 sections
 (a) Class compositions

Recordings of class and individual
 compositions.

 (b) Individual compositions for class
  ensemble

SEROCKI: Symphonic Frescoes
GERHARD: Symphony No. 4
TIPPETT: Symphony No. 3

2. Large scale forms – contrasting long
 sections, symphonic form

MOZART: Symphony No. 40
BEETHOVEN: 5th Symphony
SCHUBERT: Symphony No. 8 – following
 score
PENDERECKI: Symphony – following
 graphic reduction of score
GERHARD: Symphony No. 4
TIPPETT: Symphony No. 3

3. Open forms
 Group compositions

Recordings of group compositions:
BERIO: Concertino, Epiphanie
LIGETI: Various works
XENAKIS: Various works
STOCKHAUSEN: 'Moment' form –
 various works
STRAVINSKY: Symphonies for wind
 instruments (mosaic structure)
BROWN: Available Form I
BOULEZ: Piano Sonata No. 3
DEBUSSY: Jeux
SALLINEN: Symphony No. 3

Reproduced by permission of Tom Gamble, September 1980

Programme 2 : CSE Music Mode 3   1982 – 3

Tom Wanless, Sheldon School, Chippenham

Aims

(a) To test the candidates' knowledge of music and their aural capabilities
(b) To assess their historical background to set historical periods
(c) To test their practical ability in performance, composition and recording techniques

Syllabus

Paper 1 (Written paper, 1½ hours)

In view of the large number of candidates and the expense of procuring scores of set works it is proposed to examine the pupils' historical knowledge on two main periods. These are:
  (a) Music before 1750   (b) The 20th century
  Candidates will be tested on instruments in use during the periods, on clefs and on other relevant information. They will also be expected to be familiar with details of selected compositions and composers and with information concerning contemporary life of the times. In the study of 20th century both serious and popular music will be studied.
  Among the composers to be studied will be Ives, Penderecki, Berio, Varèse and Bartók etc. Popular groups will include Pink Floyd, Tangerine Dream, Tonto's Expanding Headband etc.

Paper 2 (Written paper, 1½ hours)

Each pupil to be familiar with the use of recording equipment (e.g. types of microphones, tape-recorders, echo machines, mixers, synthesisers etc.) and with the correct wiring of all types of plugs and sockets. It is expected that each candidate will have acted as a 'recording engineer' and will be familiar with the equipment and the use of such devices as double- and multi-tracking, and with the professional recording process, the setting up of the equipment, duties of recording engineers etc.

Paper 3 (Practical test)

The test will be in two sections of which Section 1 will be recorded in the term previous to the written examination. Section 2 will last approximately 15 minutes.
Section 1   Each candidate will be expected to take part in musical group activity and one such activity will be recorded in stereo by the group, and presented as part of the practical examination. The music used may be:
  (a) Taken from published material
  (b) An arrangement made by the group
  (c) An original composition by the group. Marks will be awarded equally for quality of performance and quality of recording.
Section 2   Candidates will be required to:
  (a) Locate and identify any errors in a melodic extract that will be performed (A correct version of the music to be printed on the examination paper. The test will be played three times.)

(b) Decide whether two single sounds in each of the three sections of music are the same as those comprising the two note chord that follows

(c) Indicate the notes omitted in a given three part piece of music played on contrasting percussion instruments

(d) Indicate the placing of chords under a given melodic series

Project File

A talk or script on a musical topic lasting approximately five minutes (complete with illustrations) to be recorded as if for a broadcast. Marks to be awarded on the Board's standard five point scale.

Mark scheme

Paper 1

Section (a) Music before 1750 – 15 questions, Section (b) The 20th century – 15 questions – 3 marks to be awarded for each correct answer.

Paper 2

15 questions – 4 marks to be awarded for each correct answer.

Paper 3

Section 1   30 marks to be awarded for performance, 30 marks to be awarded for recordings.

Section 2   Aural tests – 20 marks to be awarded.

Summary

paper 1	Section (a)		45
	Section (b)		45
Paper 2			60
Paper 3	Section 1		60
		(a)	6
		(b)	6
		(c)	4
		(d)	4
Project file			20
			——
			250
			——

Reproduced by permission of Tom Wanless

Programme 3 : Syllabus years 1 – 5

Grenville Hancox, Madeley Court School, Telford

The 'syllabus' for music education at Madeley Court is based around the principle that music should be available to all children in the school, and as such is a guide and not a formula. Given that the school is committed to mixed-ability teaching, then a music syllabus must be flexible enough to cater for children at both ends of the spectrum of ability as well as the large block between these points. Thus every child will need a specific syllabus if we are to realise the potential of our school.

Five areas of activity form the basis of music at Madeley Court:
1. The acquisition of a skill, no matter how basic
2. The use of the skill(s) to recreate other people's music
3. The creation of music, through composition and improvisation
4. Singing
5. Listening to each other's music, composition and improvisation

These activities may all take place at the same time, or only one activity might occur (e.g. singing) at one time. The notion that the teacher is a catalyst must become stronger as the years progress, the teacher becoming less of an instructor, more an enabler. Organisation of the classroom to meet individual needs is of paramount importance, and use of all available space including corridors and practice rooms, is essential.

Instrumental withdrawal will happen during music lessons and other lessons by using establishment music staff, and peripatetic staff.

Year 1

1 and 2   Skill acquisition and recreative activities

Word ostinati, monochord pieces, word games
'Shake that tree'
Learn E minor, D^7 and G guitar chords
'Zum gali-gali', 'Abram Brown', (E minor)
Trevor Wishart word games
Learn 'Tom Dooley', 'Trumpet Time', 'Orff we go'
Spanish guitar (A and D^7)
'The Sea', (E minor, D^7)
'Banks of Ohio, 'Brownsferry Blues' (D^7, G^7, A^7, D)

(The above pieces are presented in *Music at Court*, a resource book containing information on guitar fret shapes, traditionally notated pieces as above, starting points for improvisation and composition.)

3. Creative music making

Compose pieces based on word ostinati and names. Vocal sounds and body sounds. Conductor game, graphic notation.
Starting Points: Voyages, Machines, Monsters, The Sea, Weather, Water, The Wild West.
Pentatonic improvisation.
Topic work on the themes of: The Wild West and Weather to encourage a combination of skill, and recreative and creative ideas.
Aim to produce an event based on these starting points. Include known music (traditionally and graphically notated), art work, tape recording. Liaise closely with the drama department.

4. Singing

Singing for fun, pleasure, 'coach songs'
'Never get to heaven', 'Metal Cow', 'Three Crows', 'Hole in my Bucket',
'Quartermasters Stores', etc. Question and response, guitar accompaniment.
Selected parts from 'Joseph and Amazing Technicolour Dreamcoat'. Rounds.

5. Instrumental withdrawal

Use the third musician in the team to withdraw children from music lessons to give specific help instrumentally for flute, clarinet, piano, guitar, brass instruments. The aim is to reinforce all aspects of classroom work in instrumental lessons. Ensuring a peripatetic team (five hours a week!) also reinforces the classroom work.

Year 2

1 and 2   Skill acquisition and recreative music-making

Continued use of all first year materials.
Extension of chord vocabulary to include, A minor, D minor, E, B^7, C
'Music at Court' materials, as first year plus: 'Rock Around the Clock', 12-bar blues, 'Scarborough Fair', 'Sloop John B', 'Lord of the Dance', 'Lazy Bones'
Pentatonic Blues improvisation, $\frac{5}{4}$ Blues, 'Pentagon Blues'

3. Creative music-making

(a) Conductor game: the pupil conductor as composer. The pupil arranges and refines his improved game into a graphic playing score. Alternative notation schemes.
(b) Pupils create an atmospheric, descriptive composition, entitled 'The Intruder', to set a scene, plant a picture, describe a moment in time.
(c) Produce cassette tape-recording of sound environment of the school. Notate a journey from school to Madeley, following the cassette recording.
(d) Music and movement: compose a piece entitled 'Theme of a Haunted House' using reel-to-reel tape recorder, changing speeds – use music as a base for movement lessons.

4. Singing

As Year 1 with the addition of songs from 'Jesus Christ Superstar', 'Oobladi-Oobladar' etc.

5. Instrumental withdrawal

As Year 1.

Year 3

1 and 2   Skill acquisition and recreative activities

Continued use of all materials from years 1 and 2, with the addition of C^7, F^7, D minor^7, B minor,
'Music at Court' materials as for years 1 and 2 plus 'Donna Donna', 'The Last Supper', 'House of Rising Sun', 'My Dancing Day', 'Window Cleaner Blues', 'Charleston', 'When I'm 64', 'All my Loving', 'Leaving on a Jet Plane', 'Dream, Dream Dream', 'Streets of London' etc.
Clichés to be covered, I, VI, IV, V^7 etc.

3. Creative activities

(a) Song writing: use of words and music.
Starting points: confrontation, adolescent love, rebels, fashions.
Continued encouragement to pupils to express feelings and emotions through their own words and music.
(b) Number patterns: music created by patterns, suggestion of form in music.
Composition in binary and ternary forms.
(c) Extension of conductor/composer game: production of scores based on improvised starting points.

4. Singing

Increased use of Beatles songs, and emphasis upon singing for fun: Voice as an instrument. 'Sound Patterns', Bernard Rands, 'Voices and Instruments'.

5. Instrumental withdrawal

As years 1 and 2.

Years 4 and 5

(a) Music is to be made accessible to all pupils through the core subject of 'Expressive Arts'. All pupils follow the course as a Mode 3 CSE, which is continually assessed at half termly intervals. Pupils must follow the course by opting for nine choices from:

1. Electronic music   5. Instrument-making   9. Instrumental teaching
2. Play-acting   6. Film   10. Ensemble
3. Video   7. Composition   11. Television news production
4. Radio   8. Theatre crafts   12. Tape-slide sequence production

Each choice is followed for one half term. There will be two themes for the
Expressive Arts day course for each half term,   e.g. 'The Family', 'Outsiders'.
Wherever and whenever possible there will be dialogue and cross fertilisation between options, e.g. film and composition, tape-slide and electronic music.
During the fifth term of the course, students will be expected to present one piece of work that they have produced or contributed to as a final submission for the course. (Fuller details are available from the West Midlands Examination Board, Birmingham).
(b) NUJMB 'O' levels, and Associated Board theory exams may be followed in extension time by any student wishing to pursue these courses. See NUJMB syllabus, A and B.

Year 6

1. London 'A' level: emphasis upon practical music-making
2. General sixth-form course

Reproduced by permission of Grenville Hancox

Programme 4 : 'Instead of a syllabus'

Brian Loane, Boldon Comprehensive School, Tyne and Wear

The following is a plan of work for pupils at Boldon Comprehensive for the year
1981–2.

'Aims'

The aim of the department is to make music.

Principles

Music is a creative art.

There is no real distinction between musical education and musical experience.

Music-making (both performance and composition) is the core of musical
experience.

By 'music-making' we do not mean the acquisition of superficial skills, but rather a
listening, self-critical, and choosing process.

Skill learning and creativity are not two distinct areas of music education, but are
rather two aspects of the same process.

Music-making by all in class is accorded a priority equal to that of music-making by
dedicated minorities in 'voluntary groups'.

Pupils should have the opportunity to experience a wide variety of types of music,
symbolically matching the diverse and contradictory experience of late childhood
and adolescence. Within that context, however, rock music has a particularly
central role to play for the large majority of pupils.

In regard to first-, second-, and third-year classes, limitations of space at present
dictate that roughly half of each class's time is spent in large groups (classroom)
work. However, as much music-making as possible is organised in smaller groups
where the individual's contribution is distinctly audible, and therefore open to
experiment and choice.

Why not a syllabus?

Music takes diverse forms, relevant to different people in different ways at
different times. No single set of criteria for musical excellence can be drawn up.
The pupils for whose musical education the department is responsible will develop
musical interests in an ever-changing and relatively unpredictable way. It is our role
to provide the resources for pupils to follow up their interests, not to lay down in
advance what those interests should be.

The success of the teaching process should not be gauged against criteria set out
in a predetermined syllabus, but rather against those criteria (incidentally far more
demanding) thrown up by the pupils' music itself.

On the other hand, assessment of pupils' changing needs cannot be made entirely
on a week-to-week basis. This would lead to a haphazard approach to skill
learning, and so to a different block on musical experience. Moreover, the musical
skills relevant to pupils are not 100% unpredictable. Expectations can be drawn
from current experience, and detailed plans thereby constructed.

These plans, however, cannot be called a syllabus because of their permanently provisional and revisable character.

Year 1, 2 and 3 class work

Large group projects and small group projects

On the sample record sheets which appear on pages 207–9, the year is divided into six half-terms, each of which has one large group and one small group project. Space is allowed for ticking off the progress of the class.

The units on the left of the sheet are large group projects, with the class all together in the classroom. Each large group lesson contains:
(a) Nearly always, a little singing
(b) Always, work on the project (see project list)
(c) Nearly always, some work on a class performance piece – indicated in italics on the project list (In practice, (b) and (c) may be the same, or may be closely connected) and
(d) Occasionally, a little work on theory (see below).

The units on the right of the sheet are small group projects, with the class split into six groups of about five, working in the practice rooms, drama room, and hall. A series of three or four small group lessons contains:
(a) An introduction, all together in the classroom
(b) Distribution of instruments (carefully noted on each group's work-sheet), and semi-self-supervised group work in practice rooms, etc.
(c) Usually, recording of completed compositions
Where the timetable demands that two classes must share access to practice rooms, then while one class does large group work, the other does small group work, changing over by agreement after three or four weeks.

Where a class is timetabled for unshared access to practice rooms, then various modifications to the 'large group'/'small group' model become possible. For example, there could be a continuous flow between the two methods of working.

Alternatively, half the class might do a large group project while the other half works in small groups. Or, where a technique is taught which is already familiar to some pupils, they might withdraw for extra work in small groups.

(Please turn to p. 210.)

First-year project list

Large group work		Small group work	
Sound games Ostinato music *First songs*		Making a tune for given ostinato Making ostinato and tune Cumulative ostinatos	
Guitar tuition: A Strumming & picking patterns *Christmas songs*		Song writing, unaccompanied, on 'The Desert Island'	

Christmas holidays

Guitar tuition: A & E *Jumbalaye*		Music for a procession of animals	
Parallel thirds Sequence Syncopation *Caribbean carnival*		Music for a carnival	

Easter holidays

Guitar tuition A, E & D Strumming patterns *12-bar blues in A*		Making a riff for 12-bar blues Making a 12-bar blues song	
Drum kit technique (i) Bass guitar technique (i) *Rain music*		Drumming music Dialogue music	

Second-year project list

Large group work		Small group work	
Guitar tuition: A minor and E minor Ternary form *Some 16th-cent. dance tunes*		Ostinato Sandwich	
Scat singing Drum kit technique (ii) Bass guitar technique (ii) *Frankie and Johnny*		Song writing	

Christmas holidays

Keyboard Triads *Four-chord triplet ballad*		Music using triads and/or music exploring the keyboard	
Guitar tuition: A minor, E minor, and D minor *Egyptian Reggae*		Music exploring guitar picking	

Easter holidays

Music using voices *'Mist', 'Sausages', etc.*		Music using voices	
Diatonic and chromatic *Some Self pieces*		Story of a life	

Third-year project list

Large group work		Small group work	
Drum kit technique (iii) Bass guitar technique (iii) *'Sound and Silence' etc.*		Music exploring rock instruments	
Guitar tuition: A, E, B^7 *Rock Around the Clock*		Song writing	

Christmas holidays

Alternating bass and other march idioms *March of the Mods*		Music for a march	
Syncopation, ternary form, and other dance idioms *Imagine*		Dance music	

Easter holidays

Drum kit technique (iv) Bass guitar technique (iv) *A current pop piece*		Making a riff for a 12-bar blues Making a blues song	
Spare		Spare	

Singing

It is envisaged that the class should sing together briefly but regularly, in order to build up a repertoire of known songs, and also confidence in the voice. In addition, some of the large group projects involve singing and the small group projects include song writing.

Theory

Certain aspects of music theory which seem to be relevant to the majority of pupils are taught in the school. Each topic is introduced *after* pupils have experienced the relevant phenomenon in their music-making.

Conventional notation is covered for the minority to whom it is relevant by peripatetic instrument teachers, in special theory classes, and above all through the experience of playing in the school bands.

Examinations taken by pupils include a CSE Mode 3 option, GCE 'O' and 'A' level (JMB syllabus) and ABRSM Theory of Music grades 3, 4 and 5.

Bands, choirs and groups

Wind Band: The main school band, of about 50 members. Membership is by audition, and subject to there being a vacancy. (Approximate minimum standard: ABRSM grade 3)

Junior Band: About 20 members. Membership by audition. (Approximate minimum standard: a complete octave with F sharp and B flat.)

Beginners' Band: About 20 members. Membership by audition. (Approximate minimum standard: three different notes.)

Brass Band and Jazz Orchestra: 'Extra' activities open to the most accomplished and keenest members of the Wind Band.

Choir: Open to any pupil who likes singing. There is no audition.

Schola Pauculorum: A small soprano/alto/tenor/bass choir.

Recorder groups: Senior and junior recorder groups are run by pupils.

Rock groups: The school's equipment is available for pupils' group rehearsals from time to time. The 'Rock Equipment Code' must be followed.

Appendix II
Examinations and assessment

(Report of a conference held at York University 13–15 September, 1977)
Edited by Robert Bunting

1. Introduction

Many musicians, both in schools and in higher education, have been concerned
about the quality of our orthodox examination courses. This may not be the place
to discuss their weaknesses fully, but one thing is clear: the examining boards, who
construct syllabuses for the use of and in consultation with working teachers in
their regions, cannot fairly be expected to embark on radical new approaches. If
changes of this dimension are needed, they can only be carried out by individual
schools, usually working in isolation, and using the opportunities offered by Mode
3 of the CSE.

In the last few years many schools have developed Mode 3 syllabuses for CSE
Music. Where these show striking departures from orthodoxy, they tend to be of
two kinds: creative work is given a major place, and room is found for rock, folk,
jazz and *avant-garde* music.

The conference was at first intended as a sharing of ideas and materials by
teachers involved in Mode 3. But the problems of assessing creative work at this
level have never been discussed and we decided at an early stage to devote a large
part of the conference to this aspect. Following invitations to the examining boards,
we were fortunate to have the help of several representatives with experience of
assessment problems in the musical or other arts fields.

From the tapes of pupils' compositions available, a small number of pieces were
selected for detailed study and assessment. The tapes came from the following
schools:

Sheldon School, Chippenham
   (Head of Music: Tom Wanless)
Notley High School, Braintree
   (Head of Music: Phil Ellis)
Archbishop Holgate's Grammar School, York
   (my own school)
Wilbraham High School, Manchester
   (former Head of Music: Ruth Bird)
Great Marlow School, Marlow
   (former Head of Music: Clement Virgo)

In the event, only tapes from three schools were used.

As a background to our work on assessment, I prepared a document, which was
sent to conference members in advance (see section 2). A tape-recording of music
composed by CSE candidates was prepared, and all conference members were
asked to bring a cassette player as they were to be given a copy on cassette of the
tape. The five pieces in section 1 of the tape were intended for detailed assessment
studies, and since teachers from all the schools represented were to be present, we
decided to conceal the origins of these pieces.

Because cassettes copied at high speed and played back on a portable machine can lose badly in sound quality, we were all given two hearings of the five assessment pieces from the master tape. Each member then started work as an individual, using his own cassette copy to make a personal assessment. We were asked to write detailed comments on each piece, and to allocate a mark out of 10. This mark was purely in relation to the other pieces being assessed and was meant to give a rank order but also some measure of the gaps in quality between the pieces. I made a mistake here in allowing each of us to use a different spread of marks. It would have been wiser to ask everybody to use the full range from 0 to 10, without of course implying that a mark of 10 indicates perfection, or a mark of 0 that the piece is worthless.

The next stage was to work in groups, aiming at a consensus mark for each piece. Four groups of four or five people were established with our examination board representatives spread amongst them. I wish now that we had paid more attention to the work of these groups, because within a generally fair degree of consensus there were also several strong disagreements, and there was not enough time to discuss these adequately. Two people indeed found themselves unable in conscience to award marks at all, and their reasons deserve careful consideration. It might have been better to work in groups of three, or even in pairs; here the minority viewpoints would have shown up more clearly, while the scrupulous would have been under more pressure to commit themselves.

But whatever differences may have occurred *within* groups, the composite mark sheet shows that there was surprisingly little difference *between* groups. And when Richard Orton gave us his marks for the pieces, they fell into line with those of the groups.

Composite marks for assessment pieces

	Group 1	Group 2	Group 3	Group 4	R. Orton	Total	%	Rank
Vocal Piece	7	8	8	7½	8	38½ out of 50	77	1
Electronic Piece	5½	4	(7)	6	7	29½ out of 50	59	4
Zeitgeist	5	8	8	8	8	37 out of 50	74	2
Machines	5	—	4	4	5	18 out of 40	45	5
Wind on Waves	6	—	5½	7	7	25½ out of 40	64	3

But for Group 1's low mark, *Zeitgeist* would have come top in rank order, but the difference in total marks between it and *Vocal Piece* is too small to mean much.

The gap between these two, at 74 and 77%, and *Wind on Waves* with 64%, is more important. Even larger is the gap between *Electronic Piece* (59%) and *Machines* (45%). Do these gaps accurately reflect the difference in value between the pieces?

The rank orders given in the four groups and by Richard Orton are all very similar, allowing for the large number of equal marks.

Richard Orton was asked, as a composer and teacher of composition, to give us an outside point of view on our pupils' work. A transcript of his extremely valuable contribution appears in section 3.

The next task was to study the comments of individuals and groups in order to sort out a list of the criteria that we actually used in making our assessment. I had hoped for very detailed and precise comments, but in the event many people wrote in rather sketchy general terms. Partly this must be due to lack of time, but it also reflects our tendency to prefer intuitive overall judgements, which are not necessarily vague and untrustworthy, but in fact form a fairly accurate mental shorthand by which each of us sums up his own complex network of criteria and values in a few words.

Summaries of our conclusions, provisional as they are, and indicating the ground still to be covered, appear in section 4.

What we have achieved in these six sessions on assessment was only the smallest of steps, yet one of some importance. The experience we have gained would enable us to make rather more rapid progress when next assessment is discussed, but as I see it the immediate way forward is to abandon our frontal attack on assessment for a while, to look more closely at our teaching methods and our pupils' development. Any assessment, however intuitive, must be related to some framework of this kind, and a further, more extended conference devoted to these topics would in my view go a long way towards establishing a really solid basis for assessment.

2. Some Notes on Assessment (issued before the conference)

Most of us will be familiar with the distinction between *formative* assessment, which attempts to find ways of helping a pupil improve his performance, and *summative*, which tries to give a measure of his achievement compared with that of other pupils. But in studying a piece of creative work it is sometimes difficult to keep to the right track, and we may need to be rather ruthless at times. In a formative assessment, the teacher looks for seeds of promise, however small, in what may seem a completely incoherent piece; in a summative assessment, the fact of incoherence is crucial to the result.

An incoherent piece may have great value for the composer's development, marking a step forward into new territory. As teachers we shall be aware of this internal significance, but as examiners we can only assess the externals – the piece as an artistic success or failure. The amount of effort that went into it, the emotional involvement or personal growth of the composer, are irrelevant for our present purposes.

It is worth asking if this type of assessment is valuable or even desirable. There is a great danger that once external standards are established, teachers will devise slick and superficial ways of aping those standards without giving their pupils anything of inner value. In a nutshell this is what seems to have happened to the academic tradition of Harmony and Counterpoint. We must resist the temptation to follow this path, and balance any discussion of assessment with deeper thought about teaching methods and the way our pupils' minds are developing. If we can be sure of doing this, I would suggest that the assessment of externals, though not the most important part of our work, has its value, and it need not be harmful.

It would be very satisfying to establish, at this conference, a notion of the sort of standards which might be expected from 16-year-old composers. But I don't think this is going to happen. Creative work is very much more important in some of our syllabuses than in others; facilities vary widely from school to school; in some schools music is a soft option for less able children, while in others the standards are high; some pupils have had no previous experience of creative work, others have learned a great deal in earlier years; and all of us would, I'm sure, admit that we have more to learn about teaching at this level. Even if all these obstacles were removed, it would take far more than one short conference to give us a fair sample of what work is being done across the country.

So I believe we must for the present concentrate not on standards, but on *criteria* – what makes a good piece of music? Clearly the answers will relate to melody, harmony, rhythm, instrumentation, texture, form and so on. Yet these cannot be totted up crudely. For instance, a short piece for unaccompanied flute may have more merit than a long piece for full orchestra. We need to take into account the way each factor has been put to serve the overall idea of the piece. The composer of a true flute solo will purposely do without harmony and texture (in their conventional senses) in order to create the desired effect, and will exploit the other elements (melody, rhythm, attack, dynamics etc.) the more fully to compensate. We can distinguish this from the rather anonymous single line labelled 'flute' which seems to need an accompaniment of some kind, though the composer may have lacked the technique to add one.

Clearly we will not be able to discuss assessment without some reference to teaching techniques and some debate about the way our pupils' minds work. But I hope we can struggle through to the stage of making some clear statement about criteria and methods of assessment. I hope also that we shall find ourselves largely in agreement on these matters; but if different schools of thought emerge, we should welcome them rather than try to patch up a phoney consensus. After all, this is what Mode 3 is all about, and we are as yet a very long way from having to hammer out a 'creative Mode 1'.

We may, for example, find our criteria for assessing electronic or tape pieces rather different from those used for conventional instrumental music. It is worth remembering that in the Visual Arts photography or pottery are assessed quite separately from drawing and painting.

I have tried to give a fair sample of both tape and conventionally scored pieces. It has been very difficult to make the most useful selection for our purposes from the many tapes available. In the process I have made certain decisions:

(a) To exclude any piece composed by a team (two or more); any piece with a large improvised element; any piece which seems to have been composed mainly as a technical study (e.g. pieces on a pedal-note, pieces on a whole-tone scale, pieces using only three notes) and arrangements of other composers' music.

(b) To withhold scores and accompanying written material. This is rather controversial but I feel that in the limited time available we should concentrate on the essentials of sound rather than sight. It is also true that some schools have not supplied nearly as much detail as others, and their pieces might be less carefully assessed as a result.

(c) To select mainly from the upper end of the ability range. Too wide a spread of standards would distract us from the central issue of criteria.

3. Assessment: a composer's view – Richard Orton

The problem of assessment

The word 'assessment' is apparently related to the French word 'asseoir', to sit; and there must be many of us who have 'sat in' as examiners and, no doubt, many pupils who have felt 'sat upon' by examinations. However, assessment perhaps denotes a pause, a time for reflection and consideration of what is achieved. In the progress of an individual in the context of his work, the time of assessment is one when he evaluates the position he is in, in order to find out what to do next. We should note that the main concern is not the assessment itself, but what goes on before and after the assessment has been made. In other words, the assessment stands rather apart from the mainstream of life, but enables certain decisions, changes of direction, new resolves to be made. We might consider that life is a continuous process of subliminal assessment, at every moment defining our relation to the physical or mental environment; and that the kind of examination assessment with which we are concerned here is merely a heightened, conscious and social form of this everyday monitoring process.

Unfortunately, one result of this heightening, this making conscious, this socialising of assessment, is to turn the attention away from the process, from the continuity of experience, from living, to the halted fact of assessment, to the phantom 'fact', which can assume an importance, whether milestone or millstone, beyond life; related to it but not of it. It may even appear to be the zenith or nadir of the educational process – quite wrongly, in my view. In this light we see the problem of assessment as sharing that tendency of the human mind to promote irreconcilable concepts; to relate continuity and discontinuity, to wave and quantum mechanics, to analogue and digital computers, to finite and infinite philosophical and mathematical concepts, and ultimately, to their archetypes, life and death. We should recognise that of necessity we cannot say anything about death except in terms of life. Similarly, we cannot speak of assessment except in relation to the process of life, of learning, or of music, of which it is a part.

To bring this argument to its educational context, we cannot say anything about an examination mark except in relation to other examination marks – a lateral comparison of achievement with other candidates, which is socially useful; or to what the pupil has been doing, as a linear measure of his progress. This latter should merely confirm or reflect either his real enthusiasm for the subject or topic, or his apathy and lack of interest or involvement. (As an aside, we may note that examinations of factual knowledge are nowadays rather discredited because of their lacking ability to measure involvement with a subject; in turn, it has long been recognised by educational thinkers that examinations of factual knowledge do not prepare a candidate for life very well, because facts do not help an understanding of processes. And it is in recognition of this in relation to music education that this conference has been instigated.)

All assessments therefore have a double value: to society and to the individual. So, one might ask, for whom is the assessment designed? Well, we should have to answer that it is designed to help everybody, because it relies upon values standardised by consensus. But social consensus, although it does change, changes rather slowly; much more slowly than a fifteen- or sixteen-year-old person. So, as educators, we would also have to recognise that the most important thing assessment can provide for a young person is to reflect to himself or herself his or her own achievement, to show how the work relates to the work of others: other artists, thinkers, composers. For this we need very aware teachers; those who can bring to the young composer exactly the right piece of music from which to learn, or to suggest an alternative approach at exactly the right moment, when he will be able and willing to study it from his own needs. If this seems to be asking the impossible, I would tend to agree . . .

The problem, as I have outlined it, is not simply one of 'assessment'. It is one of finding the right approach to 'creative assessment'. In other words, how to find a method of assessment which will provide the necessary social consensus of standards while at the same time providing a springboard for the pupil to develop beyond what he had previously achieved by enlarging his creative horizon. For the pupil whose life is going on beyond the assessment, this is of crucial importance.

Principles of assessment

The five pieces we heard were all produced from a desire to create something new. They are all very different from each other; each composer has chosen a different medium in which to work. But I do think it is possible to outline some principles of assessment which, without being taken too dogmatically, might apply to any piece.

Variety

What control of variety has been attempted in a work? We may think initially in terms of the traditional parameters:

Pitch; melody and harmony
Rhythm; duration and tempo

But we should also consider possible untraditional, new parameters, which are becoming increasingly more important, especially in electronic composition:

Density   (and related to it, the degree of complexity: one can do a lot with a simple sound, or create a great impression with a very dense sound)
Articulation
Timbre   (because of the limitations of conventional instruments it is not always possible to work with timbre – unless you prepare or play inside a piano – but there are ways in which one can use it electronically)
Nuance   (we will need to decide whether this is intentional or not, but slight melodic or amplitude decorations might be a very significant parameter)
Location   (spatial considerations: in electronic music it is possible to 'move' a sound from one loudspeaker to another. This has also been done with instrumental music)
Familiarity   (a composer may wish to explore the differences between familiar sounds and new ones)

When one listens to a piece of music one has to decide which parameters are important. We cannot know this at the first hearing, but we have to decide what areas are being explored to make the piece. What has the composer been conscious of controlling?

Unity

What urge to unity has the composer attempted?

What intentional musical decisions has the composer taken to obtain a sense of identity for the piece?

One usually finds that the sense of identity of the piece goes along with the identity of the person who has composed it. There are many technical procedures by which unity can be reached: these can be taught (such as canon and fugal procedures), but there are many others, such as the drone in the organ piece.

Balance

Then again, we should ask to what degree these opposing tendencies, the control of variety and the urge to unity or identity, have been balanced within the work. Are the devices that make for variety over-balancing those which unite the piece? This is a very difficult question to answer, because it depends so much on what we ourselves ask from a piece of music. However, we should not be looking for a limp or loose balance, but for a dynamic balance that involves the listener in the tension of opposites.

Formal elements
How does the shape of a piece relate to its timespan? This may possibly be determined by dramatic ideas either arising from or superimposed upon the medium. I personally feel that ideas arising from the medium are more important than those superimposed upon it.

Involvement
How involved has the composer been with his material?
  This is a rather difficult question to answer, but it might be tackled by asking further questions:
  What was 'given' (or 'chosen')?
The 'given' material can be subdivided into:
  Hardware   (This can be readily ascertained: what instruments or equipment has the composer been 'given' or 'chosen' to use? Although this may have a great deal to do with his original idea for a piece, it has got nothing to do with the way he operates on his material.)
  Software   (This is much more difficult to ascertain: what ideas or techniques does the composer start from? What have been his ways of approach to the 'given' hardware? There are many possible variants here so it may be essential to have the help of the teacher who has been involved with the pupil's development: what has he 'taught' him? In what ways has the pupil been encouraged?)
What did the composer do with what was 'given'? What did he avoid doing? Has he used all the possibilities of the medium or technique, and if not, why not?
  In the end we have to recognise that the creative process is always throwing up things that are outside our experience; this, after all, is why we do it, and we should never be ashamed to admit that we cannot always provide ready explanations.

Assessment of five pieces on tape

When I heard these pieces I was provided with a tape, as we all have been, in which it was relatively easy to determine what hardware was being used. But it is almost impossible without the help of the person who is involved with the pupils to know what ideas were in their minds. This I found the most difficult aspect of assessing the pieces. It is always easier to know what a composer is getting at if one has worked with him over a period of time as I do with my composition students here at York University. Without this background knowledge it is not possible to make any assessment that is absolute. I feel as many others do, that the result is often only important in relation to the process that has been gone through to achieve it. The 'mark' is certainly not very useful to the pupil.
  When I first heard the pieces, I made what I call LDI judgements – like, dislike or indifferent judgements. They must obviously be done after the first hearing. These were the rank-order results of my first impressions:
  1. *Wind on Waves*
  2. *Electronic Piece*
  3. *Vocal Piece*
  4. *Zeitgeist*
  5. *Machines*

I am quite aware that this is very different from your considered judgements, but remember that these are not my *considered* judgements. Why did I like *Wind on Waves* best? I became aware that it followed the long organ solo and I found it very refreshing. Perhaps I rated it higher than I would have done if it was not for the order in which I heard the pieces. So the order in which we listen to the pieces may have some bearing on the initial LDI judgement. How valuable are these LDI judgements? Can they be usefully used in an examination system? My point really is that pieces must be listened to at least twice because the first impression can be so completely different from the second. The element of surprise is not there the second time. You know the areas to which you are going to direct your mind. So I rather suspect the first hearing for the purposes of assessment.

Vocal Piece
This was an electronic treatment of vocal sounds. There was a great deal of ambient sound (equipment noise, clicks etc.) which I found disconcerting and which rather spoilt what I understood to be the composer's intention.

The piece was in two sections, the first starting with breathing and odd small sounds. This was rather short and could perhaps have been extended. Tape-echo was added with a bump (I could find no reason for the bump: perhaps it was carelessness), followed by pitched vocal sounds which took up the shape of the initial breathing. It would certainly have been valuable to emphasize the connection more. Then there was an intentional sung melody plus more dramatic repeated sounds building up well, though there was some distortion and clicks which marred the effect.

Silence made a contrast with the ambient sound before the second part, which began with a long vocal melody and tape-echo. This was more lyrical than the first section, with some nice spatial effects, but the initial sound was badly edited: it was caused by a pause-button start. This section had a thicker texture than the first – more akin to a choral sound – since the melody was also imitated down an octave in pitch with increased reverberation due to the slowing down. The piece ended rather abruptly with a neat synchronization of the two voices of this 'canon'.

The intentional melodic material throughout was modal, so any harmony arising out of this material was modal rather than functional, giving a sense of timelessness, but with intended disturbances from the dramatic intervention of technical means and presumably unintentional technical faults. There was a rhythmic power which arose purely from the medium – the tape-echo. The composer used it quite well to produce a contrast to the flowing voice line. The whole piece was based on very economic means.

I did not understand why it was in two parts: otherwise the shape of the piece was satisfying. The piece immediately raises the question of *what* we are assessing: technical achievement or the inherent nature of the piece?

I gave it 8 (out of 10), but this mark does not reflect the technical mistakes.
(*Comment by Phil Ellis*   The girl who did this is not what I would call deeply involved in music. She does play the flute, but not very well. She enjoyed doing the CSE music course. That particular piece was put together rather quickly but she took a lot of time over making loops, which accounts for some of the clicks. There is a lot of unnecessary noise which I pointed out and which she could have eliminated had she wanted to. In actual fact the piece is *not* in two sections: that gap should not be there. But she lacked patience and was prepared to accept the gap rather than spend more time fading one section out and the other in, even though it was being entered for examination assessment.)

Electronic Piece

This was based on three quite distinct elements:

(1) Repetitive thumps, about 120 a minute, providing a continuous rhythmic unity but moving gradually up and down in pitch three times. These 'arches' formed the basis of the piece. This sound was produced by the positive and negative sides of the square-wave modulating an oscillator.

(2) A low square-wave oscillator producing more 'pointed' arches

(3) A high oscillator sound

Absolute pitch relationships are of no significance: the composer is only concerned about general shapes. The three different layers of sound only came together once in the piece. Technically this is much better than Vocal Piece. I gave it 7.

(*Comment by Tom Wanless*   This pupil was almost illiterate, both his reading and writing skills were of a very low level, and as a result he only obtained a very poor CSE result. He was a strange boy in many respects. He had an extremely wide knowledge of 'pop' and in particular electronic pop. As a result he knew exactly what he was trying to do when it came to composing this piece. He talked fluently about it, and although the piece was worked out by chance it doesn't sound like it because the three levels of sound were carefully worked out before he started the taping. As my syllabus insists that the quality of the recording is of equal importance with the actual composition he achieved high marks in this part of the examination. He worked on a milk round before school every day of the year to earn enough money to buy himself a VCS3. Without the Mode 3 he would have been a non-examination pupil.)

Zeitgeist

No-one had much difficulty in assessing this piece because it came closest to their own training. The musical understanding of this pupil is obviously worth a good mark: he has obviously listened to and assimilated early jazz styles, such as the extensive use of 'blue' notes. The melodic writing is quite neat: he clearly understands melodic balance, and there was a nice change of phrasing at the end. However, I soon began thinking about the limitations of this piece, which are rather severe: the simple harmonies are perpetually related to D major and passing modulations are rudimentary. It was quite witty, but not very original. I gave it 8.

(*Comment by Phil Ellis*   He wrote it very much tongue-in-cheek: he tried to spoof it as much as possible. I think he succeeded all the way along the line at what he was trying to do. This was the first time he had tried writing anything in traditional notation.)

Machines

This was performed on a solo electric organ. After an initial dissonance, there was a drone with a very quiet melody above it. This showed poor balance: the melody was almost drowned by the drone, which simply needs to be established, not overstated. There was an effective section where the composer was playing around with dynamics, articulation, swells and accents, but the swell effects palled after much use. The piece is too long for its material and would have been more effective if half the length. 5 out of 10.

(*Comment by Robert Bunting*   This was written early in the 4th year. The boy is very able, very involved in what he is doing but perhaps not very mature. He is prone to take an idea and just indulge himself in it. 'Machines' was a project for the group. We explored melodies made of constant repetitions, then they each made their own pieces. He was interested in the oppressive aspect of machines – the headache they cause.)

Wind on Waves
This was puzzling: I found it a hard piece to assess. It was for solo bamboo flute and it was very short, presumably simply evocative, with little technical thought given to it. It was poetically shaped and quite pleasant to listen to. The melodic lines were modal – a mixture of phrygian and dorian: the contrast of the two modes almost created a feeling of modulation. There was a good contrast between long notes with pauses and quick notes in runs, with nice quasi-harmonic thought in the melodic line. The opening phrase provided a paradigm for the whole piece which gradually expanded the initial balanced up-and-down movement. However the composer did not attempt to explore the instrument's potential, and the piece was not very well played. 7 out of 10.

(*Comment by Robert Bunting*   One thing that worries me about this piece is the way the player frequently cracks the top note. The boy is quite the best recorder player of his age that I know, and he also plays the oboe to Grade V standard, so he is a technically accomplished wind player. So I think he *wanted* to crack that high note. We could easily have recorded the piece again so I think it is part of the piece. However, it may be that that sound is unconvincing and perhaps it is something he should have considered more closely. The original stimulus for this piece was Mendelssohn's 'Hebrides' Overture and the idea of melodic wave patterns. But I do feel that the whole piece is very closely identified with the instrument itself, so that cracked note must be part of the composition.)

4. Criteria for assessment: conclusions

The process we undertake in judging a piece of music is largely intuitive. What must in fact happen is that we consider all the different aspects of a piece, perceive the particular way in which these aspects come together to form a single whole, and judge this process of coming together, or synthesis, using criteria we have developed from our previous listening. Spelt out like this, it may seem an intricate, lengthy and intellectually challenging business, but in practice it usually works very easily and with little need of close analysis.

This is because music is very largely concerned with synthesis and we all have highly-developed abilities in this direction. Even non-musicians have little difficulty in evaluating a new piece; their main handicap lies in their relatively narrow previous listening experience, which may distort their perception of what a piece is trying to say.

It is important to remember that our criteria have developed in parallel with our own personalities; they must by their very nature have deep psychological roots. So any attempt at evaluation must be explicit about its subjective aspect. If we feel the need to evaluate more fairly or perceptively, we cannot achieve this without to some extent developing our own personalities.

It is only to the extent that our personal values are shared with others that the evaluation of creative work has any meaning. To increase the validity of assessment we must work to bring our own values into line with those of other people, by persuasion and by being persuaded. This cannot be done without conflict at times, for in a sense any evaluation of a piece of creative work is a political statement.

Because we claim the necessity of using intuition and of making subjective judgements, it is very difficult to find words that accurately describe the methods and criteria of assessment we use. But if we are to be granted the right to work intuitively and subjectively, it seems to me that we have a duty in return to be as articulate as we possibly can.

A whole day at the conference was given over to drawing up criteria for assessment. It must be stressed that these were not meant to be imposed from some outside authority; we were merely trying to articulate what we really do during that intuitive assessment process. I had in my own mind divided our work into three stages:

1. To define the analytical techniques we intuitively use in coming to know a piece really well in all its aspects
2. To understand the varying ways in which those aspects may come together to create a unique and unified work
3. To see more clearly what sorts of value judgement we make in rating one piece of music above another, and how these express both our own individual personalities and our shared background

But before the conference I could not have defined these three stages with nearly so much clarity, and I had not realised just how difficult they were to be. In the event we succeeded fairly well in stage 1 and just began to explore stage 2. As for stage 3 I found myself out on a limb in trying to argue that value judgements are essential and need to be stated boldly.

Composing music is a complex skill to which many subsidiary skills contribute. We may be tempted to see musical literacy and performing ability as essential, and without a doubt they open up many of the most interesting possibilities for creative thought. But it seems to me confusing to assess a pupil's creative work in terms of his performance and notation skills. These can be assessed far more reliably in other ways, leaving us free when faced with a composition to concentrate solely on its creative value.

The conference seemed to have reached a fair measure of agreement on certain important practical points of assessment:

1. The composer's ability to notate his piece, or to analyze it, or to be articulate about the process of composing it, are not criteria for assessing its value as an artistic achievement.
2. If this is borne in mind, a score, background notes, and an interview with a pupil, are all useful in helping an assessor get inside the candidate's mind: they are to be used for information, not as a basis of judgement.
3. The external assessor or moderator needs to keep closely in touch with the teacher.
4. It is essential to hear the piece, on tape or live. In doing so, great efforts must be made to discover precisely which sounds are intended and which are failings of performance or recording technique. Once this is done, any performance flaws should be disregarded, unless the piece is also, and separately, being assessed as a performance.

There are however several practical points which were not discussed. These appear in section 6.

Individual comments

What follows is based very closely on the analysis of the individual comment sheets handed in after assessment of the five pieces on part 1 of the tape.

Richard Orton discussed at some length the 'parameters' available to a composer; the point being that many of them are beyond the scope of our more conventional musical styles and textbook analytical methods. We therefore tried to extend the bounds of each parameter as widely as possible, to embrace even the most sophisticated or original sixteen-year-old's work, and to ensure that unconventional approaches cannot too hastily be dismissed as mistakes. Of course, it is not necessary in practice to use this list of parameters systematically for every piece we encounter. Where we understand the composer's style well, we would probably start at once to think of general criteria. But the analysis that follows may still be useful in several practical situations, when moderator and teacher disagree, when a pupil (through either naivety or sheer originality) produces a baffling piece, or where we need to find common criteria for pieces of widely different types (for instance a pop song and an electronic piece).

So, with the warning that these are *guidelines* for *getting to know a piece*, and not in themselves criteria for judging its quality, here is our list of parameters:

1. *Form* Structure, balance, scale, sense of wholeness. Form may be established through repetition, the development of motifs, or the systematic exploration of certain techniques, yet it also has an element of pure manipulation of time. An important point to consider in coming to understand the form of a piece is the degree of *compression* involved.

2. *Medium/Instrumentation/Timbre* A piece may display the widest range of sounds an instrument can produce, or it may concentrate only on certain aspects of the instrument. Musical ideas may be shaped by the playing technique of the instrument. A composer may make the discovery of unusual sounds his main concern; or he may be almost indifferent to the medium chosen, concentrating solely on pitch and time patterns which could be played on any of several instruments.
   These remarks also apply to electronic pieces realised on tape.

3. *Melody* There are many devices of conventional melodic thinking – ornamentation, phrases of varying length and shape, repetition and sequence. It is worth looking out for unusual scale shapes (modal inflexions for instance). Yet even where melody as generally understood is less obvious, a strong sense of 'linear movement in pitch' (purposeful rise and fall) may be evident. Even a seemingly purely harmonic piece will have a linear element.

4. *Harmony* A distinction can be made between Functional and Non-Functional harmony. Functional harmony sets up certain relationships between chords in which one seems to lead to another; there is thus a grammar of harmony, and 'non-grammatical' statements can be heard as 'mistakes'. Yet in the other approach (Non-Functional) no such relationships between chords exist. A piece may show consistent use of one of these approaches or make deliberate use of both. The use of tonal centres may be flexible or intermittent. Complete absence of a tonal centre is also possible. Even a purely linear piece (e.g. flute solo) may have harmonic implications.

5. *Tempo/Rhythm* Regular tempo is a feature of most music, and choice of tempo is one of the most fundamental creative decisions. It is possible however to establish tempo of events on a broad scale without a regular pulse; or to offset passages using regular pulse against 'aperiodic' sections. Turning to rhythm patterns on the small scale, these may show considerable subtlety, in lack of symmetry for instance. Yet we must not overlook rhythm on the large scale, the sense of drive forward, overall direction to a climax. In this sense rhythm is close to form.

6. *Density* (*texture*) Layering, counterpoint. Manipulation of density may be a major interest of the composer (e.g. Ligeti).

7. *Location* May refer literally to spatial separation, either between groups of instruments or between two or more loudspeakers. There is also a figurative sense in which a piece may suggest depth, distance and nearness. In electronic music this is a particularly important parameter.

8. *Dynamics*   Level of volume – loud and soft.
9. *Articulation*   In the most conventional terms, staccato, marcato, legato, portamento and 'bending' of notes might be included. In synthesized electronic music the shape of a sound's 'envelope' can be controlled to a high degree.
10. *Mood*   A piece may be a conscious attempt to illustrate a certain verbal idea or group of ideas.

No attempt was made to decide whether some parameters should be more important than others, or whether ignoring certain parameters should be considered a weakness in a composer. Issues of this sort need to be discussed in the context of child development and teaching methods.

It is worth noting that the parameters merge into one another at many points – Harmony becomes Melody, Articulation is an aspect of Dynamics. Indeed, all the parameters are in reality merely facets of the single experience of music; thinking of Harmony or Melody as things in themselves divorced from Tempo, Rhythm, Instrumentation, Articulation and so on, is a mistake of the academic tradition which we should perhaps try to avoid rather than perpetuate. Nevertheless, any one of these facets may be our entry into a new and unfamiliar style, from which we can come to appreciate the other facets and the nature of the piece as a whole.

There was a strong feeling that we cannot assess a piece by quantifying the basic elements of music – marking it out of 10 for melodic interest, 15 for harmonic and so on. The composer may well choose to avoid melodic content or deliberately use limited harmony. Our intuitive understanding of a piece must be an awareness of how the different parameters are controlled and played off against each other to make this distinctive, unique statement.

At this higher level we found ourselves thinking about *Variety*, *Unity* (or *Economy*), *Balance*, and *Originality*. Richard Orton gave us one approach which I find particularly interesting, when he suggested that in any piece the composer is trying to resolve a tension between *Control* and *Depth*. Depth may be produced by a high degree of interest in many parameters at once, or by a very unusual approach to one or two parameters. The greater depth a piece explores, the harder it is to control the material; on the other hand, great control can be achieved if the content is rather shallow.

Unfortunately, the conference did not have time to discuss in detail the range of possibilities covered by terms like *Variety*, *Unity* or *Balance*. We did stress that *originality* could not be taken to mean 'complete freedom from outside influence'; on the contrary, one of the greatest gifts of a young composer is the ability to assimilate fully the style of music he admires. But however ill-defined at present, originality is still a term people want to use – many of us referred to 'spontaneity' or admired unpredictable turns of thought, and the term 'sincerity' was also used, though it aroused much mistrust.

The most important part of assessment trials must be to *scrutinise* the reasons why people disagree. What interested me was that even when people disagreed quite strongly, they were often agreed on all the detailed and general points so far mentioned. The differences were in *weighting* between criteria. One of us might say in effect 'this piece is a little lacking in variety and originality, yet it shows a strong control of form and clarity of texture which I value highly'. Another would say 'this piece has well-controlled form and clarity of texture, yet because it lacks variety and originality I rate it very low'. How do we interpret this? Are the differences in emphasis merely quirks (perhaps the first listener was feeling particularly benign, or the second was tired?) Or are they related to aspects of our own personalities – do they reflect deep-rooted traits of character? If the latter (as I believe), should we try to construct a system of marking which overrules personal values – say by allotting 10 marks for each of the general qualities, another 10 for technical points, and accepting the result even if it goes against our instincts? Or should we try by persuasion and discussion to adapt our personal views, each abandoning a little of our cherished independence to establish a sort of 'subjective consensus'?

5. A note on standards

Perhaps the most important information we could offer a moderator would be an indication of the sort of standards to be expected at 16+. Given this, the debate about criteria and value judgements would be less critical. Unfortunately, the situation is at present [1977] too confused for any clear guidelines to emerge. In some schools, pupils fully capable of high 'O' level grades are being taught through Mode 3 of CSE and work of great elaboration is being produced. It could be argued that every pupil of this sort should automatically receive a CSE Grade 1. Yet in other schools, Mode 3 is being used to provide courses for pupils of very average general academic attainments, with little background of musical interest.

We must also recognise that being early explorers of a very new field (creative work in examination courses), we may be a long way from realising the full potential of our pupils. The standards within one school may rise very rapidly in a few years.

Another point to consider is the amount of space, time and equipment available for creative work at this level. A school where these are severely limited must set its sights lower than a lavishly equipped school. Can different levels of attainment of this kind be defined within a Mode 3 syllabus, so that the Grade 1 of some schools is acknowledged as reflecting a lower standard than that of others? Clearly not, yet with so few creative Mode 3 syllabuses spread among so many regional boards, something of this sort must in practice be happening.

All this means that it is at present impossible to establish meaningful standards (except by hypothetical comparisons of the more orthodox qualities tested with those of Mode 1 examinations). This is not a satisfactory situation, but it is hard to see how we can improve matters except by raising the level of facilities in less fortunate schools and by detailed study of child development and teaching methods. These will give us eventually a reliable range of pupils' work on which to base our gradings.

6. Some practical questions

These were not discussed to any great extent at the conference, but they may well be very important in the process of examination assessment.
1. Is it important to assess a pupil's portfolio as a whole or should we assess each piece of work in isolation?
2. What is our attitude to the amount of teacher guidance involved?
3. To what extent should an external assessor share the burden of marking itself, in addition to the moderation between schools?

7. A possible procedure for assessment: Clement Virgo

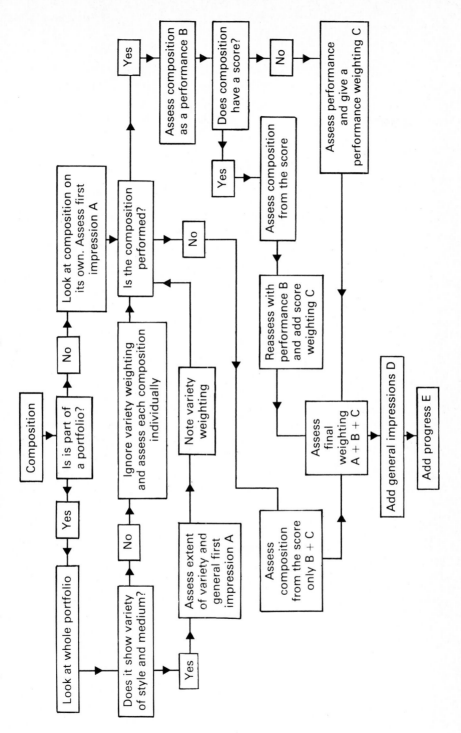

Appendix III
The evaluation of classroom music activities

Edited by John Paynter

Introduction

As part of the work of the Schools Council Project, it was felt worthwhile to list as comprehensively as possible the points which we, as educators working through music, should try to keep in mind when considering our classroom methods. As a starting point for this exercise, in May 1976 we invited teachers associated with the Project to give us their views on 'good classroom practice' for music, paying particular attention to the obvious problems that are posed by the development of 'creative music-making'. Subsequently, a digest of the teachers' replies was made. There was a strong coincidence of opinion. There were also strong indications that the small-group style of teaching had become the accepted model for many teachers who had had to devise for themselves appropriate techniques for classroom management in this new pattern of organisation.

The digest groups the teachers' main observations under four headings: *Aims and general considerations, Organisation and planning, Materials and lesson content* and *Teaching techniques*. A fifth section deals with the specific problems of *The evaluation of pupils' creative work in music*. Inevitably there is overlap, especially between the first four sections; organisation and planning cannot really be disassociated from teaching techniques or from materials and lesson content. And all are governed by the general aims for music within the curriculum.

A direct quotation does not imply that the teacher quoted was the only person to express that particular view. Many of the comments overlapped with one another or coincided exactly. Direct quotations are included principally because they aptly sum up majority opinions. Occasionally there are obvious conflicts of opinion – for example, in point 3 of *Teaching techniques* where there is disagreement about whether or not a classroom project should be abandoned if it seems to be going badly. And again with minority viewpoints, such as the correspondent who believes that 'all curriculum organisation is a sterile issue' unless it can take place within the context of a 'radically innovatory pattern of schooling'.

Notwithstanding such differences of opinion, the total impact of the teachers' response is one of unity. It would appear that teachers associated with the Project do feel that some modifications are worthwhile, in spite of limitations that might be opposed by the overall pattern for education within the school. Clearly there are teachers who have been attempting to solve the problems of music's role in the general curriculum and who have found it helpful to rationalise their own teaching techniques. It was felt that an attempt to widen the application of this rationalisation might be beneficial to many other teachers. What is needed, then, is not so much an evaluation *test* but a sequence of *suggestions*: 'points to bear in mind'.

We therefore prepared two sequenced lists of questions based upon the teachers' comments to the Project coupled with thoughts from Project team members and other sources. The first list is of a general nature and could be applied to any class music session, whatever the content. The second list is designed for work which aims in particular to develop pupils' imaginative and inventive skills. List number two is intended to be used in addition to and not in place of list number one. These suggestions are frequently expressed in the form of questions but it is important to remember that *this is not a test*. Questions clearly have different 'weighting'; a 'yes' answer to one will not necessarily have equivalent standing with a 'yes' answer to another. And again, many of the questions will not apply to teachers in certain situations. In attempting to make the lists as comprehensive as possible, within the framework of the Project's philosophy for music in schools, *it is not intended that every question should be answered*. These suggestions are to be taken merely as guidelines to help teachers to look objectively at their work and to rationalise the position of music in the curriculum.

It may be felt that the majority of points raised in the Checklists suggest an underlying current of opinion which is strongly critical of teachers and their classroom practice. *Any such criticism is most certainly not intended.* It is very hard to examine specific points of teaching technique without in some way implying criticism, but it is hoped that, since these lists of suggestions are not susceptible to 'marking' and it is accepted that it would not be possible for everyone to answer every question, much of the apparently critical effect will be dissipated.

Views of teachers on 'good classroom practice'

Aims and other general considerations

1.   Classroom music activities should involve the *majority* of pupils and should:
(a) Enable pupils to discover music – in many different forms – as a medium of expression
(b) Offer pupils opportunities to develop discrimination through personal decision-taking; 'opportunities to disagree'
(c) Develop aural perception; should be designed 'to make children use their ears'
(d) Be concerned in the main with essentially *musical* ideas (while accepting the value of integration and the 'wholeness' of educational experience – as well as the need to avoid isolating music from the rest of the curriculum, we have to remember that we are not teaching English or mathematics): 'Every lesson should contain something of *musical* worth – created, re-created or listened to'
(e) Be practical – pupils working with instruments and/or voices – and be varied and interesting
(f) 'Socialise the pupils' (working in small-groups assists the process of 'socialising') and enable pupils to experience the enjoyment and satisfaction through participation in corporate and personal music-making
(g) Enable pupils to extend their range of musical experience through their own initiative (i.e. some skills and techniques must be acquired)

2.   Music is essentially an aural *experience*. *Sound* is essential. Necessary noise levels have to be accepted. The teacher should be able to judge what is 'necessary noise'.

3.   The classroom should have a stimulating atmosphere, encouraging 'enthusiasm for experience and for learning'. There should be interesting wall display materials – posters 'geared to excitement rather than information – I often use children's paintings'.

4.   Classroom music activities should be understood as an essential part of the general education of all pupils; not merely as 'relaxation' or 'entertainment' or 'cultural' pursuits outside the real business of education. It is important too to develop 'a working relationship between pupils, teachers, parents and school governors which establishes the priority of *education*, as opposed to training for qualifications'.

Organisation and planning

1.   Careful planning is essential at all times (and is especially important when facilities and accommodation are poor). Work out in advance the optimum size for small groups, appropriate to the work to be done.

2.   Avoid 'regimented rows of desks' – 'desks are a hindrance'. Sit in a circle. There must be the possibility of 'ordered freedom of movement'; pupils should be able to move from one instrument to another. At the same time there must be discipline – teacher should control distribution and collection of books and instruments (at least, until the procedure is sufficiently established and understood for pupils to carry it out unsupervised): 'groups must put away instruments at the end of a lesson one at a time until they know where each instrument goes'. Instruments should be distributed 'fairly'. Equipment/materials should be easily available 'to avoid frustration'.

3.   Small-group work is desirable (especially in creative activities); with large or whole-class groups the teacher must 'give out' more – but with small groups the teacher can adopt more of an 'advisory role'. Groups of 3–10 pupils are most satisfactory, groups of 11–30 too large and more than 30 is 'practically unworkable'. Teacher-pupil ratio should be 'better than 1 : 15'; 'very rarely do I teach a class as a whole'. Aim for self-selecting groups choosing their own resources for music (but only after a disciplined approach has been established). Use space 'sensibly': keep potential trouble makers within sight.

4.   Keep careful records and avoid drifting through unrelated topics. Organise lessons in flexible sections: discussion, practical work, listening to music, teaching of new skills and practice of old ones.

Materials and lesson content

1.   Materials and lessons must be relevant; the teacher should assess correct needs of class age group and avoid material which is obviously too juvenile. Content should be varied and interesting to everyone. Avoid material aimed only at the musically knowledgeable or musically gifted pupils. 'My lessons tend to be composers' workshops'.

2.   There should be sufficient instruments for everyone or a means of making sounds which can be used musically (don't neglect *voices*).

3.   *Sounds* are the materials of music – any sounds can be used musically and we should not feel we are prevented from making music because we do not have conventional musical instruments, *but* those who provide financial resources should not take this as an indication that music in education can be undertaken 'on a shoe string' – equipment (good equipment) *is* necessary: good classroom instruments, audio equipment of the highest standard, books and other printed resources, so money should be available for these things: 'Lots of money!'

Teaching techniques

1.   *Before the lesson*
Good organisation and preparation (both of lesson content and of the classroom facilities and equipment) is absolutely essential. Prepare instruments and materials before the class arrives – too often discipline problems can arise because the class is inactive while teacher assembles equipment (e.g. puts bars on xylophones, looks for beaters, finds gramophone record, finds place on record, puts tape on tape-recorder, etc.). Even without discipline problems, time used in this way during a lesson period is 'time wasted on non-essentials'. The teacher must have real objectives and be aware of potential problem areas. 'Good classroom practice is all

summed up in the word "Preparation". But it must be *flexible* planning – "guide lines", perhaps, rather than a rigid structure.'

2. *Content*
Don't waste time establishing with the class 'What we did last time' and 'What we shall do today' – get on with the job. The teacher should have a clear aim, and 'the pupils should know what it is'. Music in schools must be *practical* – make sure that pupils are *'using* sounds', but allow sounds to be made only in relation to the task in hand – the materials of music (sounds) should be treated with the same degree of care and seriousness of purpose that pupils and teachers give to other materials (e.g. wood, metal). Pupils must be *taught* to have respect for sounds and not to misuse them or distort them unnecessarily. 'Get on with music-making as soon as possible.' Teacher's job is 'to stimulate imagination'; there should be 'continued exploration and discovery' in a variety of musical styles, both old and new. 'Realised forms' (existing music) can be 'matched' with pupils' own creative work. In creative work there should be a wide choice of projects. Musical knowledge (notation, history, etc.) is 'not necessarily for everyone'; it should be taught when/where it is appropriate. But tradition is important – as well as today's music. Content of lessons should 'stretch' everyone in the group – those who have already acquired instrumental skills can use them and there should always be scope for the development of imagination. There should be opportunity to listen to music (and listening can be assisted by *seeing* – e.g. use of scores where appropriate), but it is important to keep in mind the development of *aural* perception. Music is essentially an aural experience. Pupils must be aurally involved and aware of musical structures.

3. *Progress of the Lesson*
Teacher's 'opening gambit' is important – the aim should be to get the group to 'tune in to your wavelength'. There must be a clear explanation of aims. The teacher must herself/himself be convinced of the validity of the topic and the approach to be adopted, and convey that conviction to the pupils. Develop 'the ability to convey the relevance and importance of the work'. Clear introduction should stimulate pupils' imagination (especially in creative work). 'Keep talk to a minimum – clear, concise and definite explanation of what you expect group(s) will achieve.' 'Firm starting points are essential: too much initial freedom results in negative work. It is vital to start from a pre-planned point and work out parts of the project with the whole-class group. From there the children can develop their ideas.' 'Start with whole class, not small groups.' Include everyone – not merely the 'musical ones'. The teacher must be enthusiastic and also have 'specialised expertise'. He needs to be versatile in his own accomplishments but should avoid anything which is beyond his competence. The teacher must cultivate and use his own imagination and sensitivity to sounds. Avoid over-direction of pupil's work. Avoid over-projection of your own (teacher's) personality and pre-conceived ideas of how the work 'should go'. As pupils gain confidence in creative work they should be encouraged to suggest starting points and topics for exploration.

'Discuss ideas *before* instruments are fetched or distributed.' 'Adventuresome' conversation between teacher and class is an essential preliminary to creative work. There should be a 'lively, stimulating and interesting *interchange of ideas* between all the people in the room' all the time. The teacher must 'encourage the *children's* ideas', at the same time *'tactfully* discard results that demonstrate less than the best that can be offered'. *The teacher must teach* and must be able to identify problems and help to solve them. But 'avoid "inert" facts'.

After the introduction and any initial discussion and experimental activity with the whole group, the class can divide into small groups. 'Let the children take over', the teacher acting as 'an adviser and co-ordinator'. Small groups can progress at different rates (important to recognise this in mixed-ability teaching), and teacher must be aware of differences between groups – what is a correct 'method' for one group may be quite inappropriate for another. Vary the demands made in accordance with your knowledge of a pupil's ability. Is work suggested suitable for the group/individual? Teacher may wish to 'negotiate' an appropriate topic with pupils – therefore, there should be several possible lines to follow; 'children like a choice'. 'Teacher must discover pupils' interests, aptitudes and aspirations.' Give equal attention to all working groups. Important to judge when to spend time with a group and when to 'neglect' them. 'Better' groups will rise to the challenge of working with less attention from the teacher. 'Weaker' groups need more help. But *all* need encouragement – rarely 'discourage' (though it is equally important not to withhold constructive criticism).

'Don't abandon anything in "mid-flight"; work a project out to the full' but 'Don't be afraid of "failure"; abandon work not going well'. 'A topic that "works" with one group may "back-fire" with another'. ('Failure' is a built-in hazard of creative work – which is essentially a problem-solving activity; the problem may be insoluble or require several different approaches before the correct solution is found. But try to avoid too much 'failure' which can be destructive to pupils' enthusiasm. If topics are carefully chosen and clearly introduced it should only rarely be necessary to abandon something 'in mid-flight'). *All* pupils should be occupied productively (either making sounds or listening). The teacher must in some way make provision for anyone who may have been absent when vital preparatory work was done. It is also important to ensure that everyone has a *variety* of musical experience ('I've played the cow bell for the last six lessons'!). 'Feedback' is vital for pupils who must be given opportunity to perform their own pieces, though not necessarily all groups in every lesson period.

4. *Discipline and teacher/pupil relationships*
Teacher should be able to relate to pupils in a general way (i.e. 'pastorally' as well as musically). There must be a working personal relationship between the teacher and each individual; there must be *interaction* between teacher and class. 'An easy relationship with pupils is essential; nothing will work if there is difficulty in "getting on" with pupils'. But 'strict standards of conduct must be maintained – not in an authoritarian way but arising out of respect for what is being done'. 'Disciplined freedom'; it should be clear that the teacher is 'in command', though 'teacher-directed' does not have to mean 'teacher-dictated'. Pupils need guidance; a lesson must not become chaotic – 'Freedom can only arise through discipline'.

Evaluation of pupils' creative work in music

We should develop our own critical faculties and make up our minds what we are looking for – and how we can encourage our pupils to progress and to care about standards in imaginative work – 'doing something worthwhile that gives satisfaction and achieves the aims of those who have made it'.

Can they express their ideas *coherently*?
Have the appropriate decisions been taken?
Are they learning to discriminate?
Are they interested in what they have done?
Have they made good use of the given stimulus and of the selected instruments/ voices?

Is the overall organisation of the music satisfactory? Does it have 'shape' (melodic/rhythmic/harmonic/timbral) and 'wholeness'?
Is there interesting use of timbres and dynamics?
Is there care in performance of the music? (motor-coordination; appropriate use of instrumental/vocal skills).
Has the work sufficiently 'stretched' the group/the individual (does it display a range of techniques or is it severely limited)?

The evaluation of classroom music activities

Checklist 1 – General class music activities

Objectives, general philosophy of music in education – the school's policy for music
  1. Are the pupils directly involved with music as *sound*? (or if not, does the material prepared quickly lead towards such an involvement?)
  2. Are the activities likely to develop aural awareness and discrimination? Are the pupils 'using their ears'?
  3. Are there opportunities for pupils to take decisions? Opportunities to 'interpret' information and ideas?
  4. Is the material/activity likely to enable pupils to extend their range of musical experience *by their own initiative*?
  5. Is the material/activity essentially *musical*?
  6. Are there *appropriate* links with other areas of the curriculum? (or are such links planned?)
  7. Does the activity involve the *majority* of pupils in the class?
  8. Does the material contribute significantly.to the *general* education of all the pupils?
  9. Does the manner of pupil-participation contribute towards 'socialisation'?
 10. Has the teacher created a stimulating atmosphere for work in the classroom?
 11. Does the school accept the 'necessary noise' which is implied by pupils 'working with sounds'?
 12. Is musical *activity* accepted in the school as an essential part of the general education of all pupils?
 13. Is there recognition of the *educational* (as well as purely recreational or 'cultural') importance of music in the curriculum?
 14. (a) Is this recognition (13) expressed in any definite form (e.g. a written/printed statement from the Headteacher, Head of music or Head of Faculty)?
     (b) Are the curriculum implications of such a statement understood by the Headteacher? ('Is this what I expect from my Music Teacher?')
     Other members of staff? ('Do we have a common educational objective?')
     The pupils? ('Is this what we expect in music? Do we like what we do?')
     The parents? ('Is this helping my child in any way educationally?')
     The School Governors? ('Did we appoint the right person to teach music?')

Classroom organisation: preparation and planning
  1. Is there *evidence* that the teacher has prepared the material/activities carefully? (This need not necessarily imply *written* preparation.)
  2. (a) Does the teacher keep careful records of work?
     (b) Is there any overall scheme of work?
     (c) Does the scheme allow for unexpected developments? (i.e. is it sufficiently flexible?)
  3. Is the work planned relevant to the age, aptitudes, and interests of the class?

4. Is the work planned applicable to *all* pupils in the class whatever their musical background? (i.e. does the teacher's planning avoid making the assumption that certain pupils will 'carry' the lesson by means of their already acquired specialist musical skills and knowledge? *or*, if not, are such pupils to be carefully integrated into activities in such a way that everyone will be able to work at her/his own level satisfactorily?).
5. Has planning taken into account the facilities and equipment available.
6. (a) Are there sufficient instruments for the class?
   (b) If not, has the planning allowed for other sound-sources where appropriate?
7. Does the teacher's planning take account of the availability (positioning), distribution and collection (and putting away) of materials/instruments?
8. (a) Is the room suitably arranged for music-making *activity*?
   (b) Has the teacher prepared instruments/materials/audio-equipment/visual aids/class seating positions?
9. Has the teacher's preparation avoided unnecessary waste of time in finding gramophone records/tapes, setting up equipment, adjustments to instruments, music stands, etc. with the class kept waiting?
10. *Either* (a) If the work planned concentrates upon *one* area of music/*one* topic/a *single* activity: does the planning and organisation aim in any way to *compensate for lack of variety*? Has the teacher planned so that interest can be maintained?
    or (b) If the work planned is intended to have *variety* (e.g. some discussion, some practical work, some listening to music): does the planning and organisation aim in any way to give unity to the pupils' experience?
11. Is the teacher secure in what he has planned? (Does he feel that what he is doing is educationally worthwhile?)
12. Is the time-table allocation for music sufficient for the teacher to be able to realise satisfactorily his/her objectives?
13. Is there sufficient money available to enable the music teacher to carry our his/her educational policy for music in the school?

Teaching Techniques – lesson content, progress of the work and pupils' development

1. Does the teacher quickly 'get on with the job', avoiding unnecessary delays and unnecessarily long explanations?
2. Is the teacher able to involve everyone?
3. Is the teacher able to convey to the pupils the relevance and importance of what they are doing?
4. Is the teacher enthusiastic? And is enthusiasm communicated?
5. Does the teacher display musical sensitivity and imagination?
6. Does the teacher have 'specialised expertise' in music (e.g. as an instrumentalist/composer/arranger)?
7. Is the teacher versatile musically in the classroom?
8. Does the teacher *teach*? (i.e. does he, by his actions, planning etc. fulfill his role as an *educator*?)
9. Is the teacher able to identify problems encountered by the pupils as work proceeds, and does he/she help pupils to discover ways of solving these problems?
10. Is the teacher successful in making provision for anyone who may have been absent when a crucial idea was developed (one on which ability to cope with later assignments may depend)?

11. Does the teacher ensure that everyone has a fair chance to experience a *variety* of musical activities and that no-one is restricted to the same (perhaps, very elementary) role week by week?
12. Does the teacher avoid over-projection of his/her own ideas? (i.e. are pupils encouraged to develop their own reactions?)
13. Is there sufficient interaction between teacher and class? (i.e. is there a 'lively, stimulating and interesting *interchange of ideas* between all the people in the room'?)
14. Does the teacher avoid 'inert' facts?
15. Are the pupils *using sounds*?
16. Are *all* the pupils occupied productively (making sounds or listening to sounds)?
17. Do the pupils show obvious enjoyment in what they are doing?
    (a) In years 1–3?
    (b) In years 4–5 (and beyond where applicable)?
18. Do pupils have (or are they seen to be developing) a respect for the work they are doing in music/the sounds they are making/the instruments they are using?
19. Does the work develop the pupils' aural awareness?
20. Does the work 'stretch' all pupils?
21. Do pupils increase their perception of musical structures through their activity?

Teaching techniques – discipline and pupil/teacher relationships
1. Is there a good working relationship between teacher and pupils?
2. Is the teacher able to exercise control through interest and involvement of the class? Are pupils 'on his wave-length'?
3. Is there a disciplined approach to the work?
4. Is the teacher giving sufficient guidance without over-direction?

Checklist 2 – Creative music-making

N.B. This is to be used *in addition* to Checklist 1. All the points covered by the first list will apply also to sessions devoted primarily to creative music-making.

General considerations, organisation, planning, materials and equipment
1. Does the teacher's planning/scheme of work make possible the exploration of a variety of styles of music, both new and old?
2. Does the planning/method of work make it possible to develop a variety of musical skills and techniques (including the so-called 'traditional' skills) from the basis of creative activities?
3. Has the teacher thought out in advance a *strategy* for pupils' creative activity?
4. If the strategy involves work in small groups, have the optimum group sizes been determined?
5. Does the planning anticipate some form of progress or development in the pupils' work?
6. If there is a visual display on the classroom walls, is it intended primarily as a stimulus to imagination? Is it 'geared to excitement rather than information'?
7. Does the school have at least reasonable facilities (including accommodation and equipment) for creative activities in music?

Teaching techniques – pupil/teacher relationship
1. Is the teacher personally convinced about what he/she and the class are doing?

2. (a) Does the teacher have a clear aim?
   (b) Do the pupils know what it is?
3. (a) Is the teacher's introduction clear, concise and definite?
   (b) Does it stimulate imaginative work?
4. Is there sufficient discussion of the topic(s) between teacher and class prior to division into small groups?
5. Do the pupils have a choice of activities?
6. Is the teacher able to see that resources for music-making are fairly distributed?
7. Do the pupils have sufficient freedom of movement and access to instruments/ equipment they may require?
8. Is there evidence of genuine exploration and discovery in pupils' activities?
9. As the lesson proceeds, does what the teacher says and does convey to the pupils the *relevance* and importance of what they are doing?
10. Does the teacher offer constructive comments upon the music made (i.e. criticism/comment likely to help pupils progress with ideas and techniques)?
11. Does the teacher make worthwhile links between pupils' music and appropriate examples of existing music?
12. If pupils are working in small groups:
    (a) Is there a sensible use of space (including, if necessary, spaces in various parts of the school)?
    (b) Is the teacher able to spend appropriate time with all the groups?
    (c) Is the work suggested for each group suitable?
    (d) Is there evidence of the group members really *working together*?
13. Is there adequate opportunity for pupils to perform their music?
14. Do the pupils appear to derive satisfaction from performing their music?
15. In any one piece made by an individual or a group:
    (a) Is the overall organisation satisfactory and is the music coherent?
    (b) Has good use been made of the initial ideas?
    (c) Are instruments/voices used in their appropriate way?
    (d) Is there interesting use of:
        dynamics?
        timbres?
        rhythm patterns?
        harmony?
        melody?
    (e) Is there *care* in performance (motor co-ordination; appropriate use of instrumental/vocal skills)?
    (f) Is there evidence of aural sensitivity?
16. (a) In more advanced work, are pupils suggesting their own topics for creative music making?
    (b) Does the teacher encourage pupils to initiate projects?

Appendix IV
Regional centres

Here is a list of centres set up by the Project.

Mr M. Carlton
The Midland Centre for Music in Schools
Centre for Teacher Education and Training
Westbourne Road
BIRMINGHAM B15 3TN
Tel: 021 454 5106

Mr D. Hindley
East Anglian Centre for Music in Schools
Trumpington House
Homerton College
Hills Road
CAMBRIDGE CB2 2PH
Tel: 0223 47635 or 45931 Ext. 27

Mr P. Spencer
School of Education
Univerity College
PO Box 78
CARDIFF CF1 1XL
Tel: 0222 44211

Mr J. Winter
Music Department
University of London Institute of Education
Bedford Way
LONDON WC1H 0AL
Tel: 01 636 1500

Dr A. E. Kemp
Music Education Centre
School of Education
University of Reading
READING
Berkshire
Tel: 0734 85234

Mr G. Self
La Sainte Union College of Education
The Avenue
SOUTHAMPTON SO9 5HB
Tel: 0703 28761

Mrs H. Coll
Greater Manchester Secondary Music Centre
Pendlebury Hall
Lancashire Hill
STOCKPORT SK4 1RB
Tel: 061 480 8721 or 480 8099

Dr J. Paynter
Centre for Music in Schools
University of York
86 Micklegate
YORK YO1 1JZ
Tel: 0904 52910

Mr M. Waite
Bishop Otter College
College Lane
CHICHESTER
W. Sussex PO19 4PE
Tel: 0243 787911

Mr J. Wild
Bretton Hall College
WEST BRETTON
Wakefield
W. Yorks
Tel: 092 485 261

Mr B. Simms
Derby Lonsdale College
Western Road
Mickleover
DERBY DE3 5GX

Mr J. Stephens
Staff Inspector for Music
ILEA Music Centre
Ebury Bridge
LONDON WC1H 0AL

Mr B. Sargent
Keswick Hall College of Education
NORWICH NR4 6TL

Mr H. J. Sargent/Mr J. Ayerst
Music Advisers
Cornwall County Council
Education Offices
County Hall
TRURO
Cornwall TR1 3BA

Audio-visual aids produced by the Project

All these materials were designed to be used as starting points for discussion in initial and in-service teacher preparation.

Prices are correct at time of going to press.

Films

A Place for Music   16mm 44 minutes colour film. Prepared for initial and in-service teacher preparation but aimed also at a general audience (e.g. parents, Head teachers and others with an interest in the content of the school curriculum), it shows classroom work in which various approaches are adopted to encourage creativity through the age range in a variety of schools. The film audience is asked to share in the process of musical discovery and decision-making.

Available from: National Audio-Visual Aids Library, Paxton Place, Gipsy Road, London SE27 9SR. Hire: £14.84 (including VAT and postage)   Sale: £286 (plus VAT and postage), Video versions £53 plus VAT

Arrangements   16mm 20 minutes colour film. Describes interpretative work at Trinity School, Warwick, where the music teacher Kipps Horn asked groups of 5th-form pupils to devise and perform their own arrangements of a song by Alain Stivell. The project is shown from the pupil's first introduction to the recorded composition through to the final performance and critical discussion of the very varied arrangements by their creators. The film provides an excellent demonstration of the teacher's role in encouraging pupils to develop and evaluate their work collaboratively, and offers intriguing insights into the ways that pupils can work on extended group projects. The film is intended for practising and future music teachers.

Available from: National Audio-Visual Aids Library, Paxton Place, Gipsy Road, London SE27 9SR.

Hire: £8.50 plus VAT   Sale: £163 plus VAT, Video versions £43 plus VAT (no hire)

Video-tape programmes

Details of format and prices available from publisher, Drake Educational Associates Ltd, 212 Whitchurch Road, Cardiff CF4 3XF.

A Place for Music in the Curriculum   An introductory programme describing the ideas of the Project.

Starting Points   An introduction to the concept of creative activities in music expressed through the comments of teachers and pupils at some of the Project's pilot schools.

Creative Music Workshop Years 4–6   A programme showing the development of creative music making from non-examination groups through to 6th-form general studies groups. The work of three teachers working in contrasting styles is shown.

Music at Notley High School   A description of the work done by Phil Ellis through from year 1–6. The programme includes integrated work between art, drama and dance and demonstrates how children's pieces can develop.

Music at Court: Part 1 and Part 2   Grenville Hancox, the head of music at Madeley Court School, Telford demonstrates the ideas and methods he uses in teaching and the music his students produce.

Music at Manland   Tom Gamble of Manland School, Harpenden, Hertfordshire, explains the school's scheme of classroom music-making and listening to develop majority participation and understanding.

Music in Inner Urban Schools   An illustration of music teaching in two schools where the criterion is majority participation involving the use of the voice and a wide range of instruments.

The Elf: A Project in Sound and Vision   A piece composed, performed and photographed by 5th-year pupils at Madeley Court School, Telford, stimulated by the Project's own tape-slide sequences about their school. The programme expresses the boys' reaction to the destruction of the rural environment in the building of the new town.

All the above were originally produced as tape-slide programmes and are available on loan in that format through the Project's Regional Centres. The video-tape programmes incorporate the original tape-slide programme with newly recorded commentaries and additional discussion material. A ninth programme, *Materials and Instruments*, is also available on loan through Regional Centres in tape-slide format.

Appendix V
Views from the classroom

The three articles which follow – all written by classroom music teachers – extend points made elsewhere in the book.

Part 1 : Music education and industry

Grenville Hancox (Head of Music, Madeley Court School, Telford; team member, Schools Council Project, Music in the Secondary School Curriculum, 1979–80)

The notion of music as a useful/useless subject has prompted my thoughts for some time. During the past nine years, I had been part of an organisation that required an annual parade of school staff, parents and children. The options evening for the third year students reared its head with monotonous regularity, and with the expected response from most parents to music in the upper school: 'Our Justin loves his music but . . .' The need to get a job at the end of their children's school life was the main force behind the interest shown by the parents in the education of their children. As such, when compared and contrasted with physics or woodwork, or home economics, or history, etc., etc., music *appears* useless. 'What use is music to my son?' 'It won't help him get a job.' The battle cry of the parent. The epitaph of the music teacher.

Is music so useless? If music is to be given a stronger place in the curriculum, shouldn't we argue for its place in the same way that other subject areas do; that is, directly related to the acquisition of employment? Nobody would argue the need for music in everyone's lives: even the most ardent, traditional teacher will agree on 'enrichment'; 'making a person richer', 'making a whole personality', etc. Yet the parent may not see this in competition with 'useful subjects'. How to change this situation?

The thought occurred to me that employers and trades union leaders may not in fact realise what music education can offer to children and may be basing their judgements about music upon their own experience. I contacted organisations that represented these areas of employment: the CBI, Chambers of Commerce, and the Trades Union Congress, asking them if they were aware of the Project 'Music in the Secondary School Curriculum', and some of its initial conclusions; that creative, active music making encourages pupils to:

1 make decisions
2 develop self-discipline
3 co-operate with others
4 accept responsibility
5 develop an awareness and sensitivity to others

I enquired if these were not in fact qualities that we needed to encourage in our society, and that music and other arts subjects offered more opportunity to children to develop these qualities. (In mathematics, co-operation may be seen as 'cheating'.)

The initial response was favourable; positive replies were received from the CBI, and Chambers of Commerce. The former association informed me of the Understanding British Industry association, an educational offshoot of the CBI with regional headquarters throughout the country. The Director of the Birmingham branch of the UBI (Chris Hackworth) was contacted and he showed great interest in the ideas of the Project and in the implications for education and industry. As such, he put me in contact with the UBI Project Team, a group of four teachers who had been seconded by the City of Birmingham to work in various organisations for one year. This year, the team is disseminating its findings to other teachers in and around the West Midlands area, and working closely with the Schools Council Industry Project based at Sandwell. Would these teachers, all from disciplines other than music, and now hardened by one year on the shop floor, be sympathetic to the notion of music being useful? Not only were they sympathetic, they were excited by the prospect of facing employers with the idea of music's importance in the curriculum. Contacts were made with representatives of service and production industries, and a meeting held to show the film 'A Place for Music'.

Once again, the reaction was favourable – these employers could see the importance of music in relation to the qualities mentioned, as well as the 'spiritual' effect. Examination results they affirmed, in most subjects, were just part of a 'topping up' scheme: essentially, unless physics, for example, was relevant to the actual employment, they considered it just as another subject. If, then, more employers could have their attention drawn to the possibilities of music as a subject of both artistic and social importance, its *usefulness* could be argued, and pressure brought on schools to accept its importance in the upper school.

At a meeting of music teachers at the Birmingham dissemination centre, two members of the UBI team spoke of their experiences in industry, and their initial findings. They highlighted ten points that industry needs from education, suggesting that six of them (as shown by an asterisk) could be found in music education:

1. The ability to work consistently, quickly and accurately – every teacher should be encouraging these
2. Good written and oral communications – language across the curriculum
* 3. Flexibility and adaptability – willingness to accept change – a wide curriculum in schools can give the variety of experience necessary to achieve this
4. Spatial, mathematical and computational skills – understanding and application
* 5. Motor skills – coordination and control – all levels of ability need the development of these
* 6. Self-awareness and confidence
* 7. Co-operation – the ability to work as a team
* 8. Marshalling the relevant information to make a decision
* 9. The ability to use initiative in the absence of set procedures – to be creative and inventive
10. The desire to do a good job.

It would seem from these initial contacts that music education has much to offer to industry, and that we would do well to give further consideration to the connection which might in turn affect the curriculum. Continuing work is to be carried out at Birmingham dissemination centre. Music *is useful*. Music matters.

Part 2 : Music and the integration of the arts

Tom Gamble (Manland School, Harpenden)

It is generally accepted now that education in secondary schools has been over-compartmentalised; many children have suffered educationally from the 'tyranny of the subject'. But as with other aspects of education in Britain, some teachers and lecturers have over-reacted to this situation. Consequently, attitudes have become polarized into 'traditional' versus 'progressive', the latter entailing, among other things, an integrated approach to learning, particularly in the primary school. Recently, however, this integrated approach has been introduced into secondary and further education, especially in the arts, so that there are now in existence quite a few 'creative arts' departments in schools and colleges.

The reasons for this change have in many cases been economic and organizational. But the uncritical acceptance of the ideas advanced by such authors as John Cage and Marshall McLuhan has also played a considerable part. The preoccupation of many young artists, composers, and playwrights with multimedia 'events' has also had a strong influence in the establishment of creative arts 'faculties'.

Admittedly, the surface similarities of the various arts perhaps lead us to believe that there is an underlying unity in all the arts. And if we share John Cage's view that 'Music (the imaginary separation of *hearing* from the other senses) does not exist', then it may seem arbitrary to separate music from the other arts. A moment's reflection, however, will reveal that human beings are quite capable of separating, and in fact do separate, hearing from the other senses when they focus concentration on the extremely abstract organisation of sounds which we call music. Moreover, Cage's Romantic view takes no account of the importance of the intellect in perceiving music as an *object*.

Are not the various arts *naturally* separate – objects created in different media? Perhaps it is integration which is artificial; the very use of this term implies that there is something separate in the first place which demands integrating. To be consistent, proponents of integration ought to speak of *re*-integration.

Each art has a unique mode of expression; music is essentially different from the other arts because:

(i) It is more *abstract* than any of the other arts; although capable of expression, it cannot represent anything extramusical;

(ii) It exists in time – it therefore has to be 'attended to' over a constant period.

(iii) The role of the participant is radically different from the other arts. In art there is no 'performer'; in dance, drama and movement, the participant is creator, performer, *and medium* all rolled into one; in music, the participant is often creator, performer, and percipient all at the same time.

Aural awareness is an essential part of music education, and music is one of the few subjects in the curriculum which can develop listening skills. The distractions of modern society (including the mass media, muzak, etc.) have resulted in a failure to listen by the great majority of people; music is often no more than 'aural wallpaper'.

In our society music is becoming increasingly *functional*, whether as background to some activity or as an aural drug, instead of being the vital force which it can be in our lives. Music too often plays a secondary role to the other arts: when film music is considered to be most effective it is at least noticeable, and in television commercials it is the message which is most important. As a result, many children, and a considerable number of adults, are incapable of listening to a piece of music without associating it with an image. For a long time music in Europe was subservient to words and dominated by the dance. Although in the present anti-intellectual climate, when a number of composers are turning for inspiration to the relatively more 'corporeal' music of the East, I would suggest (ethnocentric as it may sound) that the development of *abstract* music in Europe is an advance – perhaps an evolutionary development in the socio-cultural sphere.

Music in an integrated arts programme will tend to reinforce this trend of music's increasingly functional role; music will be pushed to the periphery. Because of the primacy of the visual sense, music will lose out in a situation where all the arts have equal weight. The integrated approach will tend to produce superficial and mediocre music, because music is essentially about sounds. It is the *intra*-musical features of music which demand our attention and to which we must help children to respond. Music has intrinsic value and ought therefore to be completely autonomous.

It is important, however, to distinguish between 'integrated' and 'inter-related'. It does not follow that because the arts are related that they ought to be taught together. There are many ways in which music can be *related* to the other arts and indeed to other subjects. A good teacher will relate his subject to other subjects in a natural, unforced way.

Perhaps there is a place for the integration of the arts in the primary school, but in the secondary school, the integration of music into the other arts should not be welcomed unless there is extra timetable provision for such an approach, in addition to the time allocated to music alone. And even here careful and imaginative planning, along with flexibility, would be essential for the success of such a programme.

If we are not careful, music as an autonomous art form will disappear from the secondary school curriculum.

Part 3 : The absurdity of rank order assessment

Brian Loane, Boldon Comprehensive School, Tyne and Wear

Interactive and descriptive assessment

When a music teacher discusses with pupils their composition or performance, this is a process of assessment.

The teacher points out and discusses the relationship between aspects of the music, querying anomalies, drawing attention to special strengths, and suggesting extra possibilities. He or she discusses what skills are needed for the task in hand, to what extent they have been successfully deployed, how they might be perfected, what further skills might more fully realise the music, and how these might best be acquired.

The teacher tries to get the pupils to bring fully into play their own listening and self-criticism, so that the process becomes an interaction between self-assessment and teacher-assessment.

This *is* assessment in the most educationally important sense of the word. But there may also be a place for occasional descriptive documentation of a pupil's work, provided its importance is not confused with that of interactive assessment.

Although the most usual form of assessment would involve a teacher in regular contact with pupils, there may also be a place for a sort of 'examiner' coming along to bring the fresh light of an experienced outsider to bear on the pupils' work, by discussing and participating in music-making, somewhat like a visiting conductor.

Rank order assessment

But the type of assessment associated at present with the examination system is quite different. It consists of comparing pupils *with each other*, of listing them in rank order, and so of classifying them as 'distinction', 'merit', 'pass', and 'fail', or as 'A', 'B', 'C', 'D', 'E', 'O', and 'Fail', or whatever.

It seems, however, that rank order assessment is not only less important than interactive assessment, and perhaps anti-educational in wrongly concentrating pupils' attention on how they compare with each other, but also logically meaningless.

Rank order is meaningful only for quantities, and for commensurable quantities at that. We might measure the height in centimetres of all the pupils in a class, and so sort them into order of height. But rank order cannot be meaningfully assigned to incommensurable quantities. We cannot place in order twenty yards of string, three pounds of potatoes, and eight pints of milk.

Nor can any meaning be assigned to a *sum* or *average* of rank orders. We might say that such and such a pupil is third in the class in order of height, seventh in order of weight, sixth in order of length of little toe, and so on; but we can derive no 'overall class position' from such information.

Moreover, only one-dimensional quantities can be rank ordered. We may readily sort into order the numbers 5, 7, 1, and 2, but the numbers (2,3), (3,2), (0,4), and (7,1) have no rank order.

Only in a test of one very narrowly-defined task might a mark have any meaning whatsoever apart from rank order. It might answer a question like 'How many sums did the child answer correctly?' But to give an essay 6 marks out of 10 is *only* to say it was 'better than' another essay earning 5 marks, and 'not as good as' another earning 7 marks. The figure 6 answers no other question, and therefore has no other meaning. It purports to represent some sort of quantity, but in fact it is a disguised rank.

It must surely follow that adding up marks for different tasks, in order to arrive at a total on which grades may be based is an absurd procedure. It involves the summing of disguised rank orders. And these bogus quantities are not even commensurable. Spelling is as different from the imaginative use of language as weight is from height. They can have no common measure.

Moreover, any insight is of its nature at least two-dimensional. For by an act of insight a pupil transforms the relationship of *that pupil* to *reality*. Rank ordering implies quite wrongly that insight is one dimensional, for only then could we assess individuals' understanding in terms of how far along a common route they have travelled.

In addition, musical creativity is at least two-dimensional. For a pupil makes decisions about musical materials whose success can be assessed only in relation to that particular music. Rank orders can have no meaning in such a context.

If this analysis is correct, the fundamental mistake of rank order assessment is its attempt to compare a pupil's achievement not with *that pupil's* needs and interests, but with *other pupils'* achievements. In doing so, it not only distorts the education process, but falls inevitably into logical absurdities that should rob the examination system of any right to call itself academic.

It would appear that rank order assessment has nothing whatsoever to do with music education, and perhaps not much to do with any sort of education. If this leads to the conclusion that the examination system should be transformed, so that it no longer sorts and grades, but rather enters into the process of interactive assessment, let us not shirk that conclusion.

Bibliography

A. Music education (general, research, teachers' guides)

Bentley (Arnold) 1966. *Musical Ability in Children and its Measurement* London (Harrap)

Bentley (Arnold) 1968. *'Monotones' A comparison with normal singers in terms of incidence and musical abilities* London (Novello)

Bentley (Arnold) 1975. *Music in Education: A Point of View* London (NFER)

Bontinck (Irmgard) Ed. 1974. *New Patterns of Musical Behaviour of the Young Generation in Industrial Society* Vienna (UE A.G.) 1974

Brocklehurst (Brian) 1971. *Response to Music: Principles of Music Education* London (Routledge & Kegan Paul)

Burnett (Michael) Ed. 1977. *Music Education Review: A Handbook for Music Teachers* London (Chappell)

Cooper (Roy) 1969. 'What's all that noise about?' in *Music in Education* May/June

Cooper (Roy) 1976. 'Making music in school' in *Where* June

DES 1970. *Reports on Education: Creative Music in Schools* No. 63, April

Doley (Malcolm) Griffith (Diana) Tomlinson (Marie) 1978. *Music in the Curriculum 1978* Preston (Lancashire Education Committee)

Ellis (Phil) 1977. 'Creative Music at Notley' in *Music Teacher* December

Galin (David) 1976. 'The Two Modes of Consciousness, and the Two Halves of the Brain' in *Symposium on Consciousness* New York (The Viking Press)

Griffiths (Paul) 1977. 'The York Project' in *Music in Education*, Vol. 41, March/April

ILEA *Instrumental Teaching*

ILEA 1973. *Obscured Horizons: Music in Schools* NEDAL No. 11, August

Kendell (Iain) 'The Role of Literacy in the School Music Curriculum' (in Burnett (Michael) Ed. *Music Education Review*)

MANA 1974. *Report on the Training for Intending Teachers of Music* August

MANA 1975. *Spaces for Music*, Report of the Music Accommodation Panel

Merson (John) Ed. 1978. *Technology and Musical Education* (in *Investigating Music* transcripts of four ABC radio programmes) Sydney (Australian Broadcasting Commission) 1978

Mursell (James L.) 1934. *Human Values in Music Education* New York (Silver Burdett)

Mursell (James L.) and Glenn (M) 1938. *The Psychology of School Music Teaching* New York (Silver Burdett)

N.W. Regional Curriculum Development Project 1974. *Creative Music Making and the Young School Leaver* London (Blackie & Son Ltd)

OMUS 1976. *Music-Man-Society: Music Education for the Future* Gothenburg

Payne (Victor) 1979. *The Special Needs and Problems of the Musically Gifted* Unpublished MPhil thesis, University of York

Paynter (John) 1972. 'Music and Imagination' (six articles) in *Music Teacher* Vol. 51 nos. 1–6, January–June

Paynter (John) 'The Role of Creativity in the School Music Curriculum' (in Burnett (Michael) Ed. *Music Education Review*)

Plummeridge (Charles) Swanwick (Keith) Taylor (Dorothy) and Moutrie (John) 1981. *Issues in Music Education* Bedford Way Papers (University of London Institute of Education)

Sandor (Frigyer) 1969. *Musical Education in Hungary* London (Boosey & Hawkes)

Schools Council 1966. 'The Certificate of Secondary Education: Experimental Exam. Music', Examinations Bulletin No. 10 (HMSO)

Schools Council 1971. 'Music and the Young School Leaver: problems and opportunities' (Evans/Methuen Educational) Working Paper 35

Schools Council 1972. 'Music and Integrated Studies in the Secondary School' Occasional Bulletins from the Subject Committees

Scottish Education Department 1978. *Music in Scottish Schools: Curriculum Paper 16* Edinburgh (HMSO)

Swanwick (Keith) 1974. 'Class music in the secondary school – a perspective' (in *Music Teacher*)

Swanwick (Keith) 'Belief and Action in Music Education' (in Burnett (Michael) Ed. *Music Education Review*)

Swanwick (Keith) 1979. *A Basis for Music Education* Windsor (NFER Publ. Co. Ltd)

Swanwick (Keith) 1979. 'Parameters of Music Education' in *Music Teacher* January

Tapper (Karl-Herman) and Irving (Dorothy) 1978. 'New Music Education in Sweden' Report from the National Board for Universities and Colleges (Sweden)

Thackray (Rupert) 1969. *An Investigation into Rhythmic Abilities* London (Novello)

Wishart (Trevor) 1974. *Sun – Creativity and Environment* London (Universal Edition)

Wishart (Trevor) 1977. *Sun 2 A Creative Philosophy* London (Universal Edition)

B. The content of the music curriculum (Teachers' books, courses, etc.)

Attwood (Tony) 'A New Approach – Pop in the Curriculum' in *ILEA Contact* Issue 21

Barnard (Elizabeth) and Davies (Marjorie G.) *Playing with Sounds* London (Curwen & Sons)

Bennett (Roy) 1977, 1978, 1980, 1981. *Enjoying Music: Books 1, 2, 3. Enjoying Music Workshops* (Longman)

Bentley (Arnold) 1966. *Aural Foundations* London (Novello)

Brune (John A) 1974. *Resonant Rubbish* London (The English Folk Dance & Song Society)

Burnett (Michael) 1972. 'Coming to terms with pop', in *Music Teacher* November

Burnett (Michael) 'In defence of pop' (in Burnett (Michael) Ed. *Music Education Review*)

Burton (Leon) 1973. *Comprehensive Musicianship through Classroom Music* [a graded music course produced by the Hawaii Music Program Curriculum Research and Development Group, University of Hawaii] Menlo Park, California (Addison-Wesley Publishing Co.)

Callaghan (Michael) 1977. *Musical Literacy: CSE Tests*, London (Longman Group Ltd)

Chatterley (Albert) and Reynolds (Gordon) 1971. *101 Tunes to Explore* London (Novello & Co. Ltd)

Collier (Graham) 1975. *Jazz* (plus *Rhythm Section Practice Tape* and *Jazz Lecture Concert* LP disc and booklet) Cambridge University Press

Cox (Gordon) 1980. *Music of the Minorities* First Report of the Ethnic Music in Education Working Party Curriculum Development Centre, Burnley, Lancs.

Dennis (Brian) 1970. *Experimental Music in Schools* London (Oxford University Press)

Dennis (Brian) 1975. *Projects in Sound* London (Universal Edition)

DeLone (Richard P) 1971. *Music: Patterns and Style* Menlo Park, California (Addison-Wesley Publishing Co.)

Duarte (John) 1980. *Melody and Harmony for Guitarists* London (Universal Edition)

Dwyer (Terence) 1971. *Progressive Scores* London (Oxford Univerity Press)

Dwyer (Terence) 1975. *Making Electronic Music* London (Oxford University Press)

Etkin (Ruth) 1975. *Playing and Composing on the Recorder* New York (Sterling Publishing Co., Inc.)

Farmer (Paul) 1979. *Recording and Electronics*; *Pop*; *Ragtime and Blues*; *Into the Classics* 'Longman Music Topics' London (Longman)

Farmer (Paul) 1979. *Music in the Comprehensive School* London (Oxford University Press)

ILEA 1978. *Music Guidelines*

ILEA *Creative Music in Class: Project One* ILEA Learning Materials Service

John (Malcolm) Ed. 1971. *Music Drama in Schools* London (Cambridge University Press)

Johnson (Paul) *The Listening Ear* (Privately published) Manchester Polytechnic

Kendell (Iain) 1973. *A Music Desk-Book for the Class Teacher* London (J & W Chester)

Lawrence (Ian) 1967. *Projects in Music* London (Longman)

Lawrence (Ian) 1967. *Advanced Projects in Music* London (Longman)

Lawrence (Ian) 'Teaching the History of Music' (in Burnett (Michael) Ed. *Music Education Review*)

Lawrence (Ian) and Montgomery (Pamela) 1971. *An Introduction to Words and Music* London (Longman)

Leach (Robert) and Palmer (Roy) 1978. *Folk Music in School* Cambridge University Press

Loane (Brian) 1980. *How to Play the Tin Whistle* London (Universal Edition)

Mason (Bernard S) 1974. *Drums, Tomtoms and Rattles: Primitive Percussion Instruments in Modern Use* New York (Dover Publications Inc.)

Marsh (Mary Val), Rinehard (Carroll A) and Savage (Edith J) 1975. *The Spectrum of Music with Related Arts* (A classroom music course): Titles of individual books include: *Electronic Music*; *Composing Music*; *Sources of Musical Sound*; *Guitar and String Bass*; *Program Music*; *The Rock Story*; *The Arts in our Lives*; *The Choral Sound*; *Sounds of Singing Voices*; *The Materials of Music*; *Music of the Orient*; *Playing the Recorder*; *Afro-American Music* New York (Macmillan)

McMurtary (Michael J) 1972. *Group Music Making for CSE* London (Longman)

Meyer-Denkmann (Gertrud) 1977. *Experiments in Sound* London (Universal Edition)

Nordoff (Paul) and Robbins (Clive) 1973. *Therapy in Music for Handicapped Children* London (Victor Gollancz Ltd)

Nordoff (Paul) and Robbins (Clive) 1975. *Music Therapy in Special Education* London (Macdonald & Evans Ltd)

Orton (Richard) 1981. *Electronic Music for Schools* Cambridge University Press

Paton (Roderick) 1975. *Making Beat Music* (tapes and work cards) Wakefield (Educational Publications Ltd)

Paynter (John) 1972. *Hear and Now: an introduction to modern music in schools* London (Universal Edition)

Paynter (John) 1976, 1979. *All Kinds of Music* (A Classroom Course: 4 pupils' books and tapes, plus teacher's notes) London (Oxford University Press)

Paynter (John) 1978. *Sound Tracks* (4 packs of work cards plus teacher's notes) Cambridge University Press

Paynter (John and Elizabeth) 1974. *The Dance and the Drum* (integrated projects in music, dance and drama for schools) London (Universal Edition)

Paynter (John) and Aston (Peter) 1970. *Sound and Silence: Classroom Projects in Creative Music* (Cambridge University Press)

Ployhar (James) 1974. *Jazz Rock and Harmony: An Introduction to Jazz and Rock Rhythms and Styles for Young Bands* New York (Belwin Mills)

Rainbow (Bernarr) *Music in the Classroom* London (Heinemann)

Reynolds (Gordon) and Chatterley (Albert) 1969. *A Young Teacher's Guide to Class Music* London (Novello & Co. Ltd)

Roberts (Ronald) 1972. *Musical Instruments Made to be Played* Leicester (Dryad Press)

Romney (Emily) 1974. *The Musical Instrument Recipe Book* London (Penguin Books)

Sargent (Brian) 1974. *Minstrels: Medieval music to sing and play* (Cambridge University Press)

Sargent (Brian) 1974. *Troubadours* (Cambridge University Press)

Sargent (Brian) 1979. *Minstrels 2* (Cambridge University Press)

Sargent (Brian) 'Early Music for Schools' (in Burnett (Michael) Ed. *Music Education Review*)

Sawyer (David) 1977. *Vibrations: Making Unorthodox Musical Instruments* (Cambridge University Press)

Schafer (R Murray) 1969. *The Composer in the Classroom*, London (Universal Edition)

Schafer (R Murray) 1969. *Ear Cleaning* London (Universal Edition)

Schafer (R Murray) 1969. *The New Soundscape* London (Universal Edition)

Schafer (R Murray) 1970. *When Words Sing* London (Universal Edition)

Schafer (R Murray) 1975. *The Rhinoceros in the Classroom* London (Universal Edition)

Self (George) 1967. *New Sounds in Class: A Practical Approach to the Understanding and Performing of Contemporary Music in Schools* London (Universal Edition)

Self (George) 1976. *Make a New Sound* London (Universal Edition)

Southworth (Mary) 1973. *How to Make Musical Sounds* London (Studio Vista)

Tillman (June) 1976. *Exploring Sound: Creative Musical Projects for Teachers* London (Galliard)

Thackray (R M) 1965. *Creative Music in Education* London (Novello)

Tobin (Candida) 1969. *Colour Piping Books 1 and 2* Bishop's Stortford (Helicon Press)

Tobin (Candida) 1975. *Teaching Music 1*, London (Ginn & Co.)

Vulliamy (Graham) and Lee (ed.) 1980. *Pop Music in School* Second edition (Cambridge University Press)

Winters (Geoffrey) 1967. *Musical Instruments in the Classroom* London (Longman)

Wishart (Trevor) 1974. *Sounds Fun: A book of Musical Games* Schools Council Publications

Wishart (Trevor) 1977. *Sounds Fun 2: A second book of Musical Games* London (Universal Edition)

C. Books of general educational interest (including DES and Schools Council Reports and books on the arts in education)

Arts Council 1981. *The Arts Council and Education: A Consultative Document* London (Arts Council of Great Britain)

Board of Education 1931. *Report of the Consultative Committee on the Primary School* ('The Hadow Report'), London (HMSO)

Borger (Robert) and Seaborne (A E) 1966. *The Psychology of Learning* London (Penguin)

Carter (Charles), Ermisch (John) and Ruffett (Frederick) 1979. *Swings for the Schools: An Essay on Demographic Waves in Education*, London (Policy Studies Institute) Vol. XLV No. 584, December

DES 1963. *Half our Future*, A Report of the Central Advisory Council for Education (England), London (HMSO)

DES 1966. Building Bulletin 30 'Secondary School Design: Drama and Music' London (HMSO)

DES 1967. *Children and their Primary Schools.* A Report of the Central Advisory Council for Education (England), London (HMSO)

DES 1978. *Primary Education in England: A Survey by HM Inspectors of Schools* London (HMSO)

DES 1979. *Aspects of Secondary Education in England: A Survey by HM Inspectors of Schools*, London (HMSO)

DES/Welsh Office 1981. *The School Curriculum* London (HMSO) March

Ghiselin (Brewster) 1952. *The Creative Process: A Symposium* New York (Mentor)

Hadow Report. See Board of Education 1931.

Hildreth (Gertrude H.) 1966. *Introduction to the Gifted* New York (McGraw-Hill)

Holt (John) 1969. *How Children Fail* London (Penguin Books Ltd)

Jones (Richard M) 1972. *Fantasy and Feeling in Education* London (Penguin Books)

Langer (Susanne K) 1942. *Philosophy in a New Key* Cambridge, Mass. (Harvard University Press) 3rd edn 1969

Lawton (Dennis) 1975. *Class, Culture and the Curriculum* London (Routledge & Kegan Paul)

Marshall (Sybil) 1963. *An Experiment in Education*, London (Cambridge University Press)

Murdock (Graham) and Phelps (Guy) 1973. *Mass Media and the Secondary School* London (Macmillan) Schools Council Research Studies

Ross (Malcolm) 1975. *Arts and the Adolescent* Schools Council Working Paper 54 London (Evans/Methuen Educational)

Ross (Malcolm) 1978. *The Creative Arts* London (Heinemann)

Rusholme (Lord James of) 1975. *Plato's Ideas on Art and Education* York (The University of York)

Schools Council 1968. 'Enquiry 1, Young School Leavers' London (HMSO)

Schools Council 1975. 'The Whole Curriculum' Working Paper 53 (Evans/Methuen)

Schools Council 1975. 'The Curriculum in the Middle Years' Working Paper 55

Schools Council 1981. *The Practical Curriculum* a report from the Schools Council Working Paper 70, London (Methuen Educational)

Storr (Anthony) 1976. *The Dynamics of Creation* London (Penguin) (First published by Martin Secker & Warburg, 1972)

Witkin (Robert) 1974. *The Intelligence of Feeling* London (Heinemann)

D. Books of general musical interest (especially 20th-century music)

Barnes (Ken) 1973. *20 Years of Pop* (Published by Kenneth Mason)
Bornoff (Jack) Ed. 1968. *Music Theatre in a Changing Society* Belgium (UNESCO)
Boulez (Pierre) 1971. (Translated by Susan Bradshaw and R. R. Bennett) *Boulez on Music Today* London (Faber)
Cage (John) 1966. *Silence* Cambridge, Mass. (MIT)
Collier (Graham) 1973. *Inside Jazz* London (Quartet Books Ltd)
Cope (David) 1977. *New Music Composition* New York (Schirmer)
Johnson (Derek) 1969. *Beat Music* London (J & W Chester Ltd)
Judd (F C) 1972. *Electronics in Music* London (Neville Spearman)
Karkoschka (Erhard) 1972. *Notation in New Music* London (Universal Edition)
McLeish (John) 1968. *Musical Cognition* London (Novello)
Mellers (Wilfrid) 1964. *Music in a New Found Land* London (Barrie & Rockliff)
Mellers (Wilfrid) 1967. *Caliban Reborn: Renewal in Twentieth-century Music* London (Gollancz)
Mellers (Wilfrid) 1973 *Twilight of the Gods: The Beatles in Retrospect* London (Faber)
Mitchell (Donald) 1963. *The Language of Modern Music* London (Faber)
O'Donnell (Patrick A.) and Lavorni (Charles W) 1971. *Noise Pollution* Menlo Park, California (Addison-Wesley Publ. Co. Inc)
Oram (Daphne) 1972. *An Individual Note of Music Sound and Electronics* London (Galliard)
Read (Gardner) 1974. *Music Notation* London (Victor Gollancz)
Reich (Steve) 1974. *Writings about Music* London (Universal Edition)
Révész (G) 1953. *Introduction to the Psychology of Music* London (Longman)
Salzman (Eric) 1967. *Twentieth Century Music: An Introduction* Englewood Cliffs NJ (Prentice-Hall)
Schafer (R Murray) 1970. *The Book of Noise* Vancouver (privately published)
Seashore (Carl) 1967. *Psychology of Music* (Dover Publications Inc)
Shepherd (John), Virden (Phil), Vulliamy (Graham) and Wishart (Trevor) 1977. *Whose Music? A Sociology of Musical Languages* London (Latimer)
Strange (Allen) 1974. *Electronic Music Systems, Techniques and Controls* USA (Wm. C. Brown Co.)
Toop (David) Ed. 1974. *New/Rediscovered Musical Instruments* London (Quartz)
UNESCO 1974. *Music in a Changing World* (Cultures Vol 1 No. 3)
Walker (Alan) 1962. *A Study in Musical Analysis* London (Barrie & Rockliff)
Walker (Alan) 1966. *An Anatomy of Musical Criticism* London (Barrie & Rockliff)

E. Related arts and arts education

Alkema (Chester Jay) 1971. *Masks* New York (Sterling Publishing Co. Inc)
Carroll (Jean) and Lofthouse (Peter) 1969. *Creative Dance For Boys* London (Macdonald & Evans Ltd)
Grater (Michael) 1967. *Paper Faces* London (Mills & Boon Ltd)
Holbrook (David) 1967. *Children's Writing: A Sampler for Student Teachers* London (Cambridge University Press)
Laban (Rudolf) 1975. *Modern Educational Dance* London (Macdonald & Evans Ltd)
Plaskow (Daphne) 1964. *Children and Creative Activity* London (The Society for Education Through Art)
Stokes (Edith M) 1970. *Word Pictures as a Stimulus for Creative Dance* London (Macdonald & Evans Ltd)

Index